SUCCESS ORIENTED P.E. ACTIVITIES FOR SECONDARY STUDENTS

BUD *and* SUE TURNER

PRENTICE HALL
Paramus, New Jersey 07652

Library of Congress Cataloging-in-Publication Data

Turner, Lowell F.
    Success oriented p.e. activities for secondary students : pregame
sports units & fitness motivators including cooperative, interdisciplinary & critical
thinking lesson strands. / Bud and Sue Turner.
      p.   cm.
    Includes bibliographical references.
    ISBN 0-13-447434-1
    1. Physical education and training—Study and teaching (Secondary)—
United States.   I. Turner, Susan Lilliman.   II. Title.
GV365.T87   1996   95-25331
795′.071′2—dc20   CIP

Printed in the United States of America

10 9 8 7 6 5 4 3

ISBN 0-13-447434-1

ATTENTION: CORPORATIONS AND SCHOOLS

Prentice Hall books are available at quantity discounts with bulk purchase for educational,
business, or sales promotional use. For information, please write to: Prentice Hall Career
& Personal Development Special Sales, 240 Frisch Court, Paramus, New Jersey 07652.
Please supply: title of book, ISBN number, quantity, how the book will be used, date needed.

PRENTICE HALL
Career & Personal Development
Paramus, NJ 07652
A Simon & Schuster Company

On the World Wide Web at http://www.phdirect.com

Prentice-Hall International (UK) Limited, *London*
Prentice-Hall of Australia Pty. Limited, *Sydney*
Prentice-Hall Canada Inc., *Toronto*
Prentice-Hall Hispanoamericana, S.A., *Mexico*
Prentice-Hall of India Private Limited, *New Delhi*
Prentice-Hall of Japan, Inc., *Tokyo*
Simon & Schuster Asia Pte. Ltd., *Singapore*
Editora Prentice-Hall do Brasil, Ltda., *Rio de Janeiro*

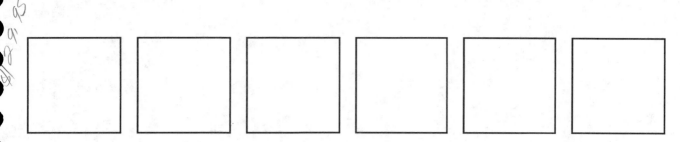

Acknowledgments

The authors wish to thank Kay Tyllia for her creative illustrations, Yuen Lui Studios for photographic assistance, and Matt Turner for typing this project.

Dedication

This book is dedicated to those teachers who are not afraid to leave their instructional comfort zones and change the course of physical education forever.

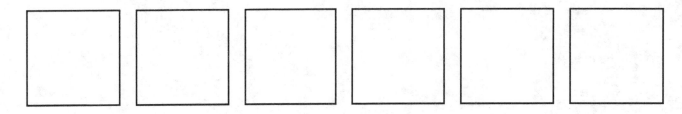

About the Authors

Bud Turner, M.Ed., is the coordinator for K–12 Health and Physical Education for the Seattle Public Schools. He regularly teaches classes for Western Washington University and the University of Washington. A national consultant, Mr. Turner is an advisor for P.E. T.V., and the recipient of AAHPERD's City and County Directors National Honor Award, Professional Excellence State Award (Western Washington University), American Cancer Society Volunteer Award, and the Excellence Award for *U.S.A. Today*. Bud has co-authored four other professional resource books.

Sue Turner, M.A., is a State Demonstration Teacher for the Seattle Public Schools, co-author of four professional books, coordinator of the Seattle School's Physical Education Demonstration Group SCATS, and a regular workshop presenter around the Northwest. She has been named Washington State Physical Educator of the Year and a Top Ten Teacher—Seattle Public Schools.

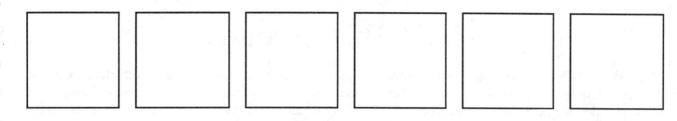

Foreword

Bud and Sue Turner continue to remind us of the endless possibilities and potential we have as teachers of physical education to improve quality of life for our students. This new resource fills a void in the literature of secondary school physical education. It provides exciting and purposeful ideas that encourage teachers and students to stretch not only their bodies and minds, but their imagination as well.

In this book, the Turners challenge us to expand our thinking about traditional curriculum and about the rules of games and how they might be modified so that all students can reach their health and fitness goals. They give us the tools and then challenge us to plan units and activities relevant to the multicultural and coeducational settings in which we teach. They give us a rich variety of unit examples that reflect what they believe physical education can and should be for students. And they state it so well: "Planned, purposeful physical education can become the PERSONAL trainer for future learning, leisure and lifetime pursuits. . . ."

This book is the fourth from these authors who have, through their teaching, writing, and research, expanded our understanding of how to define and measure success, to improve the low self-esteem of our students, and to increase student interest in physical education. They make many suggestions throughout this resource to change teaching methods to include the use of small-group situations, critical analytical thinking, peer tutoring, self assessment, and cooperative learning. They encourage us to emphasize time on task or activity learning time with their A.C.T.I.V.E. formula and give us reminders of effective teaching practices that *do* make a difference.

This is a critical time for education in the United States and especially for physical education. Many communities' response to the Educational Goals 2000 has been to cut physical education from the school day. We can show the critics with resources like *Success Oriented P. E. Activities,* that physical education makes a difference in the health and fitness of students by helping them acquire the important skills they need to continue their journey through life.

Chris Shelton
Associate Professor Exercise and Sports Studies
at Smith College, Northampton, MA.

About This Resource

Many students have great enthusiasm for their physical education classes during the elementary years but lose their zeal for participation once they enter the secondary phase of their education. The causes for this sudden lack of interest may be lack of variety in the P.E. program, overextended units, static delivery systems, and a "survival of the fittest" philosophy that promotes domination by a few and ultimately the loss of activity, self-esteem, and hope for the majority.

Success-Oriented P.E. Activities for Secondary Students offers a choice for change, including 20 stimulating pre-game teaching units and practical management suggestions to help you motivate, and better meet the needs of, all students. The five lessons from each of the pre-game units focus on scripted integral game skills presented through creative *non-threatening* small group drills, *modified* games, and *all active* delivery systems. These experiences are enhanced by challenging cooperative, interdisciplinary, and critical thinking lesson extensions, health/sport trivia, energizing "Hip-To-Be-Fit" fitness circuits, short-term alternatives, and over 100 "All-Star Motivator" activities.

For easy use, this resource is organized into the following two basic parts:

Part I: PRE-GAME TEACHING UNITS, presents 20 ready-to-use teaching units arranged alphabetically by sport, from Archery through Volleyball, plus a number of short-term alternative activities. These are preceded by an introductory section entitled "How to Use These Pre-Game Units Effectively," which offers helpful suggestions for incorporating them into your own P.E. program.

Part II: ESTABLISHING AN ENVIRONMENT FOR SUCCESS provides valuable tips, techniques, and statistics for planning and delivery of the lessons. Among these are unit duration, lesson purpose, motivation, and other topics important to all teachers today—learning styles, mainstreaming, benchmarks, and student and program evaluation.

The introduction to Part I involves a "Weekly Lesson Format" that shows how the program works at a glance and includes examples taken from the five separate sections that make up each lesson. All units are uniformly formatted, including:

- *Pre-Game Plan* with information regarding the game, its benefits, sources for further information, and the contributor(s) to that unit.
- *3 Daily Lesson Plans* for introducing and developing basic skills, with individual, partner and group practice activities, plus related cooperative, interdisciplinary and critical thinking activities.
- *Fitness Circuit*, containing a variety of individual and cooperative activities for building specific fitness components, such as upper-arm strength.
- *Physical Education Contract*, which sets specific goals related to that unit to be accomplished within in a given period and then evaluated by the teacher.
- Four or more *All-Star Motivator* activities.

All of the materials in Part I as well as the various information sheets in Part II may be photocopied by the individual P.E. teacher as needed for individual or group use. A reproducible blank contract that may be used for all units is included in the introduction to Part I.

Success-Oriented P.E. Activities for Secondary Students presents a physical education program that caters to *all* students, not just the athletic elite. It gives each individual maximum time-on-task with frequent opportunities for success. This helps elevate low skills and self-esteem, and eventually leads to increased interest in organized athletics on the part of the entire student body.

Bud and Sue Turner

HOW TO USE THESE PRE-GAME UNITS EFFECTIVELY

> "The world we have created is a product of our thinking; it cannot be changed
> without changing our thinking."
> —*Albert Einstein*

This introductory section gives you a "Weekly Lesson Format" for utilizing the 20 pregame teaching units in Part I in your own P.E. program. It also explains and illustrates the various components in each unit and includes a reproducible contract that can be used with all units.

Variety—A Key to Success

The proposed weekly lesson format described on the facing page was created to increase time-on-task, personalize physical skills, and add variety to the daily program. The process is described in five separate components:

- Daily Lesson Content
- Daily Warm-Ups
- Daily Concluding Activities
- Lesson Strands
- Motivators

Included are Monday through Friday examples to help you see the entire process within a few pages.

The Weekly Lesson Format

Day	Warm-Up	Unit*	Concluding Activity
Monday	"50"	Lesson #1	Juggling
Tuesday	Three 10-second speed jump rope trials	Lesson #2	Hoop Handstands
Wednesday	Aerobics (with music)	"It's Hip-To-Be-Fit" (Fitness/Circuit)	Cooperative Group Activities
Thursday	Long run for place	Lesson #3	Consecutive Double Unders
Friday	Cooperative Strength Training	Student Contracts	Hacky Sack

*The sample used here is the unit on Archery

Daily Lesson Content

MONDAYS   The first of these sport skills lessons occurs on Monday. The lesson features **Pre-game** skills, drills, and modified games focusing on integral game components. Each lesson is divided into **Individual, Partner,** and **Group** activities.

TUESDAY   Day two of the weekly format reviews first-day skills and offers a variety of new drills guaranteed to expedite the learning process.

WEDNESDAYS   "It's Hip-To-Be-Fit"

The main lesson content for Wednesdays is the "IT'S HIP-TO-BE-FIT" ten-station fitness circuit, including one different test from a nationally normed fitness battery each week.

Following an aerobic warm-up, partners rotate through ten unique challenges, spending from one to two minutes per station. The concluding task (fitness test) can be incorporated as a separate stop on the circuit with the instructor monitoring, or as a group practice activity.

PRESIDENT'S CHALLENGE FITNESS TEST

• ENDURANCE	1-Mile Walk/Run
• FLEXIBILITY	V-Sit and Reach
• SPEED/AGILITY	Shuttle Run
• MUSCULAR ENDURANCE	Curl-ups in 60 sec.
• UPPER ARM STRENGTH	Pull-ups or Flexed-Arm Hang

FITNESSGRAM/PHYSICAL BEST

• AEROBIC CAPACITY	1-Mile Run/Walk or PACER
• ABDOMINAL STRENGTH	Curl-up (max.) of 75 in 4 min.
• UPPER BODY STRENGTH	Flat Back Push-Up
• TRUNK LIFT	Hands under thighs—measure from floor to chin (max.) 12. in
• BODY COMPOSITION	Skin fold or body mass index (record percentage)
• FLEXIBILITY	"Back-saver" Sit and Reach (one leg at a time)

Resource: The President's Council on Physical Fitness and Sports Washington, D.C. 20001

Resource: American Alliance 1900 Association Drive Reston, VA 22091

THURSDAY The last of three **PRE-game** lessons covers the remainder of major skills necessary for productive participation. Third-day activities are usually more intensive and sport specific.

"Don't think of change as lost security."

FRIDAY Contracts Physical education contracts allow students to be creative, set short-term goals, cooperate, and specialize in areas of **personal interest.**

Under the format presented here instructors set aside 30 – 40 minutes per week for self study. Before a student contract is approved, students and instructors should consider the following questions. Is the goal:

- Attainable?
- Measurable?
- Motivational? (something a student wants to accomplish)

Benefits of Goal Setting

a. Improved skill level

b. Appropriate time on tasks

c. Increased self confidence and determination

The teacher's role is that of a facilitator moving among the various activities encouraging, offering suggestions for improvement, providing a spot on a gymnastic or circus art move, or simply guiding pupils to a higher level.

Following the initial contract writing period, some students will complete their goals during the first session. Others will require two or the maximum **three** Fridays to accomplish a goal. A very small percentage will be unable to reach their self-selected objective. Regardless of the rate of completion, the instructor has to be ready to redirect students finishing early into new, expanded, or cooperative experiences.

Contract Samples

- Juggling clubs
- Consecutive foul shots or lay-ins with opposite hand
- Badminton or volleyball serving accuracy
- Gymnastic stunts or routines
- Skateboard stunts (with appropriate safety pads)
- Disc freestyle tricks
- Unicycle stunts
- Weight training, or conditioning gains
- Etc.

PHYSICAL EDUCATION CONTRACT

Name_____

Class _____

During the next _____ weeks, I will work on accomplishing . . .

_____

_____

_____

I will need the following equipment . . .

_____

_____

_____

Teacher Approval _____Date _____

_____

Progress—Week one_____

_____

Progress—Week two_____

_____

Progress—Week three _____

_____

Goal Accomplished_____Not Accomplished _____

Teacher Comments:

Graded _____Non-Graded _____

x

PHYSICAL EDUCATION CONTRACT

Name _Jill Kimball_

Class _5th Turner_

During the next _2_ weeks, I will work on accomplishing . . .

Juggling four bags in a cascade pattern 50+ times.

I will need the following equipment . . .

Bean bags

Teacher Approval _Burns_ Date _4/21_

Progress—Week one _Best score 21_

Progress—Week two _Accomplished goal with best score of 56 & 78._

Progress—Week three _____

Goal Accomplished _X_ Not Accomplished _____

Teacher Comments:

Jill worked hard with practice sessions at home.

Graded _____ Non-Graded _X_

Daily Warm-Ups

When high school graduates were asked what they would change about their high school physical education experience, the majority responded:

"The calisthenics," "They were boring," "Did not relate to the sport being played," "Were used as a punishment," and, "We stopped doing them when the teacher wasn't looking."

There are methods of obtaining fitness without the unnecessary boredom, student sandbagging, and conditional threats. The warm-up plan that follows includes samples that have worked in several school districts. Implementing these new warm-ups WILL NOT cause **structural** failure or a **power** outage in the mind of the teacher. They will, however, increase program variety and alleviate some of the negative images associated with our profession.

MONDAY: "50"

Directions: "50" means 50 repetitions. After the signal to begin, class members complete the following exercises and sprint back to their starting spot.

Coordination	TEN jumping jacks in each of four directions
Muscular Endurance	TEN alternating sit-ups with a partner
Power	TEN standing long jumps from different lines
Flexibility	TEN alternating toe touches
Speed/Agility	TEN different wall touches

TUESDAY: Three Ten-Second Speed Trials

Directions: Students pair up with one partner (counter) sitting on the floor. The second partner stands, placing his/her rope behind and awaits the instructor's signal to begin. Once the jumper begins, the counter records each rope rotation under the jumper's feet. Scores are totaled when the instructor calls "time." If a jumper misses, he/she quickly restarts the rope and counting resumes from that point. Scores are the number of total rotations within the 10-second time frame. Partners alternate positions after each trial.

Suggestion: Posting individual and class records as well as regular entries in student journals will inspire students.

WEDNESDAY: Aerobics to Music

Directions: On this day, students warm up to their favorite music **step, bench, power, low impact, roll aerobics, water aerobics, etc.** Because of the shortened time frame, the high- or low-impact status is not so much a concern. The length of a "TOP 40" song is adequate. Since this is a student-centered program, the choice of music is often their own.

Roll Aerobics

Meany Warm-up Four Square

Step Aerobics

OUTLAWED EXERCISES

EXERCISE
- Plough
- Straight leg sit-ups
- Sit-ups with hands behind head
- Double leg lift
- Standing toe touch
- Deep knee bends

REASON
Hard on neck and back
Excessive stress on lower back
Pressure on neck and spine
Hypertension of lower back
Over-stresses lumbar area of back
Stretches knee ligaments

Source: JOPHERD, August 1987

THURSDAY: Long Run for Time

Directions: This warm-up prepares students for the various cardio-respiratory assessments, i.g., mile run included in most national fitness batteries. Practice in the gymnasium can be accomplished by establishing a set number of laps or by running for a specific amount of time. Outside, student motivation will increase by assigning points for the order of finish, i.g., a class of 25 students (first place = 25 points, 7th place = 19 points, etc.). Regardless of the methods used, it is exceedingly important to employ a slow, consistent, distance progression adequately preparing students for the actual mile run.

FRIDAY: Cooperative Strength Training

Directions: Friday's warm-up places students of equal size together for a series of partner and small-group challenges emphasizing balance, strength, flexibility, and cooperation.

The energy generated from three to four of these challenges will prepare class members for the activity of that day.

COOPERATIVE STRENGTH TRAINING

Partner Pull-ups

Push-up Tag

Hip to Hip One Arm Push-ups

Partner Walking Handstand

Hamstring Helper

Partner Leg Lifts

Sit-up Ball Exchange

Shoulder Push-ups

Assisted Backbends

Squat Thrusts

Bottoms Up

Ball On Back Chase

Daily Concluding Activities

The final portion of the lesson format is termed concluding activities. While these activities only take up the last few minutes of a lesson, their benefits are long-lasting.

These activities provide opportunities to improve fitness, promote carryover skills, elevate self-esteem, and—when practiced routinely—produce incredibly high levels of performance.

By semester's end, teachers will witness students juggling clubs, demonstrating lengthy handstands inside a hoop, consecutive double-under scores upwards of 200 and 300, and controlled kicking proficiency with the Hacky Sack footbag.

Each of the materials used can be easily transported to outlying fields of play.

Many secondary programs have attempted to implement these activities as two- three- and four-week skill units. Too often this has failed due to the frustration of learning these difficult new events. The ensuing pressures led to boredom, creating unwanted discipline problems. And, as students began to master the basics, the unit ended and the equipment was put away for another year—halting any further successes.

CONCLUDING ACTIVITY FOR MONDAY

Juggling

- Juggling is an addiction. Once you start, it's hard to stop. It's also infectious. New ideas and techniques spread quickly. Short but frequent practice sessions work best.

Equipment: Use three cubical or spherical beanbags, about the size of a tennis ball or slightly smaller, each about 3 to 5 ounces in weight.

Progression: (Cascade Pattern)

- Start by tossing one beanbag back and forth from hand to hand with a scooping underhand throw, peaking about one to two feet above the opposite shoulder. The beanbag traces an extended "infinity sign" or sideways "figure 8" pattern in the air. All throws are from the center or midline, and all catches are toward the outside. Toss to the same height on each side.

- To put two beanbags on this same path, start with one in each hand. It helps at this stage to keep beanbag number **three** "in reserve" on the heel of your dominant hand. Toss beanbag number **one** from the fingertip nest of your dominant hand along the infinity sign path and say "one"; just as it peaks toss beanbag number **two** from your subordinate hand and say "two." The two beanbags cross and end up in opposite hands, back on the fingertip nests. Pause and try again.

- Start again with two beanbags in your dominant hand and one in your subordinate. Toss number **one** from the fingertips of your dominant hand and say "one." When it peaks, toss number **two** from your subordinate hand and say "two." When number two peaks, don't say "three," say "one" again and toss number **three** along the path defined by number **one.** Catch this third beanbag on a nest formed by your thumb, pointer finger and middle finger in your subordinate hand.

- To continuously juggle, just remember to start with the hand that has two, alternate your hands, toss to the same height on each side, look at the peaks, and every time a ball peaks toss another.
- Almost all the juggling moves you will ever learn use this pattern as a building block.

RESOURCES:

The Complete Juggler, 575-page book by Dave Finnigan
Juggling Step by Step, two-hour instructional video series
These items plus a complete range of juggling equipment available from SPORTIME, 1-800-444-5700.

CONCLUDING ACTIVITY FOR TUESDAY

Handstands

For a variety of reasons, gymnastic units in secondary programs are becoming few and far between. Consequently, teaching essential skills through other formats is often the only opportunity for students to experience these important foundation skills.

A handstand is basic to more advanced movements. It's also a skill students can improve on quickly. A few minutes a week will provide impressive results.

Progression
- Raise hands straight above head.
- Take a long step forward bending the lead leg.
- As hands reach for the floor, kick the back leg upward.
- Arms should be kept straight with head up.
- To descend, lower one foot at a time and return to a vertical position.
- **Place a mat next to a wall.**
- Practice kicking up using a spotter at each side.
- Practice without spotters.
- Practice with light foot contact to the wall.
- Practice on a mat with a spotter.
- **If you overbalance, cartwheel out.**
- Now practice without a spotter with or without a mat.

Variations
- Press from a headstand to a handstand.
- Try a push-up handstand off a wall.
- Backroll into a handstand.
- Perform a handstand (tuck head) and roll out.
- Change the position of your legs while balanced.
- Statue handstands (hands are frozen).
- Challenge a friend to a handstand contest.
- Walk forward on your hands; sideways; backward.
- Balance in seconds equaling your age.
- Practice standing on your hands inside a hoop.

- Perform a cooperative handstand with feet touching.
- Create a pyramid that includes one handstand.

RESOURCES

Gymnastics for Women, Drury and Schmid, National Press Books, 1970.
Enjoying Gymnastics, The Diagram Group, Paddington Press Ltd., 1976.
Acrobatics Book, Wiley, World Publications, 1978.

CONCLUDING ACTIVITY FOR WEDNESDAY

Cooperative Group Activities

The three- to five-minute cooperative group samples below are inclusive and enlist each student's cooperation as they strive to solve a group problem.

CREW

FORMATION: Single-file lines of six or more.

DIRECTIONS: Students sit with legs draped over the lap of the person in front of them. Hands are to the sides. On the signal **"stroke,"** seats are lifted and pushed forward. The first team to cross a designated line first wins.

MINE FIELD

DIRECTIONS: Spread tennis balls and beanbags across the floor. Select partners. Partner #1 stands with eyes closed at one baseline. Partner #2 stands on the right or left sidelines and attempts to navigate (talk) #1 to the opposite endline without touching objects on the floor.

RESOURCE: *Silver Bullets*, Karl Rohnke, Project Adventure.

4 BODY PARTS

DIRECTIONS: Cooperate in moving the group of six to seven 30 feet with **only** four body parts touching the ground. All group members must be in contact.

RESOURCE: *Cowstails & Cobras*, K. Rohnke.

KNOTS

FORMATION: Students form a tight circle in groups of six or less.

DIRECTIONS: Shake right hands with someone across from you. Shake left hands with someone different. With the knot in place, the group tries to disentangle, returning to a circle.

RESOURCE: *New Games Book*, Dolphin Books.

CONCLUDING ACTIVITY FOR THURSDAY

Consecutive Double Unders

A double under is a rope-skipping trick consisting of a single bounce with a double turn. Consecutive double unders are performed with no single turns in between. Double unders require coordination, speed, and endurance. While the world record is over 10,000 consecutive jumps, a more reasonable goal for secondary students is 100. Double unders are an excellent warm-up or concluding activity.

Progression:
* Practice smooth forward jumping.
* Perform five jumps, and on the sixth, jump higher, adding a double turn.
* Use wrists, not arms, to turn the rope quickly when executing the double turn.
* Point your toes on each jump.
* As you become more successful, combine your single jump/double turns together.
* Once you can perform ten jumps consistently, work on lowering the height of your jumps and excentuate smooth, quick wrist rotations.
* Challenge a partner.
* Chart your progress.

RESOURCES:
Red Hot Peppers, Boardman and Boardman, Sasquatch Books, 1993.
Rope Skipping for Fun and Fitness, Melson, Woodlawn Publishers, 1986. American Heart Association.

CONCLUDING ACTIVITY FOR FRIDAY

Consecutive Hacky Sack Kicks

Hacky Sack, like juggling, rope skipping, and handstands, is an excellent "measurement activity." With regular practice, individuals will see daily improvement. Hacky Sack is a challenging eye-foot coordination activity with numerous possibilities for partner and group play.

THE BASICS:

First teach the basics. Start with the inside kick. Concentrate on bending the support leg and work on lifting the foot bag with the flat surface of the kicking foot. Repeat these drills with outside foot kicks as well as contacts off the knees. Emphasize the importance of kicking off each foot.

Once the basics are learned, turn on some music and try to beat your own personal record for consecutive kicks. If the rhythm moves you, clap between kicks and try to stay with the beat (kick-ercise).

Next, form a small circle (3–4) and practice cooperative kicks. Add a lowered net and play a modified volleyball/tennis game with your feet.

Inside Foot Kick

Net Shots

RESOURCES:
Mag Hughes
WE CARE
We Care Alternative Sports Program
1610 Buck Street
West Linn, OR 97068
(800) 645-4257

Lesson Strands

Examples of three different delivery systems plus a trivia question are included on the **back** of each lesson. Some of the tasks can be accomplished as a writing assignment at home while others serve as related extensions to the actual movement tasks.

Infusion of the following strands provides teachers with a tool to expand student insights, creativity, and knowledge without diminishing actual activity time.

Interdisciplinary threads illustrate curriculum links between subjects while critical thinking tasks challenge students to explore another dimension of mind and muscle possibilities. Critical thinking is the ability to "think logically on the basis of useful assumptions; be objective; weigh evidence; evaluate events and ideas critically; think independently; and synthesize information." (H.R. Buren, 1977, Jossey Bass publishers). Cooperative learning in this resource is more than simply passing the ball to each player prior to a shot. It is a vehicle allowing students to map out their own strategies, as opposed to some traditional lessons where the achievement of one student's goal is unrelated to that of another's. This negative correlation often ended in disagreement, spoiling opportunities for success.

A trivia question or fact serves as the concluding lesson activity. Health- and sport-related trivia make for interesting discussion topics.

"Think big, start small and begin."

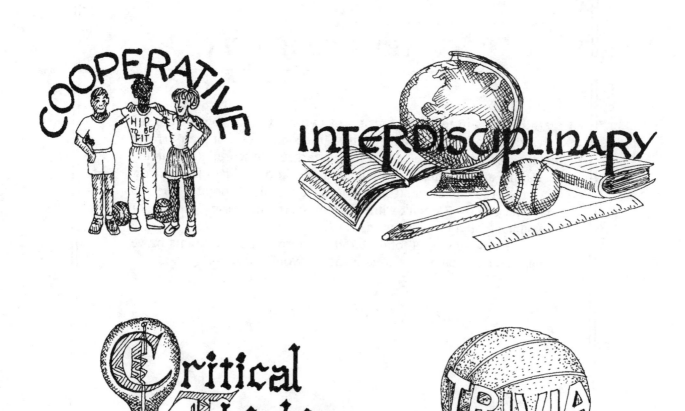

Motivators

Four to six motivators can be found at the end of each unit. Motivators serve as the "dessert" portion of the lesson menu. These games, drills, and contests provide additional repetitions on integral game skills, assisting in the skill-acquisition process. The more than 100 motivators included here will stimulate excitement and promote a further appreciation for movement.

 ## THE END RESULT

Individuals in teams of four shoot two *ends* (12 arrows) from ten yards back. All four archers have 90 seconds to shoot their arrows. Once *all* arrows have been released, targets are scored. (Reminder: waiting archers must remain behind the shooting line.) Each arrow in the gold circle counts as 9 points, red area = 7 points, blue = 5 points, black = 3 points, white = 1 point. Arrows passing through or bouncing off a target count as 7.

Teams scoring a total of 150 or more combined points move back an additional ten yards. What was your *end result?*

Teaching Goals of the Program

After participating in the program, students will:

GOAL	SUPPORT
• increase cognitive skill development	Lesson extensions
• experience numerous opportunities to work cooperatively in small and large groups	Regular lessons and extensions
• practice a variety of exercise forms	Alternating warm-ups
• be challenged by higher level thinking skills	Lesson extensions
• receive planned purposeful repetitions on integral game skills	Monday, Tuesday, Thursday lessons
• formulate, fail, and achieve self-selected goals	Friday contracts
• enhance personal fitness inventory	Wednesday's **Hip-to-Be-Fit** lessons
• increase physical skills inventory with maximal time on task through a wide variety of traditional and alternative skills	Regular lessons and extensions
• make positive health-related choices	Conditioning unit
• gain knowledge necessary for sport skill success	Monday, Tuesday, Thursday lessons
	Cooperative positive learning
• develop stronger intrapersonal skills	**All active, all successful approach**
• improve positive self concept	**Success-oriented** teaching format
	Introduction

"Physical education isn't everything, but it sure beats what's second."

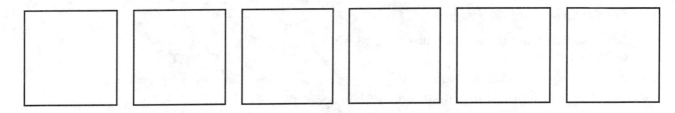

Contents

About the Authors iv

Foreword v

About This Resource vi

How to Use These Pre-game Units Effectively vii

Weekly Lesson Format vii

Daily Lesson Content viii

       Physical Education Contract (blank form)   x
       Physical Education Contract (completed sample)   xi

The Warm-Up xii

Concluding Activities xvi

Lesson Strands xxi

All-Star Motivators xxii

Teaching Goals of the Program xxiii

PART I
Pre-game Teaching Units
1

Archery *2*

       Pre-game Plan
       Lesson 1
       Lesson 2
       Lesson 3
       P.E. Contract
       All-Star Motivators

Badminton *16*

       (Same format: pre-game, 3 lessons, contract, motivators)

Basketball *30*

Bowling *44*

Conditioning *57*

Disc Sports 75
Football 91
Free Weights 104
Golf 119
Handball 133
Personal Safety 149
Soccer 163
Softball. 179
Soft Lacrosse 195
Soft Tennis. 210
Street and Line Dancing 225
Table Tennis. 238
Track and Field 252
Tumbling 268
Volleyball. 286

SHORT-TERM ALTERNATIVES
301

Adult CPR. 302
Double Dutch 304
Korfball 306
Omnikin Ball (modified) 308
Orienteering. 310
Racewalking 312
Roller Skating 314
Rowing. 316
Skateboarding 318
Small-Group Cooperative Challenge 320
Team Handball 322
Unicycling 324

Water Aerobics *326*
Yo-Yo *328*

PART II
Establishing an Environment for Success
331

Participation of High School Students in School Physical Education 332

Y.P.E. 333

Success-Oriented Physical Education 334

Problems and Solutions in Physical Education 335

Coeducational Classes 336

Lesson Purpose 337

Inappropriate Activities 337

Games and Drills That Rate an "E" 338

Safety Issues 339

Learning Compassion 340

Unit Duration 340

Learning Styles 341

Techniques for Selecting Partners and Groups 341

Mainstreaming 342

Public Relations 342

Promote 344

Motivation 345

Student Testimonials 345

P.E. Records Day Sample Poster 346

Physical Education Bill of Rights 347

NASPE Physical Education Outcomes Project 348

Student Evaluation 352

Program Evaluation 357

PART ONE

PRE-GAME
TEACHING UNITS

Part I provides 20 uniformly formatted pre-game teaching units plus a variety of alternative activities. These are preceded by an introductory section—"How to Use These Pre-Game Units Effectively."

The units include:

- Archery
- Badminton
- Basketball
- Bowling
- Conditioning
- Disc Sports
- Football
- Free Weights
- Golf
- Handball

- Personal Safety
- Soccer
- Softball
- Soft Lacrosse
- Soft Tennis
- Street and Line Dancing
- Table Tennis
- Track and Field
- Tumbling
- Volleyball

Short-Term Alternatives

- Adult CPR
- Double Dutch
- Korfball
- Omnikin Ball (Modified)
- Orienteering
- Racewalking
- Roller Skating

- Rowing
- Skateboarding
- Team Handball
- Unicycling
- Water Aerobics
- Yo-Yo

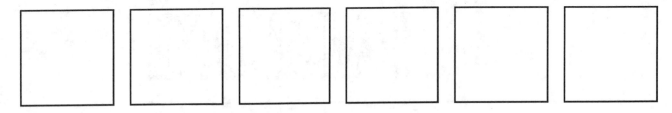

Archery

"Success is never final. Failure is never fatal. It's courage that counts."
—Winston Churchill

PRE-GAME PLAN

Archery is an activity that can capture the interest of all populations regardless of their current ability. The pleasure derived from hitting a target outweighs the quality of equipment available. Focus in this section centers around safety, shooting form, and accuracy.

HIGHLIGHTS:

M	Practice seven steps of shooting, know safety/command procedures.
T	Learn correction and scoring procedures, play "Which Way" and "Tic-Tac-Toe Archery."
W	New Hip-To-Be-Fit circuit, Endurance Test.
Th	Shoot from different positions, play "Archery Baseball."
F	Contracts.

BENEFITS:

- Lifetime activity
- Can be performed inside or out
- Sex equitable
- Compete individually or as a team

RESOURCES:

American Archery Council
23 E. Jackson Boulevard
Chicago, IL 60604

CONTRIBUTOR:

Barbara McEwan, M.A.
Seattle School District

UNIT: ARCHERY (LESSON 1)

Objectives:
- Demonstrate the seven steps of shooting.
- Adhere to safety procedures.
- Know how to remove arrows from the target.
- Recognize corrections for shooting errors.
- Understand an *end* can be either six or three arrows.

WARM-UP: "50"

Practice:

INDIVIDUAL

- From a line formation (20 to 30 feet from target) all students silently mimic each verbal command in the seven steps of shooting (bows only).
    1. **Stance**—Feet straddle the shooting line.
    2. **Nock** (put arrow on)—Place arrow perpendicular to bow, odd-colored feather pointed up.
    3. **Draw** (pull string)—First three fingers up to first joint on the string. Nock of the arrow is between the first and second fingers.
    4. **Anchor** (hold)—Elbow up and backstring near nose and chin.
    5. **Aim**—Sight with correct eye.
    6. **Release**—Allow string to slide off as you let go.
    7. **Follow through**—Hold your position until arrow impacts.
- Once students understand the safety and command procedures, each is allowed to shoot one *end* (six arrows).
- **When pulling arrows from the target, place back of one hand against target and pull out near impact point with opposite hand.**

Stance

Nock

PARTNERS

- After all bows are on the ground and the retrieval process completed, students select partners and alternate shooting six arrows. Nonshooting partners observe for the following form breaks and common errors:
    a. Make sure odd-colored feather is up.
    b. Check finger position on string.
    c. Affirm that shooter puts bow down and steps back from line.
    d. **High shots** = releasing early—bow arm up on release—arrows nocked low.
    e. **Low shots** = dropping left arm on release—arm is low—arrow not raised to full draw.
    f. **Left of target** = lowering left shoulder—bow tilted to left—sighting with wrong eye.
    g. **Right of target** = pluck string to right and release—top of bow tilted to right.
- Trade places after each **end**.

GROUP

- **"Tic-Tac-Toe Archery":** A large tagboard grid is placed over each target. Working in teams of two (groups of four), color-code arrows and see which team can place three arrows in a line first.

COOPERATIVE

In groups of three (six arrows per shooter) establish a team record for bull's-eyes. Which group was the most accurate?

"Never release an arrow aimlessly into the air, falling to earth, you know not where."
(*Archery,* E. Jaeger, Athletic Institute, 1951.)
Write two more archery jingles below.

INTERDISCIPLINARY

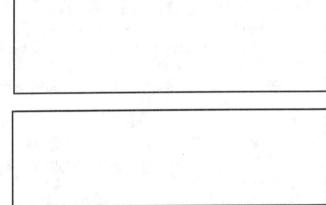

Critical Thinking

Before a lesson, have each shooting team list **ten** guidelines that will help make the shooting experience a safer one. *Possible responses* include:

- Follow established signals.
- Retrieve only when all shooting has stopped.
- Don't retrieve *dropped* arrows.
- Avoid loose clothing.
- Check equipment for excessive wear.
- Arrows point toward target when nocking.
- Never shoot arrows straight up.

TRIVIA

How many fingers are used to draw a bow?
Answer: **Three.**

UNIT: ARCHERY (LESSON 2)

Objectives:

- Learn scoring procedures.
- Review common shooting errors and how to correct them.
- Improve shooting form and accuracy.
- Work cooperatively in small groups.

WARM-UP: THREE 10-SECOND SPEED JUMP-ROPE TRIALS

Practice:

INDIVIDUAL

- Practice shooting an *end* (set of six). Remember the safety procedures and retrieval techniques.
- Explain target values and have students score their second round.
- Students try to beat their first and second rounds.
- Rebounds and arrows going through the target equal seven points.

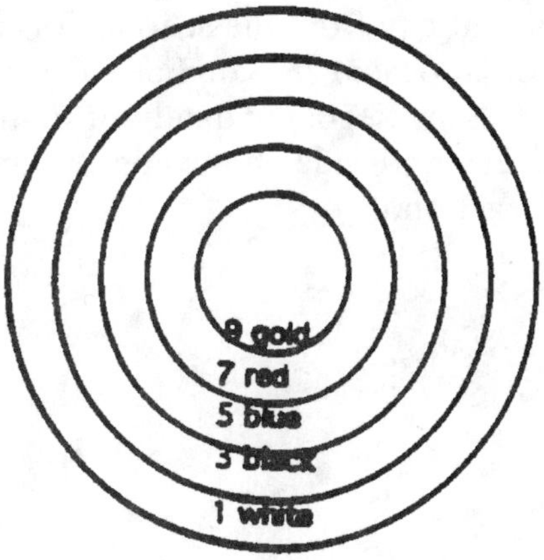

9 gold
7 red
5 blue
3 black
1 white

Sophisticated targets have inner and outer circles. Archers add an additional point when contacting the inner circle.

ARCHERY SCORE						H	Score
9	7	7	3	0	0	4	26

PARTNERS

- Challenge your partner to a best score match (three ends = 18 arrows).
- Your scoring starts after all six arrows are shot. Remove the arrows from lowest to highest in value, but *score* from highest to lowest in value (see sample card). The shooter removes arrows and calls out each score to the observer who records the *points, hits,* and *totals.*
- Option: **Students can increase the ten-yard target distance as skills improve.**

GROUP

- **"Three Bull's-eyes":** Arrange students in groups of three. Distribute 18 arrows to each target group. Archers shoot *one* arrow and return to the end of their line. This process continues until all 18 arrows are released, or one group scores **"Three Bull's-eyes."** The group's signal to stop the contest is to call **"Three,"** followed by the entire group sitting down behind the line.

There are five concentric circles on a traditional archery target. Working in cooperative teams of five (three arrows each), see how many circles your team can hit. Use regulation scoring and add ten points to your total if all five circles are hit.

"Which Way Archery": Number off students in groups of four to six. Provide each group with a set of twenty 3″ x 5″ cards. Each card contains the name of a major U.S. city, e.g., Los Angeles, Boston, Seattle, Miami. Write the name of your school over the bull's-eye. Shooter #1 draws a card and attempts to hit the quadrant representing the geographic direction of that city from the school. For instance, if the school is located in Salt Lake City and the card drawn is San Diego, the quadrant to hit would be "3 west." Teams decide on the appropriate quadrant before each shot.

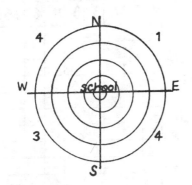

How does bow poundage equate with shooting distance?

What's the heart made of?
Answer: **Mostly muscular tissue.**

Wednesday
HIP-TO-BE-FIT FITNESS CIRCUIT

	FITNESS COMPONENTS	ACTIVITY	DESCRIPTION	RESOURCE
1	Balance	ROLL AEROBICS	From a sitting position on the ball, experiment with rolling the ball up your back and legs.	Tactile Ball, U.S. Games, 1-800-327-0484
2	Upper Arm Strength	CHAIR DIPS	With three chairs, work on lifting and lowering using arms only.	
3	Upper Arm Strength	DYNA BANDS	Find three ways to perform curls.	Flaghouse, 1-800-793-7922
4	Arm & Leg Strength	WALL PULLIN	Standing on carpet samples (slippery side down), race a partner in a wall pullin contest.	
5	Endurance	STEP TEST	Practice a dance move as you step up and over the mat.	
6	Coordination & Endurance	JUMP ROPE	How many "Jump for Heart" stunts can you perform?	American Heart Association
7	Power	PLUNGER JUMP	How many jumps can you make?	
8	Upper Arm Strength	FACE OFF	Face each other on a bar or ring. Who can hang the longest?	
9	Coordination	PASS THROUGH	Stand back to back. On "GO," #1 passes under all four legs with #2 catching in front. How many can you do in one minute?	
10	Arm & Leg Strength	WALL ROPE CLIMB	Use your arms and feet to climb above a designated mark.	

WEEKLY TEST

UNIT: ARCHERY (LESSON 3)

Objectives:

- Experience shooting from different positions.
- Concentrate on shooting form and accuracy.
- Participate in novelty shooting drills.

Kneeling Shooting

WARM-UP: LONG RUN FOR PLACE

Practice:

INDIVIDUAL

- Work on your accuracy from the following shooting positions. Shoot an *end* from each position:
  a. kneeling
  b. sitting down
  c. from a 45° angle
  d. with only a five-inch draw

PARTNERS

- Tape softball-sized balloons about the target face.
- Partners alternate shooting *ends* (six arrows) at the balloon-covered targets. Who can pop the most in one set?

GROUP

- "Novelty Shooting": Students work in groups of three. Each student is allowed two shots. The score is a *collective* effort.

CHRISTMAS TREE

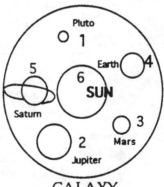
GALAXY

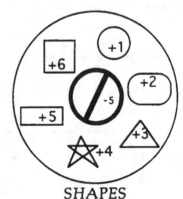
SHAPES

- **"Four Round Elimination":** Place students in even groups. Distribute three arrows per shooter. Attach faces (as shown in the illustration). Cut an extra dark-colored section for each team. On the first round place the dark cut-out over section A. Shooters aim all arrows toward sections B, C, and D while attempting to bypass the darkened area. Arrows landing inside noncovered sections count as one point. Arrows in the covered zone count a minus three. On the second round the B is eliminated.

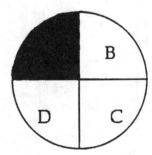

"Alpha Archery": Working in groups of three (six arrows each), try to form a letter with the 18 arrows. Groups may stop before 18 if a letter is formed.

"Archery Quiz Show": Tape 3″ x 5″ cards to the target with archery-related questions on the front and answers on the back. Once an arrow hits a card, students attempt to answer the question. Correct responses score a point for that individual or team. Play a game to ten points.

1972 marked the debut of archery as an Olympic sport. What do you think archery will look like in the Olympics of 2012?

How much hair does the body produce in a good year? *Answer:* **7 miles' worth.**

PHYSICAL EDUCATION CONTRACT

Name *Tim Church*

Class *Putnam 3rd*

During the next ___2___ weeks, I will work on accomplishing . . .

Trying to hit 3 bull's-eyes in a row from 10 and 15 yards back

I will need the following equipment . . .

Target, bow, 6 arrows, shooting glove, arm guard

Teacher Approval *Bill Putnam*　　　Date *5/20*

Progress—Week one *Made two bull's-eyes from 10 yds and one from 15.*

Progress—Week two *Could not beat two bull's-eyes.*

Progress—Week three *n/a*

Goal Accomplished _____ Not Accomplished ✓

Teacher Comments:

Improved accuracy, refined shooting techniques

Graded _____ Non-Graded ✓

10

ALL★STAR MOTIVATOR

 ## "THE END RESULT"

Individuals in teams of four shoot two *ends* (12 arrows) from ten yards back. All four archers have 90 seconds to shoot their arrows. Once *all* arrows have been released, targets are scored. (Reminder: waiting archers must remain behind the shooting line.) Each arrow in the gold circle counts as 9 points, red area = 7 points, blue = 5 points, black = 3 points, white = 1 point. Arrows passing through or bouncing off a target count as 7.

Teams scoring a total of 150 or more combined points move back an additional ten yards. What was your *end result?*

ALL★STAR
MOTIVATOR

"POP"

Establish teams and tape 10 to 12 small balloons on each target face. Place a roll of tickets behind the shooting line. After each player has shot an *end* (six arrows), he or she writes his or her name on the back of a ticket for each balloon popped. Tickets are drawn at the conclusion of the round for a cold soda **pop.**

ALL STAR MOTIVATOR

T.A.G. ("TARGET ARCHERY GAME")

Assign three to five students to a specific target. Provide each student with one arrow and one small distinctive sticker. Archers number off with #1 placing his or her sticker somewhere on the target face between the #3 and #9 rings.

One by one, group members shoot a single arrow. The closest arrow to #1's sticker scores *one point*. Retrievers cross the shooting line only after all arrows have been shot. Next, #2 places his or her sticker and takes the next shot. This process continues until all team members have had a turn to place and *T.A.G.* everyone else's sticker.

The first student to win five points becomes the T.A.G. champion.

ALL★STAR MOTIVATOR

 ## "ROUND-A-BOUT"

Form lines of equal teams behind each target. Color-code team arrows (one per target) with tape or permanent markers. Pass out a score card and pencil to each shooting line. The first student in line shoots one arrow and rotates to the end. After all students have shot once, teams rotate to their right with the last team moving across to the first target. *Arrows are left in the target.* When teams have completed shooting at all targets, the first **"Round-A-Bout"** is complete and scorers tally each scoring arrow.

Following the first rotation, see if teams can beat their original score.

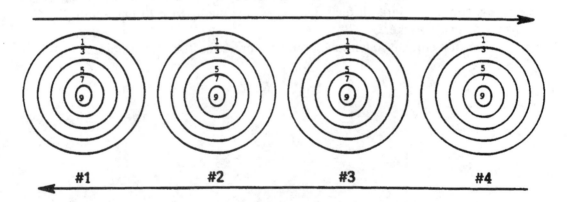

	TARGET TOTALS					
Name	Target 1	2	3	4	5	6
Bob	7	9	5	9		
Jill	0	5	3	9		
Steph	1	3	3	5		
Alex	9	9	1	1		
Hong	5	3	7	0		
Lisa	5	0	9	9		
Total	27	29	28	33		

ALL★STAR
MOTIVATOR

 ## "ARCHERY BASEBALL"

Play "Archery Baseball" with a partner. Alternate six arrows or three outs (whatever comes first). Count your cumulative runs after a three-inning game.

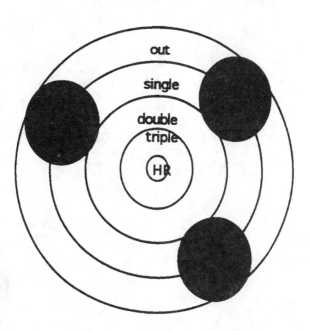

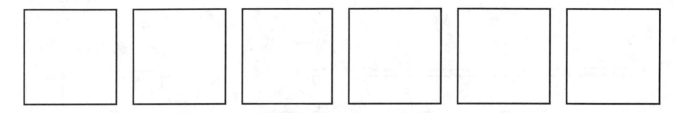

*B*adminton

PRE-GAME PLAN

Badminton is one of the world's fastest games. It is a game that can be played by young and old in gymnasiums, playgrounds, or backyards. The purpose of this chapter is to introduce students to the fundamental skills and strategies preparing them for singles and doubles play.

HIGHLIGHTS

M   Learn grips and basic strokes, play "Three Aloft" and "Badminton Golf."

T   Practice short and long service skills, clears, and basic court strategies.

W   New Hip-To-Be-Fit circuit, Flexibility Test.

Th   Improve backhand proficiency, play "Up Your Alley."

F   Contracts.

BENEFITS

- Play in small places.
- Inexpensive.
- Sex equitable.
- Lifetime activity.

RESOURCES

American Badminton Association
20 Wamesit Road
Waban, MA 02168

CONTRIBUTOR

Rob Brown
Washington Badminton Association

UNIT: BADMINTON (LESSON 1)

Objectives:

- Know basic grips for forehand and backhand.
- Improve forehand and backhand proficiency.
- Increase footspeed.
- Practice hitting toward your opponent.
- Know legal contact points.

WARM-UP: "50"

Practice

Grasping the Bird

INDIVIDUAL

- Distribute a racket and bird to each student.
- In a space with enough room to swing freely, work on forehand and backhand strokes. (Forehand) Shake hands with the racket (see illustrations) and practice hitting the bird straight up. Hit it just high enough to enable you to hit ten good contacts in a row.
- Repeat with a backhand grip.
- Alternate forehand and backhand strokes.

Grips

Forehand

Backhand

PARTNERS

- Work on forehand and backhand volleys over a line on the floor.
- Partners alternate hitting short and deep shots.
- Using lines on the floor, reduce the size of the court. Concentrate on control and accuracy.
- "Catch the Bird." This time, try to catch the return *on your racket*. Tip it up, and hit it back.
- "Straight at You." During this next sequence, try to **hit** one another with the bird.
- "Come Together." Starting on opposite back lines, partners move toward the net after each contact. Work on hitting directly to your partner.
- "Touch the Net." During legal rallies, work on moving your partner into the backcourt so that you are able to touch the net. The first one to make ten separate net contacts wins.

GROUP

- "Three Aloft." Each group challenges another to see who can keep three shuttlecocks aloft the longest. As soon as the bird hits the floor, that round ends. Set a class "Three Aloft" record.

"Backhand Madness": Much of one's success in badminton and other racquet sports is determined by the strength or weakness of the backhand. How many **collective** backhands can you and a partner score in 60 seconds? Only backhand strokes are counted. Vocalize each legal stroke and try to beat your total on the next round.

With a partner, list five courtesies that make the game more enjoyable.

You and your doubles partner are both right-handed. Opponents continually take advantage of your partner's weak backhand. What strategies can you implement to strengthen your game?

When does a person's heart start beating? *Answer:* **Six months before he or she is born.**

UNIT: BADMINTON (LESSON 2)

Objectives:

- Refine short and long service skills.
- Know basic singles and doubles offensive strategies.
- Execute consistent high clears.
- Learn the forehand and backhand net drops.

WARM-UP: THREE 10-SECOND SPEED JUMP-ROPE TRIALS

Practice:

INDIVIDUAL

- Distribute one racket, bird, and hoop to each student.
- The serve for singles is usually high and deep while the doubles serve is short and low.
- Face your hoop 20 feet back. With a forehand grip (body sideways to the hoop) work on serving toward the target hoop. As soon as you hit inside, take a step back. Repeat this backward movement each time your bird touches or lands within the boundaries. When serving, concentrate on having the weight on the back foot, with contact made below the waist line.

PARTNERS

- "Fit to Serve." Distribute three birds per player. Place both hoops 20 feet away and three feet apart. Challenge your partner to see who can place three birds in the hoop first. Encourage students to **run** between the service line and hoops. Move the hoops 15 feet apart.
- This time, partners cooperate by serving **diagonally,** alternating hoops and service lines after each serve. Which set of partners can serve all six birds in the hoops first?
- Place hoops on the short service lines. Partner #1 serves and #2 attempts to place it inside his or her partner's hoop. Alternate. Are you as accurate utilizing a backhand stroke?
- "Royal Rally." Royal Rallies are long in duration and feature clears, drives, and drop shots. Work on **running** your partner. When he or she is up—push him or her back. When back, execute a drop shot.

GROUP

- Place three hoops between the end lines of each court. Players stand in front of the hoops (near mid-court) and execute high clears on any bird hit in front of them toward the opposite hoops. Birds landing inside hoops remain until one side scores three points. Work on both forehand and backhand strokes.

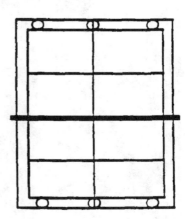

"Consecutive Cooperative Clears": In groups of three, see how many wall rebounds your group can clear in a row. Try this from a single-file line rotating to your left after each hit. If your group can hit five or more forehands in a row, try backhands.

What are three prerequisites for a good badminton player?

(Quickness, agility, coordination, reaction time)

-
-
-

Watch a classmate who is consistently able to run others about the court. Analyze what attributes or skills this person possesses.

What's another term for a badminton bird? *Answer:* **Shuttlecock.**

Wednesday
HIP-TO-BE-FIT FITNESS CIRCUIT

	FITNESS COMPONENTS	ACTIVITY	DESCRIPTION	RESOURCE
1	Upper Arm Strength	ROPE ROUTINES	Practice supporting your weight when: • Arms are bent • Legs are extended • Feet are above head • Legs do all the work	
2	Power & Reaction Time	JUMP BALL	Take turns tossing a basketball upwards and try to gain control.	
3	Coordination	UP and DOWN	Partner #1 passes a bounce pass to #2, and #2 performs a chest pass at the same time (10 to 15 feet apart).	
4	Upper Arm Strength	PUSH APART	Sit facing (cross-legged) on a scooter. Push each other apart using only your arms. Mark the distance.	
5	Coordination	CONTINUOUS CROSSES	Challenge your partner to a consecutive jump rope cross contest.	
6	Balance	TWIN TUBE BALANCE	Who can balance the longest on the thick carpet core?	
7	Endurance	BACKWARD LAPS	Complete three backward laps around the gym. Following the third lap, score a point for every forward lap you can complete.	
8	Coordination	BALOON TAP	Sitting on scooters, partners attempt to move a balloon (without touching the floor) across the gym using only the feet.	
9	Arm & Leg Strength	POWER PULL	Partners straddle a line, place outside of right feet together, grasp right hands, and attempt to pull each other over the line.	
10	Upper Arm Strength	UP TOGETHER	Sit facing (feet together), knees bent, grasp the dowel and try to pull each other up to a stand.	

WEEKLY TEST

UNIT: BADMINTON (LESSON 3)

Objectives:

- Practice short low serves.
- Increase backhand proficiency.
- Learn the overhand smash.

WARM-UP: LONG RUN FOR PLACE

Practice:

INDIVIDUAL

- Distribute a racket, bird, and hoop to each student.
- Stand your hoop against the wall and take ten steps back. Strike the bird straight up (underhand) and smash it downward at the hoop. How many times can you hit your target in ten tries? Repeat three trials. What was your best score? Remember to contact the bird in front of you.

PARTNERS

- How many backhand exchanges can you and a partner make in a row? Work on accuracy. Play a game to five points using **backhand strokes only.**
- Display a poster with the following skills and have each student work on these sequences.

Partner #1	Partner #2	Partner #1
Short low serve	Overhead clear	Smash
Long serve	Overhand clear	Underhand drop shot
Long serve	Drive to forehand side	Forehand drop shot
Short serve	Drive to backhand side	Backhand net drop

*Partners switch and repeat.

GROUP

- "Six Birds in a Nest." Arrange students in groups of three. Stand and form one foldable mat in the shape of a tube or square (nest) 20 feet from the service line. Distribute six birds per group. Following the signal to begin, groups execute high deep serves toward the targeted nest. Birds missing the nest must be retrieved by the server and returned to the service line. A point may be awarded to the group that serves all its birds into the nest first, or have the most in the target after one minute.

Practice a **shadow** game with a partner. One partner is the leader and one is the shadow (stands behind). The shadow stands a few yards away and attempts to duplicate each movement of the leader. Concentrate on good form and switch after 30 seconds.

A principle of force in badminton is **the greater the distance over which force is applied, the greater the momentum that can be generated.** What does this mean? (Use as much as possible when contacting the bird.)

Begin a rally and emphasize low drives. Why is it a good strategy to keep the bird low?

_____

_____

What are some other badminton strategies?

How many muscles does it take to smile?
Answer: **15**   Frown? *Answer:* **43.**

PHYSICAL EDUCATION CONTRACT

Name _Sue Schultz_

Class _Turner_

During the next ___2___ weeks, I will work on accomplishing . . .

Serving accuracy in badminton.

I will be able to serve 7-10 birds into a 36" hoop

from 15' away

I will need the following equipment . . .

Racquet, birds, net, hula hoop.

Teacher Approval _M. Nm_   Date _4/13_

Progress—Week one _Four of ten_

Progress—Week two _You made it — Good job (8-10)_

Progress—Week three _____

Goal Accomplished _✓_   Not Accomplished _____

Teacher Comments:

Nice effort.

_A_

Graded _✓_   Non-Graded _____

ALL★STAR
MOTIVATOR

 "ULTIMATE BADMINTON"

Directions

Form groups of three to five on an outside field. Distribute racquets and one bird to each team.

Can your group move the bird across the field:

- without a drop?
- with the bird traveling forward only?
- with each player contacting it a minimum of three times?
- with the bird contacted in a particular sequence?
- while racing another team?

Next, see if you can move your bird across while a second team attempts to intercept. If the bird hits the ground, the team striking it last loses possession.

ALL★STAR
MOTIVATOR

 ## "OVER THE LINE"

Too often schools have too few courts for too large classes. Many of the skills practiced over the nets can be performed off of walls. Simply place a piece of masking tape vertically 8´, 10˝ high on a wall. With partners 10 feet apart practice volleying the bird back and forth using forehand and backhand strokes.

ALL☆STAR
MOTIVATOR

 ## "BADMINTON GOLF"

This badminton serving motivator works like regular golf. Students count their strokes as they progress from one hole (wastepaper baskets or hoops) to the next. Birds must remain inside the target to score. Targets are placed in a large circle about 10 to 15 yards apart. Two students are placed at each hole on an 18-hole course. Rotation can be clockwise or counterclockwise.

VARIATION: Designate underhand or overhand strokes at odd-numbered holes.

ALL★STAR
MOTIVATOR

 ## "UP YOUR ALLEY"

Directions: Stroke accuracy in badminton and other racquet sports is a major determinant of success. Choose a partner, and stand 15 feet apart. Distribute racquets and birds. (If there are not enough courts available, tape alleys 20 feet long and 1-1/2 feet wide.) How many of the following skills can you check off in the time provided?

Yes

- Rally 10 consecutive birds back and forth with at least one foot inside the alley.   _____

- Hit 10 consecutive returns with both feet in the alley.   _____

- Stroke 10 consecutive backhand shots with both feet inside.   _____

- Exchange 10 consecutive shots inside while 20 to 25 feet apart.   _____

*__Consecutive__ also denotes collective. To achieve 10, each partner has to do five.

ALL★STAR MOTIVATOR

☆ "BADMINTON BASKETBALL"

The ability to perform a consistent accurate **long serve** is integral to success in badminton. Standing behind the key circle, how many birds can you contact off the backboard in a row? Can you put one through the hoop?

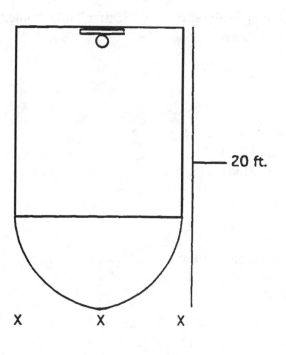

20 ft.

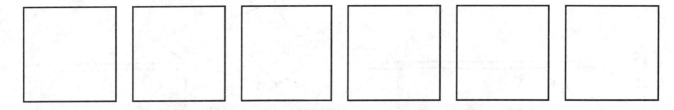

*B*asketball

PRE-GAME PLAN

"Aptitude, plus attitude determines altitude."
—Anonymous

While soccer is considered the world's most popular sport, the truly American game of basketball continues to consume the interest of middle and high school students. This section focuses on individual and partner skills with a variety of challenging lead-up activities.

HIGHLIGHTS

M   Practice ball control activities, play "Penny Push" and "Tic-Tac-Toe Basketball."
T   Refine ball control skills, play "Blanket Basketball" and "Basketball Golf."
W   New Hip-To-Be-Fit circuit, Agility Test.
Th   Increase shooting proficiency, play "Scatter," take home "Beat the Clock" homework.
F   Contracts.

BENEFITS

- Inexpensive.
- Highly aerobic.
- Play individually or in small groups.

RESOURCES

Amateur Athletic Union of the United States
231 West 58th Street
New York, NY 10019

CONTRIBUTOR

Gary Adrian
Islander Middle School
Mercer Island, WA

UNIT: BASKETBALL (LESSON 1)

Objectives:

- Practice
- Improve chest pass proficiency
- Increase free throw accuracy

WARM-UP: "50"

Practice

Arm Circles

INDIVIDUAL

Work on the following ball-control activities:
- Find a line on the floor and work on dribbling the ball close to the line using a wrist-fingertip action. Crossover (hand to hand) on each bounce.
- Dribble the ball through and around each leg using both dribbling hands.
- With your legs in a (stationary) scissor position, can you bounce the ball back and forth from side to side? Can you bounce the ball between each time you take a step forward?
- Are you able to roll the ball from one arm, across your chest, up the other arm completing the circle? How many circles can you complete without stopping the ball?
- With legs apart, toss the ball through and catch behind, flip the ball over your head and repeat this process. How quickly can you accomplish this?

Penny Push

PARTNERS

- With partners some 15 feet apart, work on exchanging the ball using a chest bounce pass.
- How many exchanges can the two of you make in 30 seconds? Repeat without the bounce.
- Place a penny between partners and work on moving the penny toward your partner using a chest bounce pass.
- (Two balls) Practice alternating chest and chest bounce passes.
- (Two and one) Have one partner toss two balls on a bounce while the opposite partner passes his or her ball between with a chest pass.

GROUP

- "Tic-Tac-Toe": Participants divide into two even teams (X's and O's). A taped or cardboard grid is placed behind the foul line, and four same-colored beanbags are provided for each team. Following the signal to begin, the first player in each line shoots from behind the foul line, retrieves the ball, passes to the next player, and moves to the end of his or her line. Players making baskets place one of their team markers on the grid. The goal for each team is to place three markers in a row (Tic-Tac-Toe). When this occurs, a new game begins.

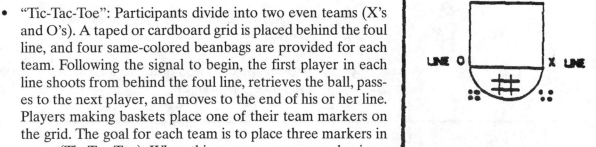

COOPERATIVE

If a standard basketball court is _____ feet long, guesstimate **how many students** it would take to lay head to foot from baseline to baseline.

INTERDISCIPLINARY

A line from an Ambrose Brazelton poem entitled "Why Must They Always Lose?" reads, **"some poor slob will be picked last, why must they always lose?"**

Devise five new ways to select teams equitably.

Critical Thinking

How can you equate losing a game with growing as an athlete?

TRIVIA

What's the diameter of a basketball hoop?
Answer: **18"**

What's the diameter of a regulation ball?
Answer: **9"**

How many balls would fit into a hoop at one time? *Answer:* **2.**

UNIT: BASKETBALL (LESSON 2)

Objectives:

- Practice ball-control activities
- Increase shooting range and accuracy
- Cooperate with a partner

WARM-UP: THREE 10-SECOND SPEED JUMP-ROPE TRIALS

Practice

INDIVIDUAL

Work on the following ball-control activities:

- From a sitting position with legs apart, practice dribbling the ball over each leg and around your back. How fast can you accomplish this circle without losing control? Change directions. Can you stand up and maintain the dribble?
- On the signal, see how quickly you can dribble, touch four walls, and return to your starting spot.
- This time, make two baskets before you return.
- Spin your ball on the floor and see if you can pick it up on one finger and continue the spin.

PARTNERS

- Partner #1 stands with legs apart facing partner #2. All #1s begin performing slow jumping jacks while the #2s attempt to dribble between as many different jumpers' legs as possible in 60 seconds. Alternate and see which partner can dribble between the most legs.

Partner Spin

- Standing back-to-back at mid-court, see who can dribble to the opposite wall and back three times.
- (Jump Ball) Alternate tossing the ball upwards, jumping and gaining control.
- Take turns working on controlling two balls. How fancy can you be?
- Can you bounce a ball in each hand, make a full turn, and regain the dribble?
- Have one partner hold a ball in two hands. Partner #2 spins his or her ball and carefully places it on top of the stationary ball. Are you able to maintain the spin?
- How long can you keep three balls bouncing?
- (Sack Ball) Place a paper grocery bag over one partner's head. Taking only verbal cues, this player attempts to dribble to the closest basket and score.

GROUP

- "Golf": Shooters shoot from each spot until they make it. Record the number of shots it takes on the form to the right.

  Eagle = 2 under par

  Birdy = 1 under par

  Bogey = 1 over par

  Double Bogey = 2 over par

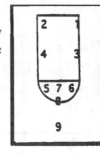

"Blanket Basketball": Organize students in groups of three to six around a blanket or tablecloth. Place a basketball in the middle of that cloth and coordinate blanket throws toward the rim.

Scoring
Backboard = 1 point
Rim = 2 points
Goal = 3 points

Which team can score 25 points first?

Cut out the box score from an NBA or college basketball game. Pretend you are a coach and this team is your next opponent. What would you do to prepare your team for this game?

You have been hired as a summer recreation assistant. Develop a unique process for teaching primary students (ages 6 to 8) one important basketball rule.

What's one way your body heats itself when cold? *Answer:* **Shivering. Your muscles contract and relax quickly, converting stored muscle energy into body heat.**

Wednesday
HIP-TO-BE-FIT FITNESS CIRCUIT

	FITNESS COMPONENTS	ACTIVITY	DESCRIPTION	RESOURCE
1	Upper Arm Strength	HEADS UP	Partners (facing) attempt to perform push-ups with a ball balanced between heads.	
2	Balance	PLAY BALL	• Can you balance on top? • Can you walk on the ball? • Push against a partner.	Marty Gilman Inc. Wa. Rep. 1-800-556-7464
3	Muscular Endurance	CHAIR CRUNCHERS	With feet on the chair practice quick "half" sit-ups.	
4	Speed Endurance	FAR WALL TOUCH	How many walls can you touch in 60 seconds?	
5	Upper Arm Strength	SNAP R BALL	How many exchanges can you make?	Flaghouse 1-800-793-7900
6	Reaction Time	penny catch	Place a penny on your elbow, lower hand and catch. Add a penny after each catch.	
7	Flexibility	YOGA BOW, PLOW	Practice stretching slowly while on your stomach. Grab your ankles and rock forward and backward.	*Yoga for Children* Warner Books
8	Agility	FOOT FENCING	With blade (plastic hockey stick) in hand try to touch your partner's toes.	
9	Leg Strength	RESISTANCE RUN	Loop a bicycle inner tube on the outside knob of a door and jog until you feel the pull.	
10	Endurance	JOGGER	Perform a slow non-stop jog.	Flaghouse 1-800-793-7900

WEEKLY TEST

UNIT: BASKETBALL (LESSON 3)

Objectives:

- Improve ball control skills
- Practice modified game situations
- Increase free throw and lay-in proficiency

WARM-UP: LONG RUN FOR PLACE

Practice

INDIVIDUAL

- Work on the following ball-control activities:

Wall Sit-up With Pass

Straddle Catch

Circle 8

- "V-bounce." Practice bouncing the ball with one hand in a V pattern. If you can do this in front, try it on each side as well as behind the back.

PARTNERS

- (Modified one on one). Partners face each other three feet apart. Following the start signal, the partner with the ball begins dribbling to any open basket. The defensive player attempts to steal the ball without fouling. If a shot is missed, the rebounding player may shoot at that goal or dribble to another. Once a basket is scored, play stops and both players return to their original starting positions. The player who scored gives the ball up and play resumes. Who can score ten points first?

- Place a ball between foreheads. Can you both bend down, touch a knee, and stand up without losing control? Can the two of you make a full turn when the ball is between backs? Stomachs? Heads?

GROUP

- "Fives": The goal in "Fives" is for each team member to make a shot from behind the foul line. The game begins with each player positioned close to the basket. As soon as their close-in shot is made, they quickly assemble in a single line behind the foul line. The first player in line shoots. If he or she makes it, all players return to a close-in range, shoot until each player scores, and return to the foul line. This same process occurs when the foul shot is missed. All shooters who score move to the end of the foul line and do not shoot foul shots again. The game ends when each player has scored from the foul line.

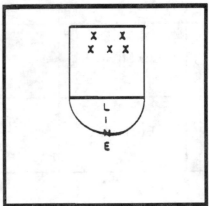

Ask a friend what will improve a specific aspect of your game and design a related skill.

Design and illustrate a piece of equipment that will make the game of basketball easier for young students.

On paper, select your squad's best player for each of the five basketball positions and tell why you made your selection.

How many people in the United States die from heart attacks each year? *Answer:* **1 million.**

PHYSICAL EDUCATION CONTRACT

Name _Matt Simpson_

Class _Team Spts. — 5th per._

During the next ___2___ weeks, I will work on accomplishing . . .

Making my age (15) in consecutive free throws.

I will need the following equipment . . .

One basketball

Teacher Approval _J. T. Nelson_ Date _1/25_

Progress—Week one _Short period — made 6 in a row_

Progress—Week two _Surpassed initial goal with 16 straight shots_

Progress—Week three _____

Goal Accomplished ___X___ Not Accomplished _____

Teacher Comments:

I knew you could do it.

Nelson

Graded ___✓___ Non-Graded _____

38

ALL STAR
MOTIVATOR

"BASKETBALL TOP GUN"

In order to qualify as a "TOP GUN," students must achieve each of the following skills within a 15-minute time frame. Each skill must be accomplished in sequence.

1. Make 9 out of 10 from any distance. _____

2. Make 6 out of 10 foul shots. _____

3. Make 3 consecutive shots with the non-dominant hand. _____

4. Make 5 consecutive baskets from outside the lane lines. _____

5. Make 1 basket from the top of the key. _____

6. Make 3 jump shots in a row. _____

7. Make a left hand and right hand hook shot. _____

8. While on the run make 3 shots in a row. _____

9. Make 3 bank shots in a row—one with the non-dominant hand. _____

10. Spin the ball on a finger for 5 seconds. _____

Gary Adrian—Islander Middle School, Mercer Island, WA

ALL★STAR
MOTIVATOR

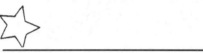

_____

Record your daily scores in the appropriate space and see how close you can come to the pro score below.

NAME_____

ROOM_____ Month_____

| BEAT THE CLOCK |
| ONE MINUTE BASKETBALL SHOOTING DRILLS |

Year_____

SUNDAY	MONDAY	TUESDAY	WEDNESDAY	THURSDAY	FRIDAY	SATURDAY
Hustle Shots Lay-up—run to foul line—return	Left Hand Lay-Up Stationary	Right Hand Lay-Up Stationary	Alternating Sides Lay-ups from right hand right side, left hand left side	Foul Shots (15 feet) Rebound-repeat	Cross Lane shots Alternate sides of lane line shooting one yard off line	Side-to-Side Shots Alternate sides following each shot from between corner of foul line and corner of court
Pro Score: 16	47	47	45	10	20	20

Courtesy of _Home Court Advantage_ by DeVenzio and Greene
Concept Sports Publications, Inc., P.O. Box 490056, College Park, GA 30349

ALL STAR MOTIVATOR

 ## "SCATTER"

Place students in lines of three behind the foul line at each available goal. (If goals are limited, more than one group can share a space.) Distribute one ball per group. Designate a penalty wall or cone about 50 to 70 feet away from each goal.

Following a signal to begin, the first person in each line shoots from behind the foul line. If the shot is missed, that person retrieves the ball, passes to the next player, and moves quickly to the end of the line. If the basket is made, non-shooting players SCATTER, touch the penalty wall or cone and try to return before a second shot is made. Each time a basket is made, players SCATTER.

Gary Adrian—Mercer Island School District, Mercer Island, WA

ALL★STAR MOTIVATOR

 ## "BINGO BASKETBALL"

Skills:	Shooting
Equipment:	One basketball per group
	One score card (same) per group
	Means of drawing numbers
Number of Players:	Any number per team
	One team per basket
Set-Up:	Each basket is marked with five different shooting areas.
	Mark each shooting area with a letter.

SHOOTING AREAS

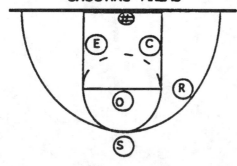

SCORE CARD

Basketball Bingo				
s	c	o	r	e
2	25	15	6	17
4	20	12	7	22
3	18	free	8	19
1	23	11	5	21
5	16	13	10	24

Rules:

- Draw a letter and number (for example, C-16), and read aloud to the class.
- Each team lines up single file behind the letter (C).
- On the signal, the players shoot in turn from behind the (C). Each player gets his/her own rebound and returns to the end of the line.
- The first team scoring 16 baskets may cover the C-16 space on its score card.
- The winner is the first team to cover five numbers in a row (horizontally, vertically, or diagonally).

Gary Adrian—Mercer Island School District, Mercer Island, WA

42

ALL STAR MOTIVATOR

"BEAT MR. ED" (INDIVIDUALIZED H.O.R.S.E.)

"Mr. Ed" is one of the greatest "trash talking" trick shot artists around. Take one shot at each of the following tricks. If you make the first shot, Mr. Ed has (H). If you miss, give yourself (H). Whoever records H.O.R.S.E. first, loses.

Tricks	Mr. Ed	You
1. Toss and "head" the ball in off the backboard.	_____ H	_____
2. Bounce it in off the floor.	_____ O	_____
3. Toss with both hands behind your back.	_____ R	_____
4. Use non-dominant hand from foul line.	_____ S	_____
5. Shoot a hook shot from a lane line.	_____ E	_____

(Game #1)

6. Release under one leg and score.	_____ H	_____
7. Score **off** the backboard from the end of the key.	_____ O	_____
8. Do a two-hand, underhand "nothing but net" shot from a lane line.	_____ R	_____
9. Toss **off** the backboard and tip it in with one hand.	_____ S	_____
10. Make a foul shot with eyes closed.	_____ E	_____

(Game #2)

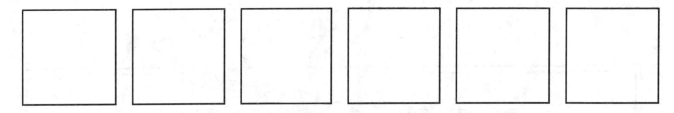

*B*owling

PRE-GAME PLAN

> "Enthusiasm is the electricity of life. How do you get it? You act enthusiastic till you make it happen."
> —*Gordon Parks*

Bowling continues to be a popular lifetime sport. With the addition of three-hole rubber bowling balls, authentic plastic pins and roll-down lane strips, the activity is adaptable to nearly any school facility. Many districts across the nation are taking advantage of the **In-School Bowling Program** sponsored by the bowling proprietors of America.

HIGHLIGHTS

M   Practice pendulum delivery and three-finger release, and play "Bowling Relay."

T   Perform one-step delivery, play "One Roll Bowl" and "Bingo Bowling."

W   New Hip-To-Be-Fit circuit, Arm Strength Test.

Th   Learn the four-step delivery, scoring procedures, and analyze partners' form, play "Clean-Up."

F   Contracts.

BENEFITS

- Accessible for special populations.
- Lifetime activity.
- Sex equitable.
- Adaptable to small spaces.

RESOURCES

Port-A-Bowl U.S.A.
192 3rd Dr. S.E.
Bothell, WA 98012

CONTRIBUTOR

Robert Rea
Port-A-Bowl

UNIT: BOWLING (LESSON 1)

Objectives:

- Learn pendulum swing-arm action.
- Know how to execute three-part finger release.
- Understand importance of good balance.

WARM-UP: "50"

Practice

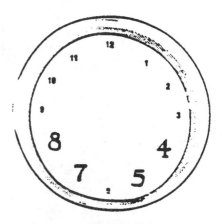

INDIVIDUAL

- Arrange students in a space where they can swing arms freely. Students assume a staggered foot position (raise hand you bowl with, move same foot back 6 to 8 inches, and relax bowling arm to side.) Practice push-relax method. *Teacher: Cut the appropriate fingers (middle, ring, thumb) out of a glove. These are the fingers used to grip the ball.

PARTNERS

- Place partners 10 to 15 feet apart. Pass out one softball and one clock per student. Students assume a kneeling position (righthanders—right knee, lefthanders—left knee).
- Set the paper clocks on the floor directly beneath the bowling arm. Softballs are placed in the middle of the clock. Fingers go on the highlighted numbers (4 and 5 righthanders, 7 and 8 left-handers).
- Slide fingers under the ball, pick it up, and practice rolling toward your partner's clock.
- How many direct hits can you make on your partner's target in a row?
- From the kneeling position (without changing feet), stand up, place a pin on your clock, and practice rolling balls at your partner's pin. How many out of ten can you hit?
- Are you as successful when moving an additional ten feet apart?

GROUP

- "Bowling Relay": Class begins with lanes set up with only the number 1 pin standing.
- The first bowler receives one delivery to knock over the number 1 pin. If that delivery is successful, students rotate and the next bowler gets a chance to knock over the number 1 pin AND the number 2 pin. If that delivery is successful, students rotate and the next bowler gets a chance to knock over the number 1 pin, the number 2 pin, AND the number 3 pin.
- This continues until all ten pins are set up and knocked over. The first team to complete this team relay is declared the "**pros for the day**."
- If, on a delivery, the student misses the pins standing, the team rotates and the next bowler must try to knock down the same amount of pins.

Port-A-Bowl U.S.A., 1993
This fun activity comes to us from Ken Ericson, P.E. Specialist from Bellingham, Washington. Since emphasis is on the bowler being accurate, good technique is maintained throughout.

Place two pins three feet apart. How many **consecutive** balls can your group roll between the pins without touching?

Abraham Lincoln was the first prominent American to spend time at bowling lanes. Write a short story describing how Abe might have promoted bowling as this country's first national sport. **Spare no details!**

What is your average after three games? Find someone who has a similar average and challenge him/her to a game.

How many bowling balls does it take to make a spare? *Answer:* **2.**

UNIT: BOWLING (LESSON 2)

Objectives:

- Learn one-step delivery into a balance position.
- Improve bowling accuracy.
- Know class rotation procedure.

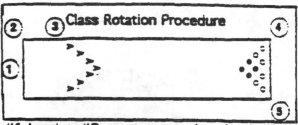

Class Rotation Procedure

#1 bowler, #2 spotter- watches for fouls, helps with form, and assists scorer. #3 scorer, #4 pin setter, #5 ball returner. Rotate clockwise.

WARM-UP: THREE 10-SECOND SPEED JUMP-ROPE TRIALS

Practice

INDIVIDUAL

- *Teacher: Teach the one-step delivery (feet together, knees bent, bowling arm relaxed at side, non-bowling arm extended outward, heel raised of sliding foot, take two practice swings and release on second swing). Remember to step forward and finish in a balanced position.
- Place 4 to 10 pins at the end of each modified lane.
- How many pins can you knock down with two deliveries?
- Work on "freezing" your balance at the end of each sequence.
- Practice a new rotation after each bowler's turn.

One step delivery

STARTING POSITION

Heel Up

PARTNERS

- In groups of two, challenge a neighboring lane to a game of "Five Strikes." The first group accumulating five strikes sits down.

GROUP

- "Bingo Bowling":
  Modifications:
  - Individual, partner, team.
  - Four corners.
  - Picture frame.
  - Strike (x) Spare (/).

"BINGO" BOWLING

Rules:
1. Bowler rolls first and second ball. Ball #1 knocks down 6 pins: Ball #2 knocks down 2 pins.
2. Bowler may mark off a "6" and a "2": or an "8".
3. To score a "0", bowler must roll ball on lane and miss all remaining pins. Any ball rolled off the lane cancels any and All pins for that frame.

Name _____

7	9	10	0	1
1	5	2	8	4
4	10	■	10	3
0	3	6	8	7
6	10	9	5	2

©1990 Port-A-Bowl, U.S.A.

"One Roll Bowl": Line up 20 to 30 pins across each end line. Two teams line up back to back at mid-court facing their pins. Following a signal to begin, each player rolls his or her rubber ball, soccer ball, or basketball at the standing pins. Points are awarded to the team knocking down the greater number of pins. Replace and repeat.

The manager of a new bowling alley has hired you to create a RULES OF CONDUCT sign for the front door. What would it say?

Bowling Etiquette
•
•
•
•
•
Larson Lanes

What are some considerations when selecting a bowling ball?

How many pounds of food does the average person eat over a 24-hour period? One? Two? Three? *Answer:* **Three.**

Wednesday
HIP-TO-BE-FIT FITNESS CIRCUIT

	FITNESS COMPONENTS	ACTIVITY	DESCRIPTION	RESOURCE
1	Balance	SNAKE BOARD	Move across the floor in circles and straight lines.	Rendezvous Trading Co. Jerry Merz (206) 780-1220
2	Endurance	SLIDE BOARD	Work on performing a cross-over slide from side to side.	Flaghouse 1-800-793-7900
3	Upper Arm Strength	ROPE EXCHANGE	Change ropes with a partner without touching the ground.	
4	Agility	DOUBLE JOGGER	How many joggers can you jump onto in the time provided?	Flaghouse 1-800-793-7900
5	Muscular endurance and coordination	WALL BALL SIT-UPS	With feet against the wall and shoulders to the floor, toss ball to wall, sit up and catch.	
6	Upper Arm Strength	HEAVY ROPES	How many jumps can you perform in the time provided?	Sportime 1-800-283-5700
7	Upper Arm Strength	EXER WHEEL	Start from knees and try to fully extend to a push-up position.	
8	Endurance	CROSS COUNTRY SKI	Practice a skating motion with cut-out rug samples.	
9	Upper Arm Strength	STICK PULL UP	Feet together, hands held in a sitting position, try to pull your partner up.	
10	Agility	AGILITY SPOTS	Hop out the following pattern ••• •• •	

WEEKLY TEST

UNIT: BOWLING (LESSON 3)

Objectives:

- Learn foot pattern and arm swing.
- Find individual starting position.
- Practice four-step delivery.

WARM-UP: LONG RUN FOR PLACE

Practice

INDIVIDUAL

- Assign students to lanes in groups of 5 to 6 and work on "out-down-swing-and-relax method." (Step Pattern) Without a bowling ball, have students mime the four-step pattern. Steps should be in a SHUFFLING style.

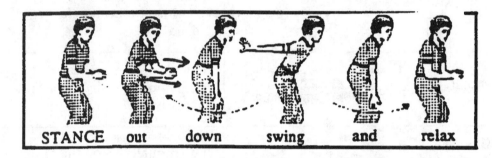

STANCE   out   down   swing   and   relax

- Take 4-1/2 steps back from the foul line and find your starting position. Pick up a ball and practice delivering your ball toward the pins utilizing this approach.
- (Tip) Ball and lead foot move together to begin the four-step delivery.

PARTNERS

- (Peer Tutoring) Partner #1 checks off #2 on the following skills.
  a. Push-away **ball and foot together.**
  b. Pendulum swing (finish balanced).
  c. Follow-through (like answering the telephone).

- "Clean-Up": Partner #1 bowls and partner #2 attempts to pick up any remaining pins. Your combined score from the two deliveries is recorded. If a strike is scored, the second bowler is allowed one throw and the two scores are added together for that frame.

10	5
	15

TOTAL

GROUP

- "Make That Spare": Use a deck of cards and deal 2. (Face cards equal ten.) If bowler #1 draws a 6 and a 5, those pins are set up and #1 tries to knock them down with one delivery.

50

Working in partners, place three pins one foot apart and 30 feet away. Each partner rolls his or her ball at the same time, trying to hit the **outside pins only.** Outside pins count one point while the middle pins carry a minus value. How many cooperative rolls does it take to score 10 points?

Score the following game.

1	2	3	4	5	6	7	8	9	10
4 2	8 1	F 6	8 —	7 /	6 2	0 9	5 3	9 /	4 1

SOLUTION

1	2	3	4	5	6	7	8	9	10
4 2	8 1	F 6	8 —	7 /	6 2	0 9	5 3	9 /	4 1
6	15	21	29	45	53	62	70	84	89

Create a new bowling game that has ties to a traditional team sport.

How much of your body is made up of water? *Answer:* **65%.**

PHYSICAL EDUCATION CONTRACT

Name _Katie Spencer_

Class _1st - Frasier_

During the next _____3_____ weeks, I will work on accomplishing . . .

Scoring 200 in at least one game in our
1st period bowling class.

I will need the following equipment . . .

Shoes - ball - glove

Teacher Approval _M.A. Frasier_ Date _2/19_

Progress—Week one _Best Score 168_

Progress—Week two _"   " 171_

Progress—Week three _"   " 170_

Goal Accomplished_____ Not Accomplished _X_

Teacher Comments:

Good Scores, still need to work on footwork.
It will come. Frasier

Graded _✓_ Non-Graded _____

ALL STAR
MOTIVATOR

 ## "EXIT TESTS"

Exit Tests are designed as a means of quickly checking information covered in daily P.E. lessons. These informal evaluations are quick and easy for both teacher and student. The "test" can be given as students "exit" class; as they pass by the teacher, they demonstrate their understanding of a particular skill.

1. STUDENT TASK: Demonstrate the fingers used to hold/roll a bowling ball.

   PROPER STUDENT RESPONSE: Student should indicate the 'thumb' and the middle two 'fingers.'

2. STUDENT TASK: Demonstrate the 'free pendulum swing.'

   PROPER STUDENT RESPONSE: Demonstrate the movement of arm with the PUSH/RELAX motion.

3. STUDENT TASK: Demonstrate the proper 'balance' position.

   PROPER STUDENT RESPONSE: Student should assume this position.

4. STUDENT TASK: Demonstrate the proper 'follow through.'

   PROPER STUDENT RESPONSE: Student should show position where the bowling arm is bent at the elbow and hand is near ear (like answering the phone).

5. STUDENT TASK: Demonstrate proper 'stance.'

   PROPER STUDENT RESPONSE: 'Stance' should look like this picture.

6. STUDENT TASK: Demonstrate the proper 'pushaway' movement with ball and foot together.

   PROPER STUDENT RESPONSE: 'Pushaway' demonstration as in picture.

7. STUDENT TASK: Demonstrate the proper 'tempo steps' for a four-step delivery.

   PROPER STUDENT RESPONSE: 'Tempo step' demonstration as in picture.

"SPEED BOWLING"

This activity is designed to give students a "workout" while still having fun, and working in a cooperative environment.

1. You may have three or more bowlers at each lane.

2. Set a time limit of 5 to 7 minutes for 'speed' bowling.

3. The bowler gets two balls when it is his or her turn.

4. All bowlers are directed to use the same number of steps (4 steps, 1 step, or from the *balance position*).

5. Pins are not reset after the first ball unless a strike has been rolled.

6. The ball returner must sprint back to the bowler and hand it off for the next delivery. The bowler may not begin the approach until the ball returner is back by the pins and has touched the gym wall.

7. After returning the ball and touching the wall, the ball returner may help set up pins.

8. When the bowler has taken two deliveries, the team members rotate to their new positions for the next frame. They will move quickly!

9. Speed bowling "Team Champion" will be the team that knocks down the most pins in the allotted time.

"SPARE MASTER"

This is a fun way for students to develop spare shooting accuracy and reinforce bowling skills.

EQUIPMENT NEEDED: Playing cards (10) for each lane (cards: 1 (ace)–10 plus the Jack and King; the only card not used will be the Queen).

SCORING: If the bowler knocks down the spare on the first delivery = **3 points**
If the bowler knocks down the spare on two deliveries = **2 points**
If the bowler does not knock down the spare in two deliveries = **one point for any pins knocked over**

HOW TO PLAY: Bowler picks two cards from the playing deck.
The cards drawn determine the pins that are set up for the spare.
EXAMPLE: If a 5 and a 2 are drawn, the 5 pin and the 2 pin would be set up as the spare to bowl for.
The bowler gets two deliveries to convert the spare.

BONUS: If a bowler draws the **KING** as one of the cards, this is a BONUS.
The bowler can choose the pin that goes up as the second pin in the spare.

STRATEGY: The bowler should choose a pin as close as possible to the other pin drawn.

TROUBLE: If a bowler draws the **JACK** as one of the cards, this results in a **PENALTY. The bowler must pick two more cards and will now have a three-pin spare to bowl for.**

SCORING: A running total each frame will determine the final score for **Team** or **Individual.**

	2	1	3
2		**3**	**6**

Port-A-Bowl U.S.A. • 19230 3rd Dr. S.E. • Bothell, WA 98012 • 1-800-767-2695

ALL★STAR
MOTIVATOR

"SPELLING BEE 'BOWLING' "

"Spelling Bee 'bowling' " is a fun way to incorporate spelling into your bowling lesson. Use bowling vocabulary, names of muscles and bones, spelling words from the classroom, etc.

EQUIPMENT: Six sets of cards with letters of the alphabet, PLUS 3 of each commonly used letter; six sets of bowling equipment.

EXAMPLE: Using the word "Quadriceps"

- each lane has cards with the letters in 'quadriceps'
- for every strike the team may lay down two letters in the word
- for every spare the team may lay down one letter in the word
- no scoring is necessary
- the first team to spell the word wins that round
- a great way to teach spelling and spares and strikes

Kristen Bradley teaches at Jackson Park Elementary in the Bremerton (Washington) School District.

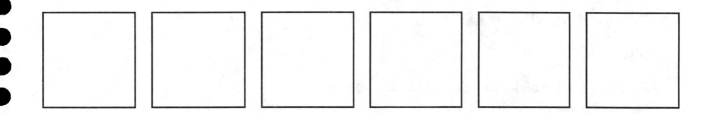

Conditioning

PRE-GAME PLAN

"You rest—you rust."

This unit serves as an introduction to lifelong conditioning and fitness. Activities included fall under the categories of upper arm strength, muscular endurance, flexibility, and cardiovascular endurance.

HIGHLIGHTS

M	Practice nontraditional fitness activities both individually and with a partner. Play "It's in the Cards" and take home a fitness motivator homework form.
T	Emphasize muscular endurance skills, figure out target heart rate, "Act Your Age" circuit.
W	New Hip-To-Be-Fit circuit, Muscular Endurance Test.
Th	Practice cardiovascular drills, play "Shadow" with a partner, attempt 1000 reps in 20 minutes.
F	Contracts.

BENEFITS

- Regular conditioning programs can improve appearance, energy, and self-esteem.
- Along with good nutrition, a planned conditioning program can help maintain wellness.
- Increase cardiovascular endurance, agility, speed, muscular strength, power, and flexibility.

UNIT: CONDITIONING (LESSON 1)

Objectives:

- Explore a variety of nontraditional fitness activities.
- Work cooperatively with a partner or small group.
- Perform activities emphasizing upper arm strength.

WARM-UP: "50"

Practice

- (One-minute circuit) How many repetitions can you accomplish?

INDIVIDUAL

- **Station—**
  1. What's your power jump score?
     Face board, reach up, take one step back, jump, and mark! The distance between the reach and jump is your score.
  2. Heavy rope jumps?
  3. Pull-ups/Flexed arm hang (sec.).
  4. Handstand push-ups.

PARTNERS

Push-up Tag: A.

Partner Pull-ups: B.

Who can score ten touches on partner's hand first?

Snap R. Ball: C.

One Arm Push-ups: D.

PARTNERS

GROUP

- "Do What You're Dealt!": Arrange students in groups of four or five. Select one student to deal the cards. This person will pass out cards to each team member. The dealer and other team members will complete the number of exercises marked on the cards drawn.

  HEARTS = Jumping jacks
  SPADES = Sit-ups
  CLUBS = Jump-rope jumps
  DIAMONDS = Push-ups

  (For example, six of hearts equals six jumping jacks)

  New hands cannot be dealt until all group members have completed their exercises. The activity ends when all cards have been dealt. Which group can complete the deck first?

"Cooperative Scream Race": Place teams of six in single formation lines in each available lane. Following a signal to begin, the first runner inhales and sprints forward screaming until that initial breath is out. The remaining "non-screaming" runners jog silently behind. When a screamer stops, he or she moves to the end of the line and the next screamer takes a deep breath and begins running. Which team can move the greatest distance after six collective screams?

Your recovery heart rate is the length of time your heart takes to return to normal following an exercise period. The higher your cardiovascular fitness level, the faster your heart rate will decrease following exercise.

What's your recovery rate?

A good indicator is, your heart rate should be below 120 beats per minute five minutes into recovery.

Source: *Lifetime Physical Fitness and Wellness, Hoeger & Hoeger, Morton Activity Series, 3rd. ed.*

Why is it unsafe to **bounce** while performing stretching exercises?

What are three ways to prevent a heart attack?
Answer: **Don't smoke, monitor fat intake, and exercise regularly.**

UNIT: CONDITIONING (LESSON 2)

Objectives:

- Practice muscular endurance and flexibility activities.
- Know that muscular endurance is how well your muscles can keep up with a particular activity.
- Know that flexibility is the ability to move joints and stretch muscles through a full range of motion.

WARM-UP: THREE 10-SECOND SPEED JUMP-ROPE TRIALS

Practice

INDIVIDUAL

- How many wall-ball sit-ups can you perform in 60 seconds?
- How far away from the wall can you be and still catch the rebound following a sit-up?

PARTNERS

- Facing a partner with a ball between you:

C
A   •Alternate sit-ups while exchanging the ball?
N
           •Reach over the ball to touch partner's hand?
   Y
           •Take the ball away while in a stretched position?
   O
   U?   •Place the ball between feet and touch the ground behind?

GROUP

- Divide the class in half. Group #1 performs either push-ups or sit-ups against a side wall while Group #2 runs the length of the gym touching each end wall as they go. After two minutes, the instructor calls time. Each group tallies its cooperative points (push-ups/sit-ups/wall touches) and groups switch places. Which group can score more collective points?

In groups of three, create a balance where all members are connected.

Research a sport that you and your family can participate in for a minimum of three times a week. What health-related fitness skills would be a product of this participation?

Why is **exercise** classified as **brain food**?

What is a proven method for safely losing body fat? *Answer:* **A program that combines aerobics and strength training may be best. If you have more muscle, you burn calories faster.**

Wednesday
HIP-TO-BE-FIT FITNESS CIRCUIT

	FITNESS COMPONENTS	ACTIVITY	DESCRIPTION	RESOURCE
1	Power/Reaction Time	TAKE CONTROL	Take turns forcibly bouncing a tennis ball straight up. The partner gaining control first scores a point.	
2	Coordination/ Reaction Time	DRIBBLE FLAG PULL	Give each partner a basketball and place 12″ to 18″ flags on hips or backsides. Partners attempt to dribble a ball and steal their partner's flag. (Limit the area in which to dribble.)	
3	Coordination	HEEL FLIP	Roll a tennis ball out in front of you. Jump, trap between heels, flip up, and catch behind. Which partner can score more points?	
4	Speed	SIDE WALL SLAP	Stand at mid-court with partners facing opposite directions. On "GO," partners run to each wall **slapping hands** as they pass. How many slaps can you accumulate?	
5	Upper Arm Strength	CROSS STRETCH	Partners face (three feet apart). Dynabands cross (right hand to right, left hand to left). Partners alternately stretch both bands back and to the side. Try from other positions.	
6	Flexibility	PARTNER STRETCH	Partners sit facing, hands held, legs apart, toes touching. Partner #1 slowly leans back and pulls #2 forward. How close can you get your chest to the floor?	
7	Power	JUMP TOGETHER	How many cooperative standing long jumps does it take to jump from one wall to the other? Partner #1 jumps out and freezes; partner #2 jumps from where his or her back heel lands.	
8	Coordination	BAG SHOWER	Take turns exchanging a beanbag at close distances. Each time you catch one, add another bag. What's the highest number of bags you can catch at a time?	
9	Leg Strength	IN&OUT	Partner #1 (inside) pushes legs out while #2 (outside) pushes legs in. Switch after 30 seconds.	
10	Flexibility/ Leg Strength	CARPET STRETCH	Stand on the slippery side of two carpet squares. Slide your feet in and out. Who can get their feet the farthest apart?	

WEEKLY TEST

UNIT: CONDITIONING (LESSON 3)

Objectives:

- Practice cardiovascular activities.
- Define cardiovascular endurance.
- Learn to racewalk.

Cardiovascular endurance is the ability of the lungs, heart, and blood vessels to deliver oxygen to the cells to meet the demands of prolonged activity.

WARM-UP: LONG RUN FOR PLACE

Practice

INDIVIDUAL

- How far can you travel in *100* steps? *1000*? How many steps does it take to cover a quarter mile? Give each student a marker.

PARTNERS

- "Shadow" select a partner. Designate partners as #1 or #2. Following the signal to begin, partner #1 tries to run away from #2. Meanwhile, #2 attempts to tag #1 as many times as possible before the stop signal is given. Points are awarded for each tag. After 15 to 20 seconds, the instructor calls **"freeze"** and both partners stop. Partner #2 reports the number of tags (points scored), partners reverse roles, the instructor says "go," and the process is repeated. The game ends after four rounds. This activity works well inside, or on a lined field outside.

GROUP

- Divide the class in half and distribute flags to one team. Flag carriers stuff them in a pocket, belt, or collar with the excess extending a minimum of 18 inches. Flags cannot be tied to other articles of clothing nor can they be guarded by the runner. Following the signal, the chase team attempts to capture and turn over to the instructor a predetermined number of the other team's flags; for example, the tenth flag collected stops the clock. Teams then change places. Boundary lines should be understood prior to beginning play.

Racewalking Work on the techniques below as you racewalk 100 yards. Quarter mile.

- Body remains upright (shoulders back and head erect).
- One foot always in contact with the ground.
- Hands swing back no further than buttocks, nor higher than mid-line of chest.
- Feet land in a straight line, hips turn with stride.

*The world racewalking record for a mile is around 5-1/2 minutes.

64

In groups of four, create a tag game where three of the players are holding hands.

Write a conditioning rap. (Sample)

"Feel the difference, look the feel. Working out makes the feeling real."

Write a paragraph explaining why young women usually score *higher* than young men in flexibility on nationally-normed fitness tests, but *lower* on upper-arm strength.

How many cells does your body contain: 10 million? 40 billion? 60 trillion? *Answer:* **60 trillion.**

PHYSICAL EDUCATION CONTRACT

Name _Jill Kimball_

Class _Conditioning 4th (Turner)_

During the next ____1____ weeks, I will work on accomplishing . . .

Do three complete overhand pull-ups.

I will need the following equipment . . .

Bar

Teacher Approval _Sue Finn_ Date _3/11_

Progress—Week one _Completed three overhand pull-ups_

Progress—Week two _n/a_

Progress—Week three _n/a_

Goal Accomplished ___X___ Not Accomplished _____

Teacher Comments:

"Great" — Let's move to five

Graded _____ Non-Graded ___✓___

ALL★STAR MOTIVATOR

"1,000 IN 20"

The goal in this high-energy activity is for each student to accomplish 1,000 repetitions while rotating with a partner through 20 one-minute stations. The circuit features a variety of traditional and nontraditional equipment. Students tally their successes following each experience. Activities can easily be substituted for when listed equipment is unavailable.

CIRCUIT	PARTNER #1	#2
1. 3–5 lbs. heavy rope turns.		
2. Spri or Dynaband (full extensions).		
3. Leg Slides (in/out) on a bath towel.		
4. Hula Hoop rotations.		
5. Hacky Sack kicks.		
6. Bench Steps.		
7. Lolo/Pogo Ball jumps.		
8. Basketball dribbles between legs.		
9. Pogo Stick bounces.		
10. Bar Hang (seconds).		
11. Wheel Chair rotations.		
12. Jogger Jumps.		
13. Backward rope skips.		
14. Basketball/or football partner passes (15–20 feet).		
15. Handstands (cumulative seconds in the air).		
16. Frisbee™ disc exchanges (15–20 feet).		
17. Tennis ball rebounds off a wall (15–20 feet back).		
18. Medicine Ball sit-up exchanges.		
19. Volleyball bumps or self sets.		
20. Juggling catches.		

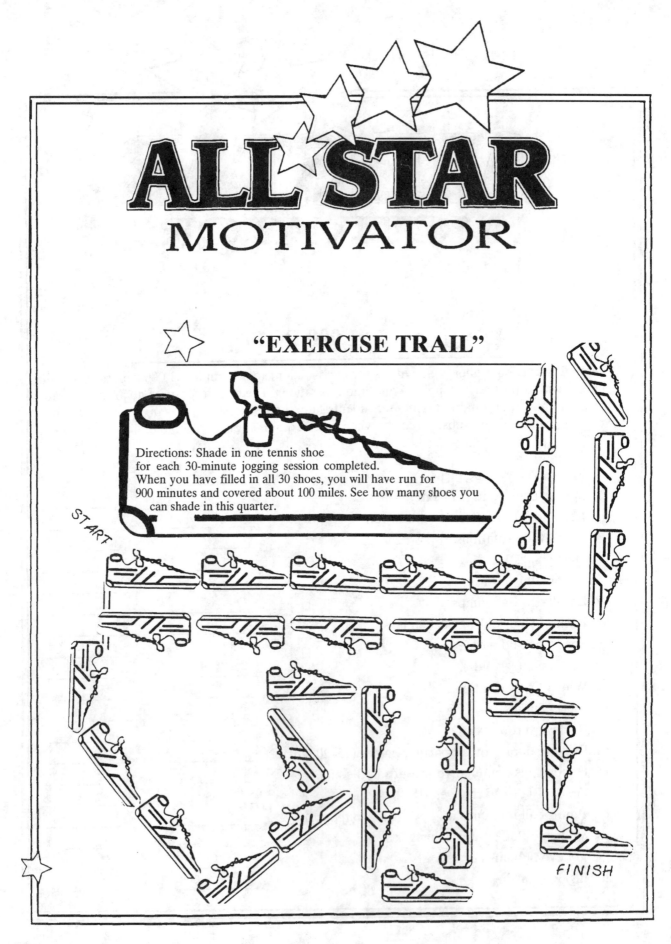

ALL★STAR MOTIVATOR

"EXERCISE TRAIL"

Directions: Shade in one tennis shoe for each 30-minute jogging session completed. When you have filled in all 30 shoes, you will have run for 900 minutes and covered about 100 miles. See how many shoes you can shade in this quarter.

START

FINISH

ALL STAR MOTIVATOR

 ## "IT'S IN THE CARDS"

Directions: *Hearts*   *Spades*   *Diamonds*   *Clubs*

- Get in groups of five and sit in a circle.
- Pass out decks of cards.
- Designate one student to be the dealer.
- Following the start signal, the dealers deal one card (face down) to each group member.
- Teams turn cards over and perform designated tasks.
- As the last group member completes his or her task, used cards are placed in the middle of the circle and new cards are dealt.
- *(Goal)* The first team completing the deck wins.

Equipment:

- 1 deck of cards, 3 jump ropes, 9 beanbags, 1 mat for each group.

Key:

Ace	=	Takes precedence over all other cards—entire group jogs the perimeter of the gym.
King	=	10 push-ups
Queen	=	10 high kicks
Jack	=	10 jumping jacks
Joker	=	10 cartwheels
Heart	=	That number of jump rope jumps
Spade	=	That number of curl-ups (sit-ups)
Diamond	=	That number of handstands
Club	=	That number of juggling throws
3 of a kind	=	Free pass for entire group—new cards dealt.

This idea is a modification of an idea shared by Chuck Ayers of the Bellingham (Washington) School District. 1987 WAHPERD Convention.

ALL★STAR
MOTIVATOR

 "ACT YOUR AGE"

Directions: Students attempt to **score their age** on each of the fifteen stations in less than ten minutes. Scores do not have to be consecutive but cumulative. If the appropriate score is not attained after two minutes, students may move ahead. A minimum of four items should be placed at each spot to eliminate waiting.

- Hang with your chin above the bar _____ seconds.
- Stroke a tennis ball off the wall _____ times.
- Jump a traffic cone _____ times.
- Kick a hacky sack _____ times.
- Pass a basketball through your legs and catch behind _____ times.
- Perform _____ cartwheels or round-offs.
- Juggle two or three balls _____ times.
- Score _____ baskets.
- Pitch a tennis ball into a 2′ x 2′ taped square _____ times (20′ back).
- Sprint from side wall to side wall _____ times.
- Self or wall set a volleyball _____ times.
- Jump rope _____ times.
- Strike a badminton bird upwards _____ times.
- Step up and off a double folded mat _____ times.
- Perform _____ sit-ups or push-ups.

ALL★STAR
MOTIVATOR

"FITNESS FREAKS"

FINISH LINE

FITNESS FREAK

BEGIN HERE

Fitness Freaks is a self-paced exercise program for students who want to move beyond regular school exercise experiences. Students chart their own daily progress by shading in the 200 15-minute cubes on the chart. Once 50 hours have been completed, they may turn their entries in for extra credit and purchase a school Fitness Freak shirt (at minimal student cost).

Any exercise completed outside of school is acceptable. Activities may include walking/jogging, skiing, skateboarding, skating, rowing, swimming, dancing, etc. The main ingredients for success are **simplicity, regularity,** and **enjoyment.**

ALL★STAR MOTIVATOR

 ## "TOWELICIZE"

INDIVIDUAL

- Sit with legs extended, loop a rolled towel between the toes and heels. Practice leaning back, extending the toes, and stretch.
- Repeat while lifting heels up to a 45° angle.
- From a standing position, hold the towel in each hand (6 to 10 inches apart). Work on pulling down with your left hand and up with your right. Switch hands. Try to hold each position for ten seconds.
- Grip the ends and roll the wrists inward.
- Place one toe on the end of the towel and pull out to the side. Switch sides.
- Lay the towel out flat and place both feet on top. See how fast you can slide across the floor without lifting a foot.
- Balance on one leg, place the towel behind one instep, and pull up slowly.
- What sport skills can you mimic with both hands on the towel? (racket strokes, batting, etc.)

PARTNERS

- Challenge a partner to a sliding race across the floor.
- Face your partner in a sitting position and hold one end. Work on alternating sit-ups.
- Who can pull the other over a line?
- Counter-balance.

GROUP

- Invent a tag (slide) game.
- Play a **slide** basketball game.

☆ "CALENDAR CALISTHENICS"

Calendar Calisthenics is a voluntary daily fitness supplement conducted outside of school. Calendars are placed on refrigerators or appropriate walls in the home, and homework checked off as completed. Daily tasks take from two to five minutes and exist merely as an extension of the regular exercise program. The box in the upper left-hand corner is for the date, while the box in the lower right is for checking off exercises completed. Small doses of creative exercises can move students toward more consistent exercise patterns.

	SUNDAY	MONDAY	TUESDAY	WEDNESDAY	THURSDAY	FRIDAY	SATURDAY
C O O R D I N A T I O N	ONE ARM DRIBBLE!	If you are looking good, you are feeling good.	FEBRUARY 1995 S M T W TH F S 1 2 3 4 5 6 7 8 9 10 11 12 13 14 15 16 17 18 19 20 21 22 23 24 25 26 27 28	While sitting (legs a-p-a-r-t), see how close you can lower your chest to the floor. GO SLOW! **1**	Practice your soccer skills. Head a ball or balloon just off your hairline. **2**	Baseball season is just around the cor-ner. Play catch for ten minutes. **3**	Bike, skate or jog a mile or more. Have a great weekend. **4**
	Practice bouncing a ball from a push-up position. (one arm) **5**	Organize a family arm-wrestling tournament **6** How did you do?	Jog in place for 5 minutes. Heart rate: Old_____ New_____ **7**	Try some elevated push-UPS while heels are on a chair. Next, with hands on a chair. **8**	Improve your best block run by 2 seconds. Before____ After____ **9**	Who in your family can do the most sit-ups in 60 seconds? **10**	Practice catching self-tossed balls ABove your your head. Try this outside. **11**
	Play a DON'T STEP on myTOE tag game. DON'T STEP ON MY TOES **12**	JOGAROUNDYOUR HOUSETENTIMES WHILELIFTING SOUPCANS. **13**	Time yourself - how many seconds does it take to run & touch: the fridge, front door, a sink, a closet, a bed. **14**	Sit on your knees and jump to your feet. Can you leanback and touch your head to the FLOOR. **15**	Dribble a ball around the block. Repeat with the opposite hand. **16**	Invent a table or chair exercise with a partner. **17**	Practice 50 ``crunches'' with feet on COUCH. **18**
	Place a ball b-e-t-w-e-e-n your ankles, jump, and catch behind. **19**	How L O W CAN YOU squat. **20**	Place a broom stick on your toe. How long can you balance it? **21**	Improve your handstand record by ONE second. Old_____ New_____ **22**	Lay a broom on the floor and JUMP OVER 100 times. **23**	Lie on STOMACH hands behind head - how high can you Lift your head? Measure inches from chin to floor with a yardstick. **24**	PLACE an ice cube on the counter and exercise until it melts. **25**
	Juggle socks for FIVE minutes. **26**	Create a dance while STANDING on a towel. ``Do the Tootsie Roll'' - new slide. **27**	Discover THREE ways to ROLL into A balance. **28**	Can you JUMP your toe? **29**	Hold a towel ABOVE your head and s-t-r-e-t-c-h. Can you HOLD for 30 sec? Try behind the back. **30**	Play a step back game. Each time you catch, move a step back. **31**	APRIL 1995 S M T W TH F S 1 2 3 4 5 6 7 8 9 10 11 12 13 14 15 16 17 18 19 20 21 22 23 24 25 26 27 28 29 30

IT'S HIP   **TO BE FIT!!**

ALL★STAR
MOTIVATOR

 "EXTRA CREDIT LOG"

Activity	Minutes	Initials

Directions: Chart the minutes that you participate in physical activities outside of school. Parents' initials are required for each activity. A completed sheet of 30 hours will be an "A," which will be averaged in with your other physical education grades.

List of Possible Activities:

Team	Individual		Alternative
Basketball	Aerobics	Juggling	Skateboarding
Baseball	Archery	Skating	Frisbee™
Football	Bicycling	Skiing	Juggling
Handball	Bowling	Swimming	Jump Rope
Soccer	Golf	Walking	Unicycling
Softball	Hiking	Racquet Sports	Recreational Sports
Volleyball	Martial Arts	Weights	

NAME _____

GRADE _____ TEACHER _____

Total Number of Hours: _____

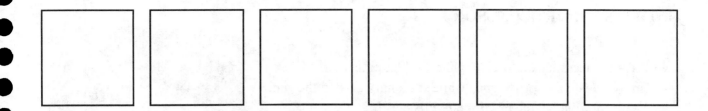

Disc Sports

PRE-GAME PLAN

Disc sports provide numerous opportunities for coed classes to improve throwing, catching, and cardiovascular skills.

HIGHLIGHTS

M   Learn the origin of the sport, practice forehand and backhand throws, play "Ultimate Keep-Away," "Catch All You Can," and "One-Minute Speed Flow."

T   Learn "Spinastics," work on increasing distance and accuracy, play "Aerobic Disc Golf."

W   New Hip-To-Be-Fit circuit, Endurance Test.

Th   Practice optional throws, skip exchanges, play "Jump" and create a **new** disc game.

F   Contracts.

BENEFITS

- Aerobic activity.
- Improves eye-hand coordination.
- Sex equitable.
- Lifetime activity.

RESOURCES

WE CARE

UNIT: DISC SPORTS (LESSON 1)

Objectives:

- Increase accuracy on forehand and backhand throws.
- Improve catching proficiency while stationary and on the run.
- Learn modified game of **Ultimate Frisbee™**.
- Cooperate with other teammates by calling personal fouls.
- Apply spin correctly.

WARM-UP: "50"

Practice

INDIVIDUAL

- Spin Jammer discs have a cone underneath (**Whatchamastallit™**) allowing novice players to spin the plate like freestyle experts. Distribute one Spin Jammer to each student. Hold the disc chest high (parallel to the ground) with fingertips pointed up on each side. Rotate your dominant hand past your nose, quickly spin it upwards, and catch. Try to apply spin to a toss that peaks just above your head. This time following the spin, work on **stalling** by placing your index or middle finger inside the cone.
- Can you move the spinning disc from finger to finger (dominant hand) maintaining the spin?
- How high can you throw it and continue to catch and stall on your finger?
- Can you toss from a standing position and catch while lying down?

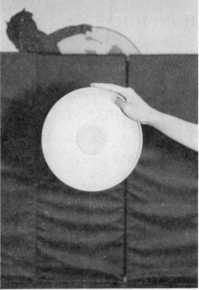

PARTNERS

- Partners face ten yards apart. Using a **backhand** throw (thumb on top, fingers underneath, disc parallel to the ground), practice tossing and catching with your partner.
- Work on level flights by stepping forward off the dominant foot and following through with a quick cross-body delivery.
- Another backhand grip places the index finger on the edge. Try this technique. With both styles snap the wrist on release.
- Work on throwing curves by dipping the disc slightly on release. Can you maintain accuracy?
- How many combined catches can the two of you make in 30 seconds? Work on two-handed (pancake) catches.
- Practice leading your partner when he or she is moving.
- Next try a **forehand** (sidearm) delivery. Form a peace sign by placing the middle finger on the rim, and the index finger pointed toward the center. Keeping your elbow in, try to make ten accurate throws so your partner doesn't have to move. Snap your wrist on release.
- "Hot Potato": From ten yards away, see who can complete a total of 20 catches first. Partners sit down when they achieve the 20th catch. Repeat using a different delivery.

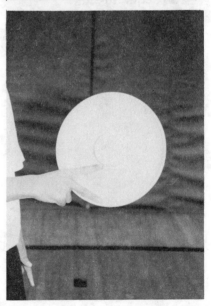

GROUP

- "Ultimate Keep-Away": Working in groups of three, challenge another group to a game of Ultimate Keep-Away. The team in possession has to complete three consecutive passes (one to each teammate) in a row. A point is scored when this occurs, and the disc is turned over to the opposite team.

In groups of three to five, form a circle 10 to 15 feet apart. Practice exchanging the disc from player to player, changing the type of throw each rotation.

"Ultimate Heart Rate": Take your pre–warm-up (resting) heart rate, a post–warm-up pulse rate, your pulse rate after a 15-minute (small group) Ultimate game, and a post-game pulse five minutes after the game.

- Pre–warm-up
- Post–warm-up
- Post-game
- 5 minutes after game

Note: Your recovery heart rate (depending upon exercise level) should be under 120 beats per minute, five minutes after the Ultimate game.

The first recognized disc was a pie tin. Invent a new disc game with another household item, e.g., plastic garbage can lid. Diagram a challenging six-hole golf course around your home and challenge each family member to a game. *Teacher*: Offer a prize for the most creative course.

What is higher in vitamin C? A 3-1/2–ounce serving of oranges or strawberries? *Answer:* **Strawberries.**

UNIT: DISC SPORT (LESSON 2)

Objectives:

- Increase throwing distance and accuracy.
- Learn the game of Aerobic Disc Golf.
- Review the forehand deliveries.
- Practice the pancake as well as trick catches.
- Create a freestyle routine.

WARM-UP: THREE 10-SECOND SPEED JUMP-ROPE TRIALS

Practice:

INDIVIDUAL

- Review spinning and finger stalls with the Spin Jammer disc. Count the number of seconds the disc remains spinning on your finger.
- "Spinastics": Can you keep the disc spinning as you perform a:
  - Roll forward and backward?
  - Cartwheel?
  - Pass under a leg?
  - Toss, jump, turn, and catch?

PARTNERS

- "Exchange": Hand your disc to a partner and take one step back. Each time a successful exchange is made, move back one big step. Which partners can be the farthest apart? *Teacher:* Emphasize a two-handed pancake catch.
- Can you catch a partner-thrown disc:
  - Skipping off the ground?
  - While you are lying on the ground?
  - Between your legs?
  - With one finger in the cone? On the rim?
  - Behind your head?
- "Freestyle": Cooperate with a partner in creating a freestyle routine.

GROUP

- "Aerobic Disc Golf": Set up and number nine traffic cones inside hula hoops (zigzag pattern) some 50 to 100 yards apart. Begin with three to five students per hole. Following the signal to begin, students run from hole to hole throwing toward the next numbered target. Your final score equals the number of minutes and seconds it takes to touch your disc to each of the nine cones. The game can be played by using individual times, or by combining the total times of each person starting at a particular hole. Sit down when you complete the course and remember your completion time.

Select a partner and practice exchanging two discs at a time. How many collective catches can the two of you score? Next, have one partner throw both discs at once. Can the receiver catch both?

Describe briefly how a disc can stay in the air as long as it does. In your description mention the factors of air, spin, frictional force, etc. What gives the disc stability? *Answer:* **Spin.**

Discover a way to make your disc hover in the wind and return to you like a boomerang. Experiment with different release angles.

What was originally called the Pluto Platter? *Answer:* **The Frisbee™.**

Wednesday
HIP-TO-BE-FIT FITNESS CIRCUIT

	FITNESS COMPONENTS	ACTIVITY	DESCRIPTION	RESOURCE
1	Power & Coordination	SPRINGBOARD TO HOOP	Work on running, jumping, and landing inside the hoop. • Increase height • Add a turn	
2	Balance	BEAN BAG BALANCE	Place a beanbag on your head and try to touch a knee to the floor.	
3	Arm & Shoulder Strength	arm wrestling	Lie on stomachs facing each other. Have an arm-wrestling contest with each arm.	
4	Coordination	DOUBLE DRIBBLE	Practice dribbling to a designated point and back while controlling a ball in each hand.	
5	Wrist & Forearms	WRIST ROLL UP	Tie one end of light rope to a 5-lb. plate and the other to a 1-foot piece of dowel. Extend the arms and slowly wind it up.	
6	Balance Arm & Shoulder Strength	HAND WALK THE MAT	From a handstand position, let your legs swing slightly past your head as you walk forward on your hands.	
7	Power	BUMP JUMP	Partners face each other two feet apart. Bring arms inward, bend, and jump to the right. See if you can make a 360° turn.	
8	Arm & Leg Strength	WATER SKI	Partner #1 squats and leans back on a carpet square while #2 pulls waterski style.	
9	Balance & Coordination	HONKER HAWSER	Partners stand on carpet squares 15 feet apart holding a long rope. The object is to pull or fake an opponent off his or her mat.	
10	Arm & Shoulder Strength	ROLLER SKATE STRETCH	From a push-up position, work on stretching in four different directions.	

WEEKLY TEST

UNIT: DISC SPORT (LESSON 3)

Objectives:

- Learn to tip the disc.
- Perform an overhand wrist flip delivery.
- Practice self-caught flights.
- Review skip exchanges.

WARM-UP: LONG RUN FOR PLACE

Practice:

INDIVIDUAL

- Explore two or three deliveries that allow you to toss the disc, get under it, and catch.
- What's the longest period of time you can keep the disc aloft and still catch?
- "Tipping": Spin your disc upwards and practice tipping it back up each time it descends. Use your index or middle finger. On discs without cones, tip slightly off center.
- What other body parts can you use to tip the disc? (knee, head, toe, elbow)

PARTNERS

- Face your partner on a hard surface 30 to 50 yards apart. Practice throwing off the ground by aiming at an imaginary spot between you and your partner. How many skip exchanges can you throw in a row?
- Experiment with the **Overhand Wrist Flip** delivery (thumb under edge, forefinger and middle finger alongside on the lip of the disc, hold the disc behind your back, raise your arm and release with the elbow just above your shoulder). Remember to snap your wrist as you release.

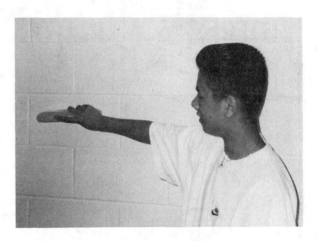

GROUP

- "2 vs. 2 Disc Minton/Tennis": Using the same rules and lines for badminton or tennis, play the game with a disc.
- "Keep Away": Number off students in groups of three. Players #1 and #2 play catch, while #3 tries to intercept. In 30-second segments, see how many catches #1 and #2 can complete. Player #3 can either intercept or knock down. Non-catches result in a point for #3, catches count as a point for #1 and #2. Throwers have three seconds once they catch the disc to release. Switch places every 30 seconds.

Place a disc between two partners on a smooth surface. From a distance of 20 to 30 feet, see how many cumulative hits each partner can score in one minute.

After learning the game of Ultimate, write an **Ultimate Rap.**

Sample: "Frisbees flyin', players skyin',
                 fakin', shakin', body achin',
                 flat out divin' . . . **Score!**"

Invent a new disc game that can be played in the confines of a tennis court.

What does the MTA mean to Disc Sport players?
Answer: **Maximum Time Aloft.**

PHYSICAL EDUCATION CONTRACT

Name _John Toby_

Class _Kay Tylia (6th) Alt. Sports_

During the next _____2_____ weeks, I will work on accomplishing . . .

Increasing my MTA (Maximum Time Aloft)
By keeping my disc in the air for (6) seconds
and catching the same throw.

I will need the following equipment . . .

One spinjammer disc.

Teacher Approval _Kay Tylia_ Date _4/21_

Progress—Week one _Five seconds_

Progress—Week two _Four seconds_

Progress—Week three _Five seconds_

Goal Accomplished_____ Not Accomplished _X_

Teacher Comments:

You needed a bit more wind.

Graded _____ Non-Graded _X_

ALL★STAR
MOTIVATOR

"JUMP"

Directions: Partners face 20 to 30 feet apart. Partner #1 throws directly to partner #2 who must **jump, catch,** and **release** the disc before touching the ground. How many can you perform in a row? Try different catches and throws while in flight.

Variation: Receivers must be moving.

Randy Silvey, Olympic Windjammer Frisbee™ Team.

ALL★STAR
MOTIVATOR

 ## "DISC MASTER"

Directions: To be a **Disc Master** you must be able to execute:

- 2 consecutive self-caught flights (minimum throw of ten yards).
- 5 consecutive spin tips.
- Land within 5 feet of a hoop 15 yards away.
- 10 consecutive passes to a partner 10 yards away (receivers cannot move feet).
- Complete **one** accurate overhand, backhand, and forehand delivery to a partner running 10 yards away.
- Catch a partner-thrown disc between the legs and behind the back.
- Throw 50 yards.

ALL STAR
MOTIVATOR

 "DISC TENNIS"

This activity focuses on high-speed catching skills and throwing accuracy.

Directions: Place six students on each side of a tennis court (four for badminton). Other than the additional bodies, nearly all other tennis/badminton rules apply. Start with a serve from behind the baseline. Receivers attempt to catch the disc and return it (without moving feet) to an unoccupied area on the opposite side of the net.

Throws appearing to travel outside the doubles line should go untouched. Tipped throws caught before hitting the ground are good. Once a player drops a disc he or she moves to the sideline until only two players remain on each side. Untouched discs landing inside the court eliminate the closest person. The remaining foursome plays out one point for the win. All waiting players return and a new game begins.

ALL STAR MOTIVATOR

 ## "M.T.A."

MTA (Maximum Time Aloft) is an outdoor activity sure to challenge your students. Arrange partners in a large space, 20 to 30 yards apart. Distribute discs to one line.

The world record for MTA is around 15 seconds. This is computed from the time of release to the moment of the catch. Experiment with different deliveries, angles, and heights while trading throws. How many seconds can you keep your disc aloft? Change places so both of you have opportunities to throw with the wind behind you. Generally, the stronger the wind, the lower you throw.

TIPS:

- Run (2 to 3 steps) to the line.
- Use a backhand delivery.
- Turn your back to the target.
- Use your whole body.
- Bend arm and snap wrist on release.
- Follow through.

ALL★STAR
MOTIVATOR

☆ "OFF-THE-WALL FRISBEE™"

Directions: Teams of three face each other from side wall to side wall. Discs are distributed to players along one wall. Strips of masking tape are placed 10 feet high and 15 feet apart forming a target zone on each wall.

The goal of this **five**-minute nonstop game is to throw discs past opponents, striking inside the box. Discs landing within this area count as one point. **Throwers** keep track of their own points and totals can be assessed at the end of the five-minute period.

Discs caught in the air, off the ground, or rebounding off the wall are classified as saves and returned immediately. All throws must be executed behind the middle restraining line.

Target	Zones	10′ high ↑	15′ wide →
Restraining Line			

ALL★STAR
MOTIVATOR

 ## "CATCH ALL YOU CAN"

Player #1 (with a stack of discs nearby) begins the contest by throwing a catchable disc to player #2. If #2 catches the first disc, a second is thrown followed by a third, fourth, fifth, etc., until that partner can no longer hold or catch further incoming discs. Allow no more than one to two seconds between throws.

Randy Silvey, Olympic Windjammer Frisbee™ Team.

ALL★STAR
MOTIVATOR

"ONE-MINUTE SPEED FLOW"

Directions: Players stand 20 to 30 feet apart and practice exchanging throws directly to each other. Play a one-minute game using the following guidelines:

Scoring:
- One point is scored for a one-handed catch.
- Two points are scored if a player makes a **restricted** catch (behind the back, under the leg, behind the head, etc.).
- Three points are scored for **spinning** catches.
- Zero points if player drops the disc.
- The player with the most points scored in one minute wins.

Randy Silvey, Olympic Windjammer Frisbee™ Team.

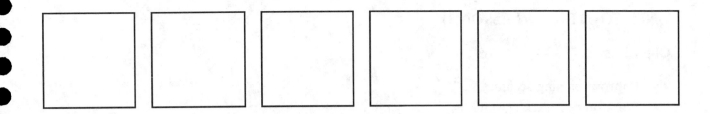

*F*ootball

PRE-GAME PLAN

"There is no strength where there is no struggle."

Modified, touch or flag football—played in small groups of four to six—provides an activity where everyone is active and able to improve on the basic skills of throwing, catching, running, and kicking.

HIGHLIGHTS

M   Increase passing accuracy, play "Bombshells" and "4 Straight."

T   Work on kicking and centering skills, play "Puntdown" and "Snaps."

W   New Hip-To-Be-Fit circuit, Flexibility Test.

Th   Practice defensive skills, play modified games in small groups, and take the "Pass Pro" contest.

F   Contracts.

BENEFITS

- Aerobic capabilities when games are minified and rules modified.
- Improve eye, hand, and foot coordination.
- Enhance speed and agility.

RESOURCES

The Athletic Institute
805 Merchandise Mart
Chicago, IL 60654

UNIT: FOOTBALL (LESSON 1)

Objectives:

- Improve passing accuracy.
- Work on eye-tracking skills.
- Practice fumble recoveries.

WARM-UP: "50"

Practice

INDIVIDUAL

- Practice tossing the ball down so that it bounces straight back to you.
- Read the direction of the bounce. Spike the ball downward and see how quickly you can gain control.

PARTNERS

- ***While you are stationary, pass to a partner who is:***
- running away at a 45° angle, to your right, left, full speed down field.
- ***pass to a stationary partner while you are:***
- moving to the right, left, back-pedalling.
- practice passing when both players are on the run.

"BOMBSHELLS"

GROUP

- In groups of five, number off "1, 2, 3, 4, 5." All players but #1 place a ball by their feet. #1 shouts **"pass"** and spirals an underhand pass straight up. One of the other four players must catch the ball before it hits the ground. If the pass is caught, it is returned to #1 and the player catching picks up his or her ball. On the next signal **"pass"** the first two balls are thrown simultaneously. If both are caught, a third ball is added. The goal for the group is to throw all five balls and have different players catch them. Whenever a sequence is broken, the groups starts over at one.
- **"2 vs. 1 (three-second pass limit)":** Player #1 centers to player #2 (quarterback) while player #3 attempts to intercept. The passer must count seconds and pass before three seconds elapse. If the ball is caught, players continue in their present roles. Players rotate positions each time an incomplete pass is thrown.

With four players per team, which team can center the ball from player to player, and one end zone to the other without a miss? Following each center, that player runs to the end of the line. Whenever a ball is dropped, the entire team must return it to the start line.

You have been hired to coach the Zoo's football team. Match eleven positions with the most appropriate animal and tell why you made this selection.

POSITION	ANIMAL	REASON
1. Quarterback		
2. Halfback		
3. Halfback		
4. Wide Receiver		
5. Fullback		
6. Tight End		
7. Tackle		
8. Tackle		
9. Guard		
10. Guard		
11. Center		

What football rule is limiting?

How would you change this rule to increase your success?

How many bones are there in your body? *Answer:* **206.**

What is the most common college football team nickname? *Answer:* **Tiger.**

UNIT: FOOTBALL (LESSON 2)

Objectives:

- Practice receiving the ball under pressure.
- Increase punting distance and accuracy.
- Improve short route passing proficiency.
- Practice defensive techniques.
- Improve centering proficiency.

WARM-UP: THREE 10-SECOND SPEED JUMP-ROPE TRIALS

Practice

INDIVIDUAL

- Practice tossing high spirals. Can you catch it with two hands above your head? Below your waist?
- Work on catching, quickly placing in a carrying position, and sprinting ten yards.
- Can you catch with your right hand only? Left?
- Can you catch while on one knee? While on your back?

PARTNERS

- "Puntdown": A coin toss determines which partner will punt first. The partner winning the toss punts first from mid-field toward the opponent's goal line. The second punter catches the ball and attempts to punt it at an angle past or over the head of the first punter. The punter is allowed two steps on each kick. The game ends when the ball crosses a player's goal line.
- Practice centering spirals back to a partner. After each successful exchange, the receiver takes a step back. How far back can you be and still receive the ball chest high?

GROUP

- "Distractor": Successful receivers must have great concentration. Place players in groups of three or four as shown in the illustration. Distractors stand a few feet from the receiver. They wave their arms, attempting to distract the person about to catch. At no time may distractors touch the ball. Distractors become passer/ receiver after ten passes.

"Consecutive Completions": In groups of three or four, challenge a similarly sized group to see who can complete the most consecutive passes. Change of possession occurs when the ball is intercepted or dropped. While teams are confined to a designated playing area, there is no line of scrimmage. Passes may be completed in any direction.

Visit a library and compare the high-tech uniforms of today with those of decades past.

Write about a personal skill in football you are unhappy with (passing, catching, running) and describe how you can turn it around.

James Naismith invented the game of basketball. What piece of sports equipment was he also credited for inventing? *Answer:* **The football helmet.**

Wednesday
HIP-TO-BE-FIT FITNESS CIRCUIT

	FITNESS COMPONENTS	ACTIVITY	DESCRIPTION	RESOURCE
1	Power & Coordination	TIP	With one partner directly behind the other, take turns tipping the ball off a backboard. How many tips can you perform in a row?	
2	Upper Arm Strength	WALL CLIMBER	Partner #1 holds the back of a chair 3 feet from a wall. Partner #2 places hands on the seat and climbs the wall with feet. Add a push-up at the highest elevation.	
3	Leg Strength & Flexibility	STAND UP	Stand back to back and place a ball between you. See how many times you can stand up and sit down without using hands or losing the ball.	
4	Flexibility & Coordination	LIMBO	Who can limbo the lowest?	
5	Endurance	SHADOW	Partner #1 holds a ball on the back of partner #2. #2 jogs for 1 minute while #1 attempts to keep the ball on #2's back.	
6	Coordination	BAT TIPS	Hold a bat with the fat end pointed up. Practice bouncing a ball off the end. Which partner can score more consecutive tips?	
7	Flexibility	TOE TOUCH	Partners lie on backs (heads close together). Grab hands and raise and lower feet. Touch together and touch the floor.	
8	Coordination	STICK FLIP	Using a track baton or a dowel, challenge your partner to see who can produce more rotations on a single toss and still catch.	
9	Arm & Leg Strength	PUSH BACK	Sit facing your partner, feet together, heels touching a line. Try to push your partner backwards. The first partner able to touch the line with hands scores a point.	
10	Coordination	PASS UNDER	Partners face 3 feet away. Partner #1 reaches under his/her legs, tosses a beanbag backwards to #2. Repeat and see how many catches you can perform in a row.	

WEEKLY TEST

UNIT: FOOTBALL (LESSON 3)

Objectives:

- Improve agility through related running/dodging activities.
- Improve tackling (deflagging skills).
- Increase passing range.
- Participate in a modified game.

WARM-UP: LONG RUN FOR PLACE

Practice

INDIVIDUAL

- With the ball carried in your dominant hand, how many seconds does it take to run from one end zone to the other?
- Repeat with the non-dominant hand.
- On your final run, practice shifting the ball from side to side each time you change direction.

PARTNERS

- Place partners with different colored flags at opposite ends of the field or gym. Following the signal to begin, the designated offensive side attempts to run across the field without losing flags. Players who are deflagged become members of the defensive team. Allow four opportunities for the remaining offensive players to score before alternating. (Captured players return to the original team following the fourth down or a score.)
- Partners face each other 30 feet apart. How many exchanges can you make in 60 seconds?
- How many total passes does it take to move from one end zone to the other?
- How many centers (hikes)?

GROUP

- "2 vs. 2": Using a shortened field, play a mini game allowing each team four chances to score following a kick, punt, or pass off.

Practice running parallel with a partner up and down the field lateralling the ball backwards on each exchange. *Remember,* the receiver must be one or more steps behind the person passing.

"Change the Count"
As you are doing sets of calisthenics, or center-to-quarterback snap counts, change the language. Try some of those listed below, or research some of your own.

	Spanish	Sounds Like	Chinese	Sounds Like
1.	Uno	Oono	_____	_____
2.	Dos	Dose	_____	_____
3.	Tres	Tre's	_____	_____
4.	Cuatro	Cuatro	_____	_____
5.	Cinco	Sinko	_____	_____
6.	Seis	Seis	_____	_____
7.	Siete	See-a-tay	_____	_____
8.	Ocho	Ohcho	_____	_____
9.	Nueve	Noo-a-vay	_____	_____
10.	Diez	D-ez	_____	_____

Exaggerate your performance in a class flag football game. How good were you?

What are the chances that a high school football player will play in a future Super Bowl?
Answer: **1 in 2,351.**

How many seams are on a football?
Answer: **Four.**

PHYSICAL EDUCATION CONTRACT

Name _Rommel Rios / Tim Church_

Class _Team Sports_

During the next ___2___ weeks, I will work on accomplishing . . .

Improving my passing accuracy with my partner.
I will throw 15 completions — 30 yards

I will need the following equipment . . .

Football — Space outside

Teacher Approval _Kay Tyler_ Date _10/15_
Add - receptions are to be caught when running.

Progress—Week one _Accomplished — this may have been too easy._

Progress—Week two _n/a_

Progress—Week three _n/a_

Goal Accomplished _X_ Not Accomplished _____

Teacher Comments:

This was a good practice activity.
By adding a defensive player it would have been more realistic. _KT_

Graded _____ Non-Graded _X_

ALL STAR MOTIVATOR

"SNAPS"

Arrange students behind a goal in single-file lines of four (two feet apart). Distribute one football per line. Following the signal to begin, the first person in line bends down, **snaps** (hands) the ball between his or her legs to player #2 and runs to the end of the line. This process continues until the ball crosses the opposite end line.

During the second race, have students receive the ball 5 to 10 feet back from the snapper. If the ball is dropped, the entire team runs back to the start line and begins again.

"4 STRAIGHT"

Directions: This activity is best suited for a large outdoor field. Divide students into groups of four. Designate one group as *offense* and one as *defense*. Distribute one nerf™, junior, or regulation football to each offensive group. The goal in "4 Straight" is to complete a pass to each of the four offensive players prior to an incomplete or intercepted pass by the defense.

Once the game begins:

- No contact is allowed.
- Players have five seconds to pass once they receive the ball.
- Receivers sit down and "freeze" after completing the next pass.
- Once an incomplete pass occurs, all sitting players stand and the process begins again.
- **Teams have three chances to score** "4 Straight."

Teacher: Remind offensive players to find clear zones and defensive players to enact a one-on-one or two-on-one coverage once a pass is completed.

ALL★STAR
MOTIVATOR

 ### "TOUCHDOWN"

Directions: Select two teams. One team will begin on offense and carry a hidden coin. The other team plays defense and tries to tag all members of the offense. Prior to the start signal, the offense huddles around the instructor at midfield. It is here that he or she chooses the player to carry the marker. Five yards away, the defense creates a barrier and awaits the call to **break.** Following this signal, the offense scatters with fists clenched. Remaining inside established boundaries, runners attempt to run untouched across their opponents' goal line. As these players are tagged, they freeze and open both hands. If the marker is stopped, the offense has three remaining downs (from that point) to score. After a score, teams return to midfield and change places.

Variations:

- Limit teams to one down.
- Use two coins.

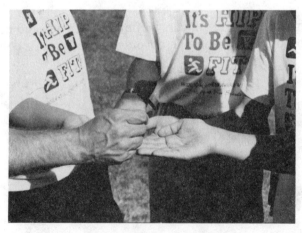

Taken from *Alternative Sports and Games*, Turner and Turner, Ginn Press, 1989.

ALL★STAR MOTIVATOR

 "PASS PRO"

Directions: Work through the following skills and try to reach the "pass pro" level.

Can you pass to a partner:

- Standing 10 yards away? _____
- Running to your right 10 yards away? _____
- Running to your left 10 yards away? _____
- Running toward you? _____
- Kneeling 10 yards away? _____
- Over his or her right shoulder 20 yards away? _____
- Over his or her left shoulder 20 yards away? _____
- On his or her back 10 yards away? _____
- On the run without breaking his or her stride? _____
- While you are running parallel to that partner? _____

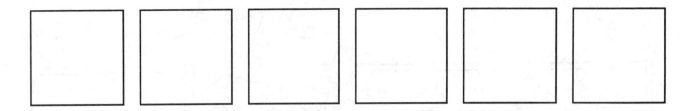

*F*ree Weights

PRE-GAME PLAN

"I don't have time to exercise." WRONG. "You don't have time to *not* exercise!"

This unit includes safety and lifting techniques to be used when strengthening the legs and back, chest and shoulders, triceps and biceps. The three lesson samples utilize light weights and alternative exercise props such as Dynabands.

HIGHLIGHTS

M   Work on legs and back. Learn safe spots, rotate through the "Super Set," begin "Pumping Up" contest.

T   Emphasis on chest and shoulders, practice partner resistance activities, rotate through group stations, and learn about dangerous exercises.

W   New Hip-To-Be-Fit circuit, Agility Test.

Th   Work on "Pumping Rubber" progression, concentrate on biceps and triceps, practice "Bottoms-Up," and participate in the "Triceps Race."

F   Contracts.

BENEFITS

- Increase muscular strength, flexibility, and power.
- Learn lifetime safety and stretching techniques.
- Know unsafe exercises.

CONTRIBUTOR

Yueh Chun Chang
3-Time World Drug-Free Powerlifting Champion

UNIT: FREE WEIGHTS (LEGS AND BACK) (LESSON 1)

Objectives:

- Understand that with hard work all bodies can make positive changes.
- Learn proper spotting techniques.
- Know that stretching should precede all lifting.
- Strengthen back and legs.

WARM-UP: "50"

Practice

INDIVIDUAL

Rotate through the following four individual exercises:

- "Good Mornings": Utilizing a bar (maximum of 50 pounds), bend to a bow, legs straight, lift, straightening your back, lower and repeat for two sets of ten reps.
  Variation: "Dumbbell Shrugs."
- "Lunges": With dumbbells held on each side, lunge slowly forward with both legs bent. Your weight is balanced between the front and back toes. Alternate walking forward with right and left legs leading. Complete 20 steps with slow bends. What muscles do you feel working?
- "One Arm Rows": With the inside knee and hand supported on a bench, row upwards with the outside hand. Remember to keep the back straight. Raise dumbbells upward to the armpit. Alternate ten on each side.
  Variation: "Calf Raises."
- "Bent Over Rows": Using an underhand grip, legs shoulder-width apart, and knees slightly bent, lift the bar (maximum of 45 pounds) up to stomach and repeat.
  Variation: One dumbbell from a straddle position, back bent, free arm held on same knee.

Good Mornings

One Arm Rows

PARTNERS

- "Squat Spots": Select a partner of equal size. Load the bar to approximately half of your body weight. Spotter stands directly behind lifter. From the squat rack, using an overhand grip, lifter moves under the bar, lifts, and steps back slowly. Spotter places hands under the bar near the shoulder area. Spotter must be alert and prepared at all times in case the bar slips. Mimic the lifter as he or she bends to a squat position.

UNIT: FREE WEIGHTS (LEGS AND BACK) (LESSON 1) (CONT'D)

- "Super Set": In groups of four, rotate through each of the following four stations. Rotate after each set. "Lower Back Flex Test."

Chin-up

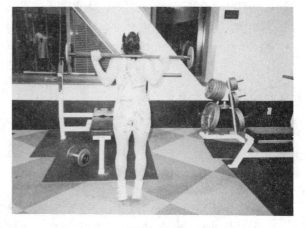

Calf Raise

Bar Bows

Resist

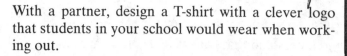

COOPERATIVE

With a partner, design a T-shirt with a clever logo that students in your school would wear when working out.

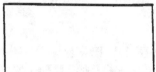

Your idea

INTERDISCIPLINARY

Assume the roll of a newspaper advice columnist. Write an appropriate response to this 15-year-old student.

Dear _____,

I am fifteen years old and, no matter how hard I try, I can't get rid of the baby fat around my waist. What can I do?

Dear _____,

Critical Thinking

"Sport Rebus": Sometimes called a pictograph or anagram, a rebus is a puzzle representing an athletic word or phrase by either letters, numbers, or pictures. Look at the rebus samples below and create some of your own.

(ANS) "Safe Spot"

(ANS) "Bench Press"

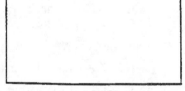

(ANS)

TRIVIA

What are cramps? *Answer:* **Cramps are when muscles contract on their own. This happens when they lack minerals and when muscles are tired.**

UNIT: FREE WEIGHTS (CHEST AND SHOULDERS) (LESSON 2)

Objectives:

- Increase upper body strength.
- Understand that trial weight totals vary among individuals.
- Know the names of the muscles being worked and their locations.

WARM-UP: THREE 10-SECOND SPEED JUMP-ROPE TRIALS

Practice

INDIVIDUAL

TEN REPS (2 SETS)

Distribute dumbbells to each student (10 to 20 pounds each). Complete each of the following four exercises with two sets of ten repetitions.

- "Dumbbell Flies": Lie back on a bench with a dumbbell in each hand. Extend arms upward (palms facing). Lower to side in a semi-circular motion. Elbows are slightly bent. Lower as far as possible. If you can perform this on your back, try it from a front lying position. This exercise works your deltoids. Where are they located?
- "Lying Dumbbell Chest Press": Use the same position as "Dumbbell Flies," palms face out.
- "Dumbbell Military Press": With dumbbells held at shoulder height (back straight), lift upward above the head.
- "Upright Rows": With dumbbells held together, (as pulling a rope) raise each upwards to the **ear** level. What muscles do you feel working?

Chest Press

Upright Rows

PARTNERS

- "Partner Resistance": Partner #1 (elbows in) pushes out while partner #2 pushes in.
- Can you invent two other partner resistance activities that will strengthen the chest and shoulders?

GROUP

- Rotate through each of the four stations performing ten reps with dumbbells.

Front Raises	**Pec Flex**	**Bend Over Raises**	**Triceps Extension**
Alternate raising dumbbells to eye level with palms facing.	Move dumbbells outward with "elbows in-elbows out" movement.	Bend back forward and raise arms outward to the side.	Have back on bench, head near the end, and raise dumbbells upward and lower over head.

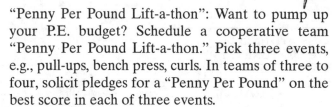

"Penny Per Pound Lift-a-thon": Want to pump up your P.E. budget? Schedule a cooperative team "Penny Per Pound Lift-a-thon." Pick three events, e.g., pull-ups, bench press, curls. In teams of three to four, solicit pledges for a "Penny Per Pound" on the best score in each of three events.

		Sample			
Name	Weight	Pull-ups	Bench	Curls	Total
Susan	105	11X105=$11.55	65=.65	40=.40	$12.60

Diuretics are used to eliminate excess water. What are some of the dangers of these non-prescriptive dehydrating drugs? What is the more natural way to rid the body of water?

These two exercises are described by many exercise physiologists as dangerous. Research a safer alternative that will accomplish the same thing.
- Deep Knee Bends
- Standing Toe Touch

ALTERNATIVES:

1. _____

2. _____

If push-ups with hands placed far apart are good for the chest, what are push-ups with arms close together good for? *Answer:* **Triceps.**

Wednesday
HIP-TO-BE-FIT FITNESS CIRCUIT

	FITNESS COMPONENTS	ACTIVITY	DESCRIPTION	RESOURCE
1	Upper Arm Strength	ONE ARM DRIBBLE	From a push-up position, support yourself on one hand and dribble a ball with the other. Switch support arms as you dribble under.	
2	Speed	DON'T STEP ON MY TOES	Partners face with fingers interlocked. See who can touch an opponent's foot 10 times first.	
3	Upper Arm Strength	INVERTED ROPE CLIMB	Find 3 ways to raise your feet above your head.	
4	Balance	TWO PART WAND BALANCE	Balance a wand on your toe, flip it upwards into a balance on one hand.	
5	Flexibility	NO TOUCH	Lie on the floor with shoulders down. Holding a dowel with both hands, tuck your knees and shoot both feet under the wand without touching it.	
6	Upper Arm Strength	BACKWARD PUSH-UP	From a sitting position on the floor, place heels on the front of a chair and see how many backward push-ups you can do.	
7	Balance	4 SQUATS	From the end of a beam, walk forward and perform 4 one-legged squats before reaching the other side.	
8	Agility	ZIG ZAG JUMP OFF	Partners face (5 feet apart) on the same side of a rope or line. With feet together, jump back and forth across the line. Who can reach 25 first?	
9	Upper Arm Strength	STEP BACK MEDICINE BALL EXCHANGE	Partners stand 3 feet apart. Exchange the medicine ball 5 times. Each time you exchange take a step back.	
10	Endurance	DUMB BELL	Jog around the gym for 2 minutes. Exaggerate upper arm movements with light dumbbells.	

WEEKLY TEST

UNIT: FREE WEIGHTS (TRICEPS AND BICEPS) (LESSON 3)

Objectives:

- Increase strength for throwing and pulling.
- Learn the dangers of anabolic steroids.
- Practice some alternative exercises.

WARM-UP: LONG RUN FOR PLACE

Practice

INDIVIDUAL

Rotate through the following exercises performing three sets of ten on each.
- "P-Bar Dips": Dips will improve your ability to throw and pull. Take turns performing dips off both ends of the parallel bar.
- "Wall Push-ups": From a handstand position (feet against wall), practice lowering and raising your body.
- "Dumbbell Curls": (Alternating) Stand with feet shoulder-width apart. Arms are to the side with palms up. Alternate right and left curls. Can you do three sets of ten on each side?
- "Concentration Curls": Seated on a bench with elbow on inner thigh, curl upwards. Can you feel your biceps working? Which side was easier? Why?

PARTNERS

- "Bottoms Up": Find a partner of equal size. Sit facing with bottoms of feet touching. Hands are placed outside and behind buttocks. Use your triceps as you and your partner push together and lift seats off the floor.

GROUP

- "Triceps Race": Divide the class into two teams. One half sits next to a wall while the other half lines up beneath a goal on one end line. Following a signal to begin, students on the floor walk their feet up the wall (seats off floor) and runners sprint from end line to end line. One point is scored for each line touched. Runners continue until the last wall sitter comes down.

COOPERATIVE

In groups of three to five, plan an evening Health Fair for your school. Assign groups for various responsibilitiese, .g., potential speakers, fees, space requirements, promotion, etc. Possible contributors and topics are listed below:

Topic	Presenters
Diet/Nutrition info.	Local dairy councils
Smoking	Cancer Society, Heart and Lung Associations
Exercise	Local fitness clubs
Self defense	Police and martial arts clubs
CPR	Local fire deptartment

INTERDISCIPLINARY

Anabolic steroids are synthetic male hormones. Research these drugs and list five negative mental and physical risks/effects caused by these short-cutting drugs.

Critical Thinking

What are some safety concerns when working with a partner on cooperative stretching exercises? (*Possible answer*) **You can't feel your partner's pain.** Communicate with each other.

TRIVIA

In a lifetime, your heart might pump 77 million gallons of blood. That would fill all the tanks in the New England Aquarium 150 times!

Source: American Heart Association

PHYSICAL EDUCATION CONTRACT

Name _Danny Bibbet_

Class _Cond/weight control_

During the next _____3_____ weeks, I will work on accomplishing . . .

Firming arms and legs while losing three pounds

I will need the following equipment . . .

Free weights – bench

Teacher Approval _Kay Tillis_   Date _2/11_

Progress—Week one _Weight 138 (beginning) 1st week 138_

Progress—Week two _Weight 136 – lost two pounds_

Progress—Week three _Weight 136_

Goal Accomplished_____ Not Accomplished _X_

Teacher Comments:

Good job – you worked hard

Kty

Graded _____ Non-Graded _X_

MOTIVATOR

 ## "POWER PUSHES"

To excel in most sports, **power** is essential. Try the power pushes pictured below and see your own power improve.

Jump the Stick

Knee to Feet Jump

P-bar Jumps

Push-up With Clap

Heavy Rope

Play ball push

Mat Jump

Hoop Jump

Door Jammin'

One arm push-up

ALL★STAR
MOTIVATOR

 ## "DOING THE TWIST"

The Twist was a famous dance from the 1960's. The Twist below is an exercise designed to firm the external oblique muscles located at the sides of the waist. It is also good for the lower back. A broom stick or long dowel is the only equipment required. The movement can be accomplished from a standing, sitting, or kneeling position. In all of these positions, the **feet and hips** must remain **stationary.**

Directions: Place a stick across the shoulders behind the neck and roll both wrists along the ends. Twist the body as far to the left as possible and follow with a twist to the right. Perform twenty repetitions to each side, rest, and repeat. Next, move to your knees and experiment with some other twisting possibilities. Can you touch the ends of the stick to the floor?

ALL STAR
MOTIVATOR

 ### "PUMPING UP"

Pumping Up is a physical education competition where the top 25 pull-up scores from **each** class are accumulated and compared. All pull-ups are performed in an overhand fashion and numerical scores rather than names are charted. This way, individuals can work on self-improvement without losing self-esteem. In many classes there will be students who will record a zero score initially. The goal for those pupils is to complete one pull-up.

Pump Power Rating	
Super	125+
Good	100-124
Average	75-99

Hahler

Period	Score
1	114
2	90
3	*136
4	83
5	101

Bowen

Period	Score
1	93
2	97
3	*141
4	76
5	81

Frazier

Period	Score
1	76
2	128
3	84
4	110
5	*129

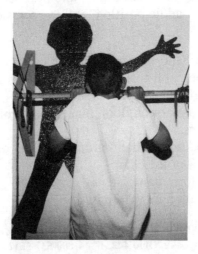

School Record Holder
Roberto Chavez
52 pull-ups

ALL STAR MOTIVATOR

"PUMPING RUBBER"

Dynabands are portable thin latex sheets cut into three-foot lengths used to strengthen and tone muscles. The Dynaband possibilities have just begun to be tapped. At your desk, on the phone, or when relaxing in front of the television, the Dynabands resistive exercises can be employed.

When using the Dynabands:

- Go through a full range of motion with every exercise.
- Pace yourself.
- Keep your back straight.
- To increase the difficulty, simply double the band to double the tension.
- Exhale after each repetition.

Exercise Samples

Standing	•Perform ten curls under right foot with right arm.
	•Perform ten curls under left foot with left arm.
Sitting	•Place under both feet and curl ten times.
	•Repeat with legs lifted slightly.
(Lats)	
Sitting	•Place band under feet and pull back (2) sets of ten.
Standing	•In straddle position, pull to each side (inside and outside).
(Abduction)	
Lying on side	•Tie band in circle. Place band around knees. Lift upper leg ten times, roll to the opposite hip and repeat. Move band down to ankles and repeat lifts.
Sitting	•At desk or on floor, place band around ankles and move apart ten times.
	•Tie knotted band around the leg of your chair and pull over the back of the chair.
Standing	•Perform dance steps.
	•Invent a new exercise.

Resource: **FITNESS WHOLESALE**   **A Division of Future Dynamics, Inc.**
3064 West Edgerton   Silver Lake, Ohio 44224   1-800-537-5512   FAX 1-216-688-1021.

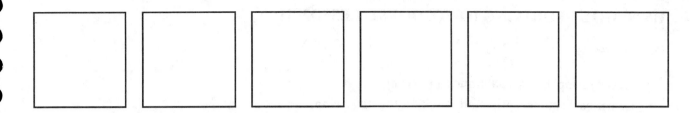

Golf

PRE-GAME PLAN

"Golf is a good walk spoiled."—Mark Twain

Golf is a leisure sport for all ages and abilities. It's a game where size is not a factor. Practice is what is most important. Whether swinging on world-class courses or high school football fields, the skills and thrills are the same.

HIGHLIGHTS

M Activities in this lesson sequence center upon the grip, stance, and swing, with a variety of modified experiences.

T Learn basic grip, stance, swing, and scoring terms. Play "Over the Line" and "Bocci Golf."

W Practice driving and chipping skills, know which clubs work best for specific shots, play "Chip Off the Old Line" and "Pop Shots."

New Hip-To-Be-Fit circuit, Arm Strength Test.

Th Increase putting accuracy through a variety of nontraditional holes, play "Nine Hole Target Golf" and "Penny Putt."

F Contracts.

BENEFITS

- Lifetime activity.
- Sex equitable.
- Handicapping balances competition.
- Play individually or in small groups.

RESOURCES

PGA of America
100 Avenue of the Champions
Palm Beach Gardens, FL 33418
407-624-8400

CONTRIBUTOR

Mark Lynch
Pacific Northwest Section PGA
Junior Golf Coordinator

UNIT: GOLF—DRIVING (OUTDOORS) (LESSON 1)

Objectives:

- Know group safety techniques and swing signals.
- Learn basic stance, grip, and (back-and-forth) swing.
- Understand golf courtesies.
- Score a hole.

WARM-UP: "50"

Practice

INDIVIDUAL

- While all clubs will work, try to collect as many 5's, 7's, 9's, and putters as possible. Emphasize a STOP, LOOK, and SWING rule prior to each swing. Establish a "Swing Line" and signals for starting, stopping, and retrieving. (Place non-hitting participants 10 to 20 feet away). Waiting players place their clubs on the ground.

PARTNERS

Stance
- Place feet shoulder-width apart with arms close to chest.
- Knees are slightly flexed and relaxed.
- A slight forward bend in the hips allows the arms to hang down.
- Ball placement is at the midpoint between feet.

Overlap grip (right-handers)
- Grip club with left hand, placing the thumb down the center of the club. Next, place your right hand on the club so that it covers your left index finger.
- The V's formed by the forefingers and thumbs are pointing to the right shoulder.
- Maintain *soft hand pressure* throughout the swing.
- Practice short and full swings, brushing the grass and following through.
- Partner #1 practices hitting ten tennis or perforated plastic balls toward a hoop 50 feet away.
- Partner #2 checks for grip (finger alignment), shoulders parallel, and swing follow-through.
- Score one point for each ball landing within one club length of the target. Switch places and repeat.

GROUP

- **"Know the Score"**: Establish a par 3 hole and alternate hits toward that hole. If your ball lands inside the target one stroke under par, you score a *birdie*. Two strokes under par is an *eagle*. One stroke over par is a *bogey,* and two over is a *double bogey*. A hole in one is also called an *ace*.
- **"Over The Line"**: Working in groups of three count the *collective strokes* it takes to move each of the three team balls from one end of a large field to the other. The low group score wins. Remember, every contact counts as a stroke and only swing when the area is clear.

COOPERATIVE

Proper etiquette is expected in the sport of golf. Examples include not talking when another player is hitting, and replacing all divots. In groups of three, create a list of at least ten other golf courtesies.

Look at the picture of the golfer. Describe a safer way to place a tee.

_____

_____

_____

INTERDISCIPLINARY

Critical Thinking

As the number of the club increases (3, 4, 5, etc.), the length of the shaft decreases in length. Why can you expect to hit the ball further with lower numbered clubs?

TRIVIA

What outdoor sport is the hardest to master? *Answer:* **Pollsters put that one to 1,500 physical education teachers. Remarkably, they agreed:** *Golf.*

UNIT: GOLF—DRIVING AND CHIPPING (OUTDOORS) (LESSON 2)

Objectives:

- Review grip, stance, swing, and safety procedures.
- Practice driving and chipping skills.
- Know which clubs work best for particular shots.
- Determine length of arm swing and position for specific shots.

WARM-UP: THREE 10-SECOND SPEED JUMP-ROPE TRIALS

Practice

INDIVIDUAL

- Divide available tennis balls among students.
- Practice contacting the ball with a *full* swing.
- "Your hands and arms swing the club; your body pivots."
- Draw your club back slowly so that your back is toward the target.
- On the down swing the club head returns to the starting position and swings through the ball.
- Pick an imaginary target directly down range and see how close you can drive your ball into the target area.
- *Instructor:* Emphasize accuracy and form over distance.

PARTNERS

- Exchange tennis balls for perforated plastic balls.
- Select partners and distribute one ball per pair.
- Face each other in an open area, 15 to 30 feet away.
- Using one-third of a full swing, practice chipping back and forth.
- Score one point if your partner can catch your chip shot.
- *Increase* the range of your swing from one-third to one-half and see if partners can continue to catch hit balls. (Remind students not to run in front of others.)
- How do you obtain height? Experiment with placing the ball left of center.
- **"Chip Around":** Place nine hoops 50 to 100 yards apart in a zigzag pattern. Distribute one tennis ball per pair. From a clear hitting area, partners alternate chipping from one hole to another. Partners are allowed a total of two strokes per hole. Balls landing inside a hoop count as one point.

GROUP

- **"Pop Shots":** Have each student print his or her initials on a ball. Students drive their ball toward a large hoop or cone 50 yards down field. The closest ball wins a soda "pop."

"Chip & Win (fundraiser)": Chip & Win is a cooperative fundraiser enabling a class, department, or school to raise money in a short period of time. Select a student committee. Each member is in charge of one of the following tasks:

Set-up
- Collect as many golf balls as possible.
- Contact local sporting goods for donations.
- Bring a 3, 4, or 5 iron.
- Number off each ball.
- Make a chart with contestants' names and ball #.
- Locate a hula hoop for the target.
- Sell chances (balls) at 50 cents to $1.00.
- Advertise the event.

Directions
- Place a hoop 75 to 100 yards from the hitting line.
- Locate one (helmeted) student behind a standing foldable mat near the target hoop.
- Call students up to hit one at a time.

Call a local golf course and arrange a video interview with one of the club pros. What does his job entail? Share your story with the class.

You have just been asked to participate in a Junior National Golf Tournament. In one day you are scheduled to play 36 holes (six to eight hours). What types of food could you carry that would supply the needed energy?

Why do many top golfers line up the ball at the heel of the club? *Answer:* **The club pulls toward the body on the down swing resulting in the club moving slightly inward.** *Source: P.E. Digest,* **Summer 1994.**

Wednesday
HIP-TO-BE-FIT FITNESS CIRCUIT

	FITNESS COMPONENTS	ACTIVITY	DESCRIPTION	RESOURCE
1	Leg Strength	MEDICINE BALL WALL PUSH	One partner moves the ball up, the other down and up again.	
2	Upper Arm Strength	PEG BOARD	How many holes can you fill?	GOPHER 1-800-533-0446
3	Coordination	NYLON HOOP EXCHANGE	Practice cooperative exchanges of a ball using hoops covered with nylon pantyhose.	
4	Balance & Coordination	CHUCK EM FENCE OFF	Challenge your partner to see who can stay on the beam the longest.	Chuk-em Enterprises (206) 244-7049
5	Endurance	HEAVY HAND JOG	Alternate arm curls as you jog the gym.	Sportime 1-800-283-5700
6	Coordination	360° PARTNER ROLL BACK	Place a ball between you (chest high) and work on turning and rolling the ball from front to back to front.	
7	Power and Speed	CONE ROPE HURDLES	Work on clearing each hurdle with the same leg.	
8	Flexibility	EXERSTIK	Create ten different stretching exercises.	1-800-Exerstik
9	Balance	SEAT SPINS	From a sitting position, tuck knees, push off with hands, and see how many rotations you can make.	
10	Balance	BALANCE ROPE	Work on walking the rope forward and backward.	

WEEKLY TEST

UNIT: GOLF—PUTTING (INDOORS) (LESSON 3)

Objectives:

- Know that putting is an abbreviated swing using minimal wrist and body action.
- Work on aim and body alignment.
- Increase putting distance and accuracy.

WARM-UP: LONG RUN FOR PLACE

Practice   *Directions*: Set up a nine-hole putting course around the gym floor. Holes can consist of broken hoops, PVC pipe, chairs, beams, jump ropes, mats, etc. Place one ball and putter at each hole. Pass out score cards.

INDIVIDUAL

- **"Putt Putt Golf":** Students rotate through each hole, recording the number of strokes it takes to hole out each hole.

PARTNERS

- **"Search and Destroy":** Like the old game of marbles, partners face from 15 to 20 feet away. Alternating strokes, they putt toward their opponent's ball. The object is to strike your partner's targeted ball before your own is hit.

GROUP

- **"Penny Putt":** Space students evenly in a large circle (20- to 30-foot diameter). Place a crown of ten pennies in the center of the circle. Players have one putt to see how close they can come to the pennies. Closest balls win.

Distribute one whiffle ball, hoop, and iron to each set of partners. Challenge another set of partners to an **Alternating Chip** game. Place team hoops 50 yards away and 10 to 15 yards apart. Partner #2 stands in the field behind the hoop and serves as the counter for partner #1. When the ball lands in the hoop, players switch places. Players' strokes are combined and later checked with the team that was challenged.

Using the chart, compute par for each of the nine holes.

Computation of Par

Par	Men	Women
3	0–250	0–210
4	251–470	211–400
5	471–690	401–590
6	691+	591 +

Hole	Yds	Par
1	210	
2	315	
3	475	
4	205	
5	350	
6	340	
7	290	
8	450	
9	195	

Experiment with slicing the ball. What do you have to do to make the ball curve to the right? Left?

When was the tee invented? *Answer:* **1899.**

PHYSICAL EDUCATION CONTRACT

Name _Shannon Scanlan_

Class _3rd_

During the next _____2_____ weeks, I will work on accomplishing . . .

Increasing the distance I can drive the ball.
I will also make some trips to the driving range.

I will need the following equipment . . .

Driver — regular and perforated balls.

Teacher Approval _Kay Tyler_   Date _5/3_

Progress—Week one _Needs to work on form (Best Drive 125 yards)_

Progress—Week two _Best Drive (160 yards)_

Progress—Week three _n/a_

Goal Accomplished___X___   Not Accomplished _____

Teacher Comments:

The extra work paid off.

Graded ___X (B)___   Non-Graded _____

ALL★STAR MOTIVATOR

"NINE-HOLE TARGET GOLF"

Nine-Hole Target golf is an individualized golf motivator emphasizing putting accuracy.

Directions: Draw five concentric chalk circles 12 to 18 feet apart on a flat surface. Mark a square 20 feet back from the closest circle. Each player finds an open spot and takes nine putts. Scores are tabulated after each putt. Putts rolling and stopping outside the circle are marked as a six. The lower the total, the better your game.

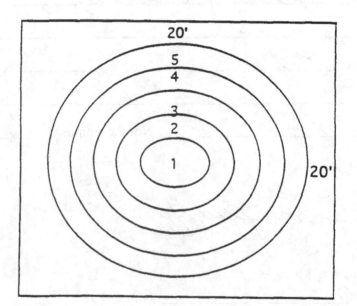

"CHIP OFF THE OLD LINE"

Directions: Distribute one whiffle ball and iron per student. Divide the class in half with players facing from opposite goal lines. As space is available, students chip forward to the ten-yard line. One shot is allowed per line. The area between the 40- and 50-yard lines serves as a safety zone. Students reaching this point turn around and chip back toward their own goal line.

Scoring: Balls landing within one shoe length of a line count one point. Who can score the most points during one eight-shot rotation?

Group #1 ↓

Turn Around Zone

Group #2 ↑

ALL★STAR
MOTIVATOR

"BOCCI GOLF"

Directions: Arrange students in groups of three. Place a golf ball 15 to 30 feet away. Each student putts his/her ball toward the targeted ball. The object is to come the closest without touching the target. The closest ball scores one point. Play a game to ten points.

ALL STAR MOTIVATOR

 ## "GOAL GOLF"

The object in Goal Golf is to strike the ball over or under a football or soccer goal post. Students form three lines (five yards apart) 30 feet away from a football or soccer goal post. One club and a basket of large plastic balls are placed at the head of each line.

One by one, players approach their tee and attempt to chip a ball into or between the goal posts. Balls rolling under the goal score **one** point. Balls travelling above and between the post score **three**. Teams vocalize their collective points as they occur. The first team scoring 50 points wins.

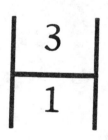

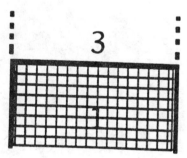

ALL★STAR MOTIVATOR

"PPPPUTTAG"

Remember the game of marbles where one player's marble would chase another? It was a basic tag game. Contact your opponent's object before your own is touched.

Players place their balls on a smooth surface 15 to 20 feet apart. Partner #1 putts softly toward partner #2's ball, and partner #2 does the same. Each player strategizes on how close to come before actually putting directly at the targeted ball. Count one point each time you touch your partner's ball first.

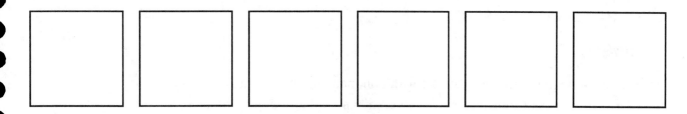

*H*andball

PRE-GAME PLAN

"The best angle to approach anything is the try-angle."

Handball is a simple game easily modified for nearly any size ball or wall surface. It's a game of quick reactions, coordination, and strategy. Play can be strictly recreational or highly competitive. Focus in this chapter emphasizes game situations with the dominant and non-dominant hands.

HIGHLIGHTS

M   Practice serves (throwing) with dominant and non-dominant hands and play "Synchro Serv."

T   Strike rebounding balls with multiple stroking actions, play "Position Rally" and "Handball Bingo."

W   New Hip-To-Be-Fit circuit, Muscular End Test.

Th   Improve returns in a timed sequence, learn singles strategies, try for the "Ace Award."

F   Contracts.

BENEFITS

- Aerobic activity.
- Lifetime activity.
- Play individually or in small groups.
- Inexpensive.

RESOURCES

United States Handball Association
930 North Benton Avenue
Tucson, AZ 85711
(602) 795-0434

U.S. Handball Association
4101 Demster Street
Skokie, IL 60076

CONTRIBUTOR

Dr. Lea Ann Tyson
Western Washington University
Former National Champion

UNIT: HANDBALL (LESSON 1)

Objectives:

- Perform overhand throwing stroke with dominant and non-dominant hands.
- Perform sidearm throwing stroke with dominant and non-dominant hands.
- Recognize angles of rebound.
- Catch a thrown ball rebounding off a wall before it bounces twice.

WARM-UP: "50"

Practice   Distribute one racquetball to each student. Find a clear space 15-20 feet back from the wall. How many times can you:

INDIVIDUAL

- Throw overhand (dominant hand) and catch the racquetball before it bounces twice?
- Perform an overhand throw with the non-dominant hand and catch it before it bounces twice?
- Throw sidearm with the dominant hand and catch it before it bounces twice?
- Repeat with the non-dominant hand?
- Move a few steps back and experiment with different throws?

PARTNERS

- With your partners six feet apart and approximately 20 feet from the wall, have partner #1 throw the ball (dominant hand) and partner #2 catch it before it bounces twice.
- Repeat practicing serves to a partner utilizing overhand and sidearm deliveries with both the dominant and non-dominant hands.

GROUP

- In groups of five or six, form a line 20 feet from the wall. Using an overhand throw and the dominant hand, the first person in line throws the racquetball to the wall and the next person catches it before it bounces twice. The second person throws to the wall and the third person catches it before the second bounce. This continues until all line members have contacted the ball. How many catches can the group make in one minute?
- Repeat using opposite hands and different deliveries.

134

"Synchro Serv": In groups of three, form a triangle (6 to 10 feet apart). Each partner drops a ball and executes a "one-bounce serve" to the person on his or her right. Serves must be synchronized. Score a point each time a successful round is completed.

If a handball player wants to improve his or her overall conditioning, what exercises would be appropriate for the following body parts?
Write a recipe for improvement:

- **Legs**
- **Torso**
- **Arms**

Number off in groups of three. Players #1 and #2 play a modified game to five points. Player #3 analyzes the strengths and weaknesses of the first two players and creates a game plan when he or she rotates in.

Why do humans have fingernails? *Answer:* **The nail acts as a shield and helps us pick things up.**

UNIT: HANDBALL (LESSON 2)

Objectives:

- Strike a racquetball with an overhand stroke using both the dominant and non-dominant hands.
- Strike a racquetball with a sidearm stroke using both the dominant and non-dominant hands.
- Strike a thrown or hit ball rebounding off a wall before it bounces twice.
- Recognize angles of rebound.

WARM-UP: THREE 10-SECOND SPEED JUMP-ROPE TRIALS

Practice Distribute one racquetball to each student.
Position yourself 15 to 20 feet from the wall and see how many times you can:

INDIVIDUAL

- Drop and hit the racquetball to the wall using the dominant hand and sidearm stroke, catching it before it bounces twice.
- Repeat with the non-dominant hand.
- Throw the ball to the wall, hit it back with any stroke, and catch it before it bounces twice.
- Try this last task with each hand.

PARTNERS

- With partners six feet apart and 15 to 20 feet from the wall, practice throwing the ball to the wall so that your partner can hit it with any stroke and either hand before it bounces twice. Do this ten times before switching.

GROUP

- **"Position Rally":** In groups of four, position yourselves so that two people are in the court (marked by cones) and the other two are behind the court (about 25 feet from the wall). Divide the court in half (right and left sides). One court player begins the rally by dropping and hitting the ball to the wall. Whichever side the ball rebounds to, that player attempts to hit it back to the wall before the ball bounces twice. Players need to stay on their respective sides to avoid hindrances. The two players behind the court also stay on a side and serve as the retrievers when the ball is missed by a court player. After a minute, rotate clockwise one position.

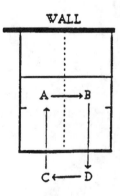

136

Working in pairs, alternate setting each other up for "kill shots." Kill shots are shots hit low and hard, making returns difficult.

Research the regulation game of handball.

In what countries is participation high?

Invent a half-volley game. A half volley is striking the ball just as it starts to bounce off the floor. Play a game to ten points.

What percentage of your brain is water?
Answer: **85%.**

Wednesday
HIP-TO-BE-FIT FITNESS CIRCUIT

	FITNESS COMPONENTS	ACTIVITY	DESCRIPTION	RESOURCE
1	Upper Arm Strength & Flexibility	KIP UP	From a squat position, roll onto the back of your neck. With legs straight and hands on mat by ears (hips up), rock back, extend legs and push up to a squat position.	
2	Arm and Leg Strength	TOWEL PULL	Stand back to back with a towel held between you. Try to pull your partner over a designated line.	
3	Agility and Coordination	HOOP LA	Slowly roll a 36" hoop across the floor and see which partner(s) can get through it without touching.	
4	Leg Strength	ANKLE PUSH	Partners face in a sitting position. Place a heavy medicine ball between ankles and move the ball back and forth.	
5	Power	JUMP YOUR TOE	Lightly hold one foot with the opposite hand. Raise the toe and jump through the circle.	
6	Coordination	KNEE CATCH	Assume a squat position. Place a beanbag on your head. Tilt your head forward and trap the falling bag between your knees.	
7	Balance	BALANCE THE SCALE	Stand side by side. Balance on one foot, lean forward, and extend your back leg straight out. Who can balance the longest? Change feet.	
8	Balance Coordination	BUDDY BOARD	How far can you and a partner go and remain in balance?	GOPHER 1-800-533-0446
9	Balance and Coordination	HIGH JUMP	How many consecutive rope skips can you perform on a low balance beam?	
10	Power and Coordination	180°	Practice performing a 180° jump-rope trick.	

WEEKLY TEST

UNIT: HANDBALL (LESSON 3)

Objectives:

- Strike a rebounding racquetball with an overhand stroke (dominant hand).
- Strike a racquetball that is rebounding from the wall with an overhand stroke (non-dominant hand).
- Strike a rebound with a sidearm stroke (dominant hand).
- Strike a rebounding ball with a sidearm stroke (non-dominant hand).

WARM-UP: LONG RUN FOR PLACE

Practice   Distribute one racquetball to each student.
Find a clear space 15 to 20 feet from a wall.
How many times can you:

INDIVIDUAL

- Drop, hit, and return the ball to the wall before it bounces twice?
- Hit the ball back to the wall in one minute?
- Hit the ball back to the wall with your dominant hand only?
- Hit the ball back to the wall with your non-dominant hand only?
- Hit the ball back to the wall while alternating the dominant and non-dominant hands?

PARTNERS

- **"Cooperative":** Standing six feet apart (20 to 25 feet from the wall), rally with a drop and hit to the wall. See how many times you and your partner can alternate hitting the ball back to the wall with any stroke and either hand. You must cover the entire court. When a legal return is not made, re-start the rally with the other person dropping and hitting. **Next, time each other in one-minute sequences.**
- **"Competitive":** With partners six feet away (20 to 25 feet from the wall), begin the rally with a drop and serve to the wall. The other partner attempts to return the ball. Each time the receiver cannot return the ball, you score one point. You can only score when you serve.

GROUP

- **"Cooperative":** In groups of four, position yourself so that one person is in the court, and the other three are in a line behind the court. The player in the court drops and hits the ball to the wall, and the first person in line returns it to the wall and moves to the end of that line. The player in the court hits that shot and the next person in line returns it to the wall. In other words, the player in the court is hitting every other ball and the players in line play the ball only if they are at the front of the line. Rotate after one minute.
- **"Competitive":** In groups of three, position yourselves so that two players are in the court and one is behind the court acting as the retriever. The in-court players begin to rally with a drop and hit. The rally continues until one player commits an error. The loser of the rally goes behind the court to retrieve, the winner of the rally gets to serve (drop and hit), and the original out-of-court player moves into the court to return serve. Each time a player serves and wins the rally, that player scores a point.

COOPERATIVE

In groups of three, face a wall 15 feet away. Player #1 serves, #2 plays the rebound with a "friendly" return, and #3 does the same. Count a point for your group when you can sequence three consecutive hits with the dominant and three consecutive hits with the non-dominant hand. All hits must be in player order (1, 2, 3).

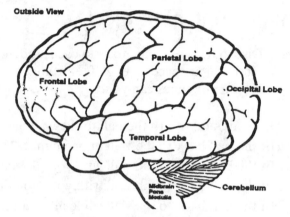
Outside View

Frontal Lobe

Parietal Lobe

Occipital Lobe

Temporal Lobe

Midbrain
Pons
Medulla

Cerebellum

INTERDISCIPLINARY

Different areas of the brain control various body functions. For instance, the *frontal lobe* is responsible for making predictions and processing new ideas. The *occipital lobe* is where vision is processed. The *parietal lobes* process all touch, pain, and temperature. The *temporal lobes* integrate sensory input from the ears and eyes. The ability to play handball is controlled by the part of the brain dealing with balance and coordination. Identify this center. **(Cerebellum.)**

Critical Thinking

Cardiovascular fitness activities raise the heart rate. Develop two new handball exercises that turn a usually inactive drill into an aerobic one.

TRIVIA

How many gallons of fluid does your heart deliver throughout the body each day? *Answer:* **2,000.**

140

PHYSICAL EDUCATION CONTRACT

Name _D. J. Patterson_

Class _4th period — McEwan_

During the next ___1___ weeks, I will work on accomplishing . . .

Improving my consistency with the opposite hand — Hit 25 consecutive strokes (one bounce)

I will need the following equipment . . .

One racquetball — wall space

Teacher Approval _Adrian 2nd Per._ Date _3/10_

Progress—Week one _Best Trial 35 consecutive hits . . . . . ._

Progress—Week two _n/a_

Progress—Week three _n/a_

Goal Accomplished ___✓___ Not Accomplished _____

Teacher Comments:

Good job — Your form is improving too.

Graded ___X___ Non-Graded _____

"PLAYING THE ANGLES"

Objective: Serve with control and accuracy.

Directions: Partners stand 15 feet apart facing the wall (10 to 15 feet back). Partner #1 serves a ball off the wall *directly* to partner #2. If the receiver catches the ball *without moving feet,* he or she takes one step back and serves at an angle back to #1. The secret to success is hitting at the right angle. **See how far back both of you can get.** Return to the starting point when a partner moves his or her feet.

MOTIVATOR

"PASS"

Passing shots are balls hit past an opponent. They usually occur as cross-court passes. Place 3 to 8 players in two separate lines behind the short line at mid-court. Set 3 to 5 empty 2-liter soda bottles in each marked side alley.

Directions: *Lines alternate serving.* Player #1 starts by dropping the ball and underhanding it to the middle of the wall. Player #2 in the opposite line attempts to hit the rebound cross court to knock down one of the plastic bottles. If player #1 can play this rebound, he or she hits it cross court towards the opponent's bottles. When a rally ends, players return to the end of their line and the next two step forward. The first team striking a bottle wins a point.

```
        WALL
5'|                      |5'
0 |                      | 0
0 |       short line     | 0
0 |_____| 0
0 |    X          X      | 0
0 |    X          X      | 0
0 |    X          X      | 0
  |   #1          #2     |
```

ALL★STAR MOTIVATOR

 "HANDBALL BASEBALL"

In handball, a round of play where both players have an opportunity to serve (until put out) is called an inning. Play a three-inning game attempting to score 100 collective runs. An inning begins with a **friendly** serve followed by partners alternating hits. Each hit is a run and should be counted aloud. With both partners serving three times until a mistake is made, an average of 35 good strokes per inning are needed to reach this goal.

ALL★STAR MOTIVATOR

"60-SECOND HOOP HANDBALL"

Control is crucial in handball. Putting the ball where and when you want to is more important than pure speed and power. Put the ball into play with a *self* serve and see how many balls you can hit inside the hoop in 60 seconds. Partners count **good hits** and then try to beat partner #1's score on the second round.

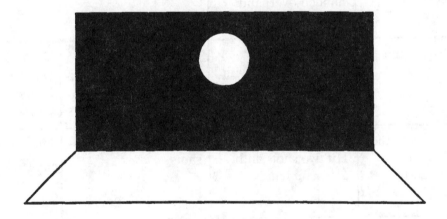

ALL★STAR MOTIVATOR

"COOPERATIVE HANDBALL BINGO"

Hit 4 legal serves	Return the ball with a left-handed overhand stroke	Throw 5 balls to the wall with a right-handed overhand stroke	Return the ball with a right-handed overhand stroke
Return the ball with a right-handed sidearm stroke	Throw 5 balls to the wall with a left-handed overhand stroke	Rally with self for 4 shots	Hit a serve and return it to the wall
Hit two overhand shots in a row	Return the ball with a left-handed sidearm stroke	Hit a trick shot	Throw 5 balls to the wall with a right-handed sidearm stroke
Throw 5 balls to the wall with a left-handed sidearm stroke	Hit two shots and alternate hands	Rally with self for 8 shots	Hit two shots and alternate strokes

1. Find a classmate to watch you.
2. Perform the task in the square.
3. Have the classmate sign the square after he or she watches you.
4. Obtain signatures of classmates as quickly as possible.
5. A classmate may sign your bingo card no more than two times.
6. When your card is filled in with signatures, shout "BINGO!" and turn your card in to the teacher.

* All hits (except serves) are made on a ball rebounding from the wall after a self-throw.

* If it is not designated, you may use any hand or any stroke.

ALL STAR MOTIVATOR

 ## "ADD 'EM UP"

Equipment: Masking tape, chalk, racquetballs, and dice.

Objective: The object of this handball activity is for serve receivers to hit the correct combination of squares as they compete to "Add 'em Up."

Directions: The server rolls the die. The number that is shown is the targeted number for the receiver. Next, the server hits a friendly serve and the receiver attempts to score the targeted number (1, 2, 3, 4, 5, or 6) by hitting rebounded balls into the appropriate squares. If a six is rolled, the receiver might hit the **(1), (2),** and **(3)** in succession, or the **(3)** twice. A point is scored for that player and he or she becomes the new die roller and server. Play a game to ten.

Variation: Alternate hits following the serve.

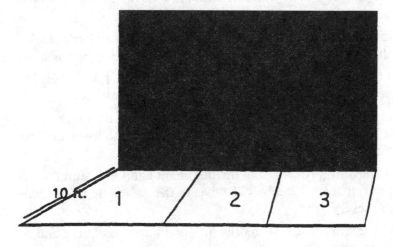

147

MOTIVATOR

 "ACE AWARD"

* Have a class member or the teacher initial when each "letter" has been completed and witnessed. Use any wall space available, but do not interfere with anyone else.
The "letters" can be completed in any order.

GOOD LUCK!

Initials

H = High Stroke: Using either hand, hit 21 overhand strokes to the wall. Hits do not have to be consecutive.

_____

A = Alternate Hands: Using the overhand stroke, alternate using right hand and left hand to hit the ball 21 times to the wall. Hits do not have to be consecutive.

_____

N = Non-Dominant Hand: Using the non-dominant hand only and any stroke, hit the ball 21 times to the wall. Hits do not have to be consecutive.

_____

D = Dominant Hand: Using the dominant hand only and any stroke, hit the ball 21 times to the wall. Hits do not have to be consecutive. _____

B = Ball Contacts: Using any stroke and either hand, hit the ball 21 consecutive times to the wall (a 21 contact self-rally).

_____

A = Alternate Hands: Using the low sidearm stroke, alternate using right hand and left hand to hit the ball 21 times to the wall. Hits do not have to be consecutive.

_____

L = Low Sidearm Stroke: Using the dominant hand only and the low sidearm stroke, hit the ball 21 times to the wall. Hits do not have to be consecutive.

_____

L = Low Sidearm Stroke: Using the non-dominant hand only and the low sidearm stroke, hit the ball 21 times to the wall. Hits do not have to be consecutive.

_____

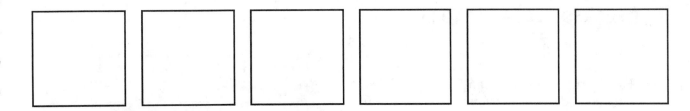

*P*ersonal Safety

PRE-GAME PLAN

"The more you celebrate life, the more there is to celebrate."

- "Homicide is the leading cause of death among young black males and the second among young white males."
- Battering is the number one cause of injury to women in this country.
- One out of every three females and one out of every six males will be victims of sexual assault before age 18.
- 16,000 crimes a day occur on or near school campuses.

In summation, more than ever before, students need a personal safety plan. The information that follows will increase awareness for such a plan. (*Source*: FBI)

HIGHLIGHTS

M   Practice "Kick Circuit," play "Toe Fencing" with a partner, learn personal safety procedures, record emergency numbers.

T   Learn safety rolls, points of vulnerability, partner holds and counters. Play "Give and Take."

W   New Hip-To-Be-Fit circuit, Endurance Test.

Th Work on basic strikes and blocks with rolled newspapers, play "30-Second Block Tag." Complete the "Tunnel."

F   Contracts.

BENEFITS

- Learn personal safety techniques.
- Increase speed, agility, coordination, and reaction time.
- Know how to make home safety plans.

CONTRIBUTOR

Charles Bernasconi
Rainier Beach High School
Seattle School District

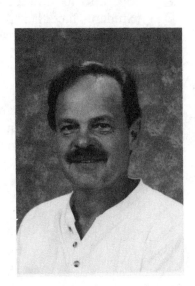

UNIT: PERSONAL SAFETY (LESSON 1)

Objectives:

- Hear crime statistics and know difference between defending yourself and criminal assault. (See introduction.)
- Learn front, side, and heel kicks.
- Increase kicking accuracy.
- Improve coordination and reaction time.

WARM-UP: "50"

Practice

INDIVIDUAL

- **"Kick Circuit":** Run to each of the ten stations, perform the designated kick, replace the equipment when necessary, and move to the next station.
  1. Side kick a medicine ball with the right foot to one wall, left to the other.
  2. Front thrust kick a suspended ball (nerf™ ball in nylon sock).
  3. Side kick (over), than replace a free-standing foldable mat.
  4. Back heel kick a soccer ball off a wall three times in a row.
  5. Side kick a softball off a batting tee (without touching the tee).
  6. Perform three different kicks on a self-tossed balloon before it touches the ground.
  7. Lie on your side ten feet from a wall. Place a ball near your foot and practice kicking and catching the rebound.
  8. Back heel kick a balloon on a string taped low to the floor.
  9. Face a wall. How high can your heel touch on the wall?
  10. Jump and perform as many **heel clicks** as you can. Do five jumps.

PARTNERS

- **"Toe Fencing":** This is a game of quick reflexes. Distribute equipment (one yardstick *or* piece of 36″ to 40″ dowel 1/4″ thick, plastic hockey stick, *or* thin piece of PVC pipe) for each student. Students face their partner and, following the signal to begin, try to touch opponent's feet ten times before their own feet are touched ten times.

GROUP

- **"Three vs. One Tag":** Good defensive tactics call for speed and agility. Number off students in groups of four. Students #s 1–3 hold hands forming a triangle. #4 calls a number (target) and the other two numbers in the triangle attempt to protect that number by keeping #4 from touching the target. At no time can hands separate in the triangle.

"Be Aware—Not a Target": Create a safety plan for the following uncomfortable situations.

Situation	Potential Problem	Your Solution
• Boxed in at intersection	_____	_____
• Crossing a park at night	_____	_____
• Followed by another car	_____	_____
• Sitting on a crowded bus	_____	_____
• Alone in an elevator	_____	_____

Look up, fill in, and post the important numbers below:

- Police—Fire _____
- Electric Company _____
- Poison Control Center _____
- Family Physician _____
- Dentist _____
- Gas Company _____
- Parents' Work _____
- Other _____

Every year around 6,000 people die from drowning. What would you do to assist an individual struggling in deep water?

How many children are treated in emergency rooms each year for bicycle-related head injuries? *Answer:* **50,000.**

UNIT: PERSONAL SAFETY (LESSON 2)

Objectives:

- Understand importance of getting away from attacker(s).
- Learn points of vulnerability (knee, nose, neck, eyes, groin).
- Break kicking fundamentals into slow motion.
- Practice basic stance.

WARM-UP: THREE 10-SECOND SPEED JUMP-ROPE TRIALS

Practice

INDIVIDUAL

- *Safety*: Distribute mats. Assume a squat position and work on tucking chin to chest while rolling both forward and backward.
- Once you attain proficiency, repeat from a standing position, falling and rolling.
- *Teacher*: Chalk human outlines on foldable mats. Place small circular targets on **points of vulnerability** and stand mats against the wall.
- *Stance*: The basic stance has the student's weight on the back foot, body turned sideways to attacker, lead hand (sword) with palm up—backhand (dagger) palm down.
- From this stance, work on performing three quick strikes utilizing the following kicks and body targets.

POSITION	KICK	TARGET
Facing	Front	Groin
Back to mat	Back kick	Ankle
Sideways	Side thrust	Knee

PARTNERS

- Select a partner of equal size and practice the following defensive techniques. Remember to walk through each movement in slow motion before changing places.

PARTNER #1 EXECUTES:	PARTNER #2 COUNTERS WITH:
Bearhug from behind _____	Ear slap—runs away
Bearhug from behind _____	Stomps on instep—runs away
Bearhug from behind _____	Bends finger back—runs away
Arm grab _____	Twists out—runs away

GROUP

- Students number off in groups of three. Distribute two soccer, nerf™, or rubber playground balls to each group. Students #2 and #3, on backs with heads three feet from the wall, place a ball between both feet and lift the ball just off the ground. #1 moves between and **heel** kicks each ball and tries to catch the rebound off the wall. After balls are retrieved, #s 2 and 3 follow. On the second round, legs are raised for the side thrust and front kicks.

  Note: Remind students that accuracy is the key. Only the ball is kicked.

COOPERATIVE

In groups of three to five, design a **15-second** television ad emphasizing sports safety.

INTERDISCIPLINARY

Locate a Red Cross or American Heart Association CPR manual.
What is the main difference between adult and infant CPR?

Critical Thinking

Devise a fire safety plan for your home that includes adequate smoke alarms, a fire escape plan for each room, and an agreed upon meeting place outside.

How many teenage girls start smoking each day?
Answer: **1,600.**

TRIVIA

Wednesday
HIP-TO-BE-FIT FITNESS CIRCUIT

	FITNESS COMPONENTS	ACTIVITY	DESCRIPTION	RESOURCE
1	Upper Arm Strength & Endurance	PORTABLE STAIR MASTER	Work on coordinating arm and step patterns.	Quantum Marketing INT. 801 Candelaria Rd. NE Albuquerque, NM 87107
2	Speed & Agility	CONE RACE	Race your partner through the cone course.	
3	Upper Arm Strength	TIGER BANDS	Alternate upper arm curls.	Perform Better 1-800-556-7464
4	Flexibility	DOUBLE ROLLS	Holding each other's ankles, practice smooth double rolls.	
5	Speed	SPORTS RADAR	Time the speed of your sprints at 30, 40, and 50 yards.	Flaghouse 1-800-221-5185
6	Upper Arm Strength	PARTNER SHOULDER PUSH UP	Partner #1 assumes a handstand position with feet on shoulders of #2. #2 takes a step back and tries a push-up.	
7	Power	BENCH POWER JUMP	Stand sideways to the bench, jump up to the top and down. Repeat.	
8	Upper Arm Strength	POWER PUSH	Practice push-ups with arms held at different angles.	Perform Better 1-800-556-7464
9	Speed	SPEED CHUTE	Work on short and intermediate sprints to open the attached chute.	Perform Better 1-800-556-7464
10	Balance & Upper Arm Strength	HANDSTAND WALL PUSH-UP	From a handstand position (feet against the wall) work on lifting and lowering.	

WEEKLY TEST

UNIT: PERSONAL SAFETY (LESSON 3)

Objectives:

- Review stance with basic kicks and blocks.
- React quickly to teacher commands.
- Increase fitness and coordination.
- Learn strategies to help avoid being a crime victim.

WARM-UP: LONG RUN FOR PLACE

Practice

INDIVIDUAL

- Distribute two rolled (taped) newspapers to each student.
- Work on individual **shadow** moves from the stance described in Lesson 2.
  Practice the following:
- Block up with lead hand and strike with backhand toward an imaginary opponent's nose.
- Block down and kick toward the knee area.
- Increase your speed and focus on good form with low-, medium-, and high-level kicks with a recoil action.
- Create a smooth slow-motion kicking routine.

PARTNERS

- Select a partner of approximately the same size and designate as #1 and #2. While facing three feet apart, practice the following in slow motion first.

PARTNER #1 (newspapers)	PARTNER #2 (hands)
• Left-hand strike high	• Wrist block
• Right-hand strike high	• Wrist block
• Left-hand strike low	• Wrist block
• Right-hand strike low	• Wrist block

SWITCH   PARTNERS

- After each student has had numerous opportunities to practice the strikes and blocks, speed of the movements may be increased.
- This time, try not to let your partner penetrate your defense.
- **"30-Second Block Tag":** (Teacher calls off a body part, e.g., "knee." Partner #1 has 30 seconds to try to tag the knees of #2. Points are scored for each legal hit. Switch after every 30 seconds. Try not to move outside your space.

GROUP

- **"The Tunnel":** Arrange students shoulder to shoulder (push-up position) in lines of six. This activity will increase upper arm strength. Following a signal to begin, the first person quickly crawls under the rest of the line, comes shoulder to shoulder with the last person in line, and yells "GO." This process continues until all six have crawled through the tunnel. A point is scored if **all** students can hold the push-up position for the duration. Join with other groups and set a goal for the entire class to traverse **one** tunnel.

With a partner, create a catchy jingle for radio, promoting either the heart attack signals or steps to reduce your risk.

SAMPLE
Don't smoke—and watch your fat. Reduce the chance of a heart attack. EXERCISE, have some fun, and we won't have to dial 911.

What are five signs of a heart attack?
- **Pain in chest for two minutes or more.**
- **Pain spreading to arms, neck, and shoulder area.**
- **Dizziness.**
- **Shortness of breath.**
- **Nausea, etc.**

Good Samaritan laws are established to encourage people to assist others in emergency situations. When acting in a **reasonable manner** these laws protect the rescuer from liability. An example is moving an injured person away from traffic. What actions could occur that would negate this protection?

How can couch potatoes cut their cholesterol level?
Answer: **Turn off the tube. Couch potatoes watching three or more hours of TV a day are nearly twice as likely to have high cholesterol levels.**

PHYSICAL EDUCATION CONTRACT

Name *Darcy Hepburn – Rob Ricci*

Class *Self Defense 1st Per.*

During the next _____2_____ weeks, I will work on accomplishing . . .

Rob and I will work on refining our escapes and counters culminating in a routine for the curriculum night in mid January

I will need the following equipment . . .

Mats

Teacher Approval *Kay Tyler* Date *12/1*

Progress—Week one *Good Progress – Need to smooth out your breakfalls.*

Progress—Week two *Nice Job – you both will look great on curriculum night.*

Progress—Week three *n/a*

Goal Accomplished___*X*___ Not Accomplished _____

Teacher Comments:

your routine is outstanding

Graded _____ Non-Graded _*X*_

ALL STAR
MOTIVATOR

 ### "GO BEHIND"

With regard to personal safety, success can be measured by one's ability to maintain control. "Go Behind" is an activity that stresses foot speed, strength, and coordination.

Directions: Face a partner and place both hands on your opponent's shoulders. Following a signal to begin, attempt to escape and get behind to place your partner in a bearhug position. Score one point each time you are successful.

Starting Position

Group

ALL★STAR
MOTIVATOR

 ## "SLAP-REACT"

Quick reactions are essential for personal safety. *Slap-React* is a partner activity that will improve balance, coordination, and reaction time.

Directions: Face each other from a catcher's position 2 to 3 feet apart. Both *palms* are up (facing partner) and are the only means of upsetting your opponent's balance. Following a signal to begin, partners slap palms or perform a feinting movement (drawing hands back) to cause the opposite partner to move his or her feet. When feet move, a point is lost. Play a game to ten points.

ALL STAR
MOTIVATOR

 "THREE WAY ROLLS"

"Three Way Rolls" is an excellent exercise for improving agility, coordination, and reaction time.

Directions: Form groups of three on separate mats. Students number off "1, 2, 3 . ." and assume a position on all fours (facing the same direction) three feet apart.

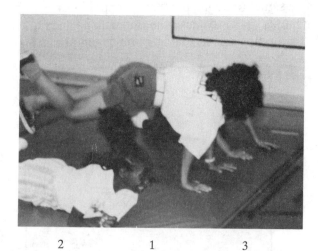

2   1   3

    Action begins as the middle person rolls to the right and #2 jumps over. Student #3 then jumps up and over #2. This sequence continues with all movements occurring in the middle of the mat.

ALL STAR MOTIVATOR

 ## "GIVE AND TAKE"

Slow motion give-and-take sparring is an unrehearsed minimal contact sequence of blocks and counters between two partners.

Partners face each other and alternate being the attacker and defender. For safety's sake all attacks, blocks, and counters are controlled and should always begin in slow motion.

Variation: Use rolled newspapers as in Lesson 3.

ALL★STAR MOTIVATOR

"BREAKFALLS"

With every throw there is an appropriate fall. Breakfalls are rolling movements meant to reduce injuries from throws. Practice the following rolls on mats with the aid of a partner.

STARTING POSITIONS	TECHNIQUE	RECOVERY
1. Squat down. Have a partner push one shoulder.	Roll sideways with the outside arm across the chest and knees tucked.	Push from knees to feet.
2. Squat down. Have a partner gently push your forehead back.	Roll slowly backwards with chin to chest. (Place a tennis ball between chin and sternum). Relax as you complete the movement.	Return to squat position.
3. Repeat the rolls above with the arms (hands) acting like a shock absorber. Beat the hands forcefully as you land. Practice stopping your roll with a resounding pound on the mat.		

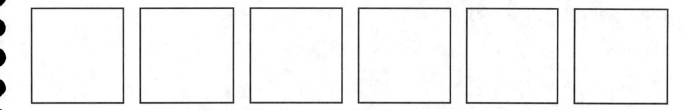

*S*occer

PRE-GAME PLAN

"Don't be content with being average.
Average is as close to the bottom as it is to the top."

Called the world's most popular sport, participation continues to grow in this country. The three lessons in this chapter concentrate on the basic soccer skills of dribbling, trapping, passing, heading, kicking, and juggling.

HIGHLIGHTS

M   Work on juggling, trapping and passing, play "Shadow Dribble," complete "Minute Master" drill, and participate in a modified two vs. one game.

T   Practice heading, agility dribbling drills, play "Beach Blast" and "Four-Ball Soccer."

W   New Hip-To-Be-Fit circuit, Flexibility Test.

Th   Increase passing accuracy, tackling ability, play "Bone Head Soccer."

F   Contracts.

BENEFITS

- Aerobic activity.
- Improve eye-foot coordination and agility.
- Social aspects of team play.

RESOURCES

National Collegiate Athletic Assoc. (NCAA)
Box 757, Grand Central Station
New York, NY 10017

UNIT: SOCCER (LESSON 1)

Objectives:

- Improve soccer juggling skills.
- Practice trapping and kicks on goal.
- Increase dribbling agility.
- Work on passing accuracy.

WARM-UP: "50"

Practice

INDIVIDUAL

"Can U's?": (Distribute one ball per student.)
- From a lying position, can you place a ball between your feet, raise overhead, and touch the ball to the floor behind? Repeat five times?
- Perform a push-up with both hands on the ball?
- Place a ball between ankles, jump, flip over shoulder, and catch?
- In a clear space, practice the following **juggling sequence.** Toss the ball up and tap it off your head, thigh, and foot.
- Can you reverse the sequence?
- What is the highest number of consecutive contacts you can make before losing control?
- **"Quick Kicks":** Face a wall 10 to 15 feet back. Toss the ball upwards, trap, and quickly kick off the wall. Work on kicking it so that it comes straight back to you.
- **"Run the Lines":** Place your ball on the baseline, dribble to the foul line, back to the baseline, out to the mid-court line, and back over the baseline.

PARTNERS

- Select a partner and face each other on opposite baselines. Challenge your partner to a *Run the Lines* contest. Who can dribble back to the baseline first?
- **"Shadow Dribble":** Using the same partner, the leader dribbles in different directions, while the other partner attempts to shadow the leader's movements with his or her ball.
- **"Two at Once":** Partner #1 assumes a kneeling position with a ball in each hand. Partner #2 stands ten feet away. The kneeling partner rolls one ball after another while the standing partner attempts to trap and quickly return each incoming ball directly back to the kneeling partner. Change partners after ten balls.

GROUP

- **"Two vs. One":** (Groups of three in a confined area). Players with the ball attempt to keep it away from the defensive player. Alternate after three passes.
- **"Human Goals":** Players #1 and #2 act as goals (legs apart) while #3 and #4 try to score through their legs.

In partners, alternate exchanging soft tosses to one another, permitting the receiver to practice **heading** the toss back to the tosser. Work on setting a cooperative record.

Draw an offensive play for your soccer team in the box below.

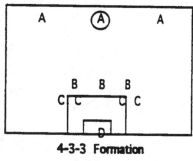

4-3-3 Formation

A = Forwards
B = Mid-fielders
C = Defenders
D = Goalkeeper

Find three ways to move a ball from the ground to your head without using your hands.

The brain of a five-year-old is (1/2, 2/3, or 9/10) of its adult weight. *Answer:* **9/10.**

UNIT: SOCCER (LESSON 2)

Objectives:

- Improve passing accuracy.
- Increase ball-control and trapping skills.
- Practice kicking and goal-keeping techniques.
- Work on front and side tackling skills.

WARM-UP

Practice

INDIVIDUAL

- Distribute one ball to each student. Practice moving slowly, keeping your ball close (one to two feet) to your feet as you dribble among the group. Work on changing directions (feinting) as you go. When your hear "FREEZE," see if you can trap the ball within three seconds. Use the sole, inside, and outside of your foot. After each freeze, increase the speed of your dribble (remove one ball on each freeze). Those without a ball attempt to make a legal steal.
- **"Foot Taps":** Place your dominant foot lightly on top of the ball. Can you alternate the right and left foot on top without moving the ball? Next, practice moving the ball backwards, forwards, and side to side by lightly stroking the top of the ball with the dominant and non-dominant foot.
- **"Quick Trap":** Toss your ball ten or more feet in the air and see if you can trap it (no hands) with a foot on top in less than ten seconds. Eight? Six? Four? This time, incorporate the chest, thigh, inside, and outside of your foot.
- Place a small cone or pin near a wall. From 20 feet back, how many times can you knock it over and retrieve the ball in 60 seconds? Can you match the score with your opposite foot? Concentrate on inside foot kicks.

PARTNERS

- How far away can you and a partner be while passing through cones three feet apart? Alternate passes with left and right feet.
- **"Pin Down":** Using good throw-in techniques (two-hand release from back of head to the front without either foot leaving the ground), practice exchanges with each partner moving one step back on each successful catch. How far apart can the two of you be while maintaining good technique?

GROUP

- Play begins after selected players scatter their pins on one side of the floor. Balls are distributed to a majority of the pin guards and remaining class members form a single-file line on the opposite side of the court. Following the signal to begin, participants possessing a ball use correct throw-in or kicking techniques to move the ball toward other players' pins. When pins are toppled by balls or one's own feet, players leave the pin in the down position and immediately run to the end of a single-file line. Players in the line shout "Pindown" and the player at the head of the line resets the fallen pin and begins guarding it.

What are some safety concerns when working with a partner on cooperative stretching exercises? (Possible answer) **You can't feel your partner's pain.** Communicate with each other.

A simile is defined as "a figure of speech in which two essentially unlike things are compared, the comparison being made explicit typically by the use of the introductory *like* or *as*." For example, "Like ancient trees, we die from the top." (**Gore Vidal).** Create a **SOCCER SIMILE.**

You have been asked by your instructor to select teams for tomorrow's soccer tournament. Your selection process should produce:

- Equal-ability groups.
- Sex-integrated teams.

How will you accomplish this?

If you placed the blood vessels in your heart from end to end, how many miles long would they stretch? *Answer:* **60,000 miles.**

Wednesday
HIP-TO-BE-FIT FITNESS CIRCUIT

	FITNESS COMPONENTS	ACTIVITY	DESCRIPTION	RESOURCE
1	Arm-Leg Strength	CHUK-EM PULL	Partners facing away, attempt to pull their partner over a line.	Chuk-Em Enterprises 11080 Arroyo Beach Pl. S.W. Seattle, WA 98146 (206) 244-7049
2	Balance & Coordination	BATAKA BEAM	Compete to see who can maintain balance the longest.	Flaghouse 1-800-793-7900
3	Upper Arm Strength	4 BACK PUSH UP	Complete 4 quick push-ups on different parts of your partner's back.	
4	Leg Strength	WALL SIT	With back against the wall (knees bent), challenge your partner for the longest wall sit.	
5	Coordination	ROOSTER SOCCER	Challenge your partner to a game of "Rooster" (one-leg) soccer. (Beanbag)	
6	Leg Strength	RESISTANCE RUN	Tie two bicycle inner tubes together and place around partners' waists and begin a slow jog apart.	
7	Endurance	POGO STICK	How long can you keep jumping?	Gopher 1-800-533-0446
8	Arm-Leg Strength	SPRI XERCISE TUBES	How many exercises can you create?	Gopher 1-800-533-0446
9	Speed	WALL TO WALL BEAN BAG SHUTTLE	Race a partner to see who can collect and replace the most bags.	
10	Upper Body Strength	QUICK-FIT TONER	Focus on wide slow stretches	Sportime 1-800-283-5700

WEEKLY TEST

UNIT: SOCCER (LESSON 3)

Objectives:

- Improve dribbling and passing accuracy.
- Work on heading skills.
- Moving the ball utilizing **all** parts of the foot.

WARM-UP:

Practice

INDIVIDUAL

"**Alpha Dribble**." Tape a different letter of the alphabet on each of 26 cones scattered about the floor and assign one or two students per cone. Distribute one ball per student. In 60 seconds, see if you can perform a **controlled** dribble gently touching each cone in alphabetical order.

- Reverse the order and see if you can touch as many cones.
- Practice using each part of your foot as you
  a. Spell your name.
  b. Spell the month in which you were born.
  c. Dribble around four different cones.
- From a sitting position (legs together) try to move a ball from your lap to your feet by alternately raising and lowering your feet and buttocks.

PARTNERS

- Distribute one ball to each set of partners. The partner without the ball assumes a wide stance (legs apart). Following the signal to begin, students with ball dribble between as many different legs (goals) as possible in 60 seconds. After the stop signal dribblers report the number of goals and partners change positions.
- During the second round have stationary partners perform slow jumping jacks making goals more challenging.

GROUP

"Heads-Up"

In lines of four, see which group can be the first to move the ball from one end of the line to the other with one contact (head) per player enroute.

"Keep It Up"

Assign four to five students per mat, and distribute one beach ball. Teams lie on their backs positioning themselves to cover the entire space. Which mat team can keep the ball in the air the longest?

Note: In the beginning lessons nerf™ or similarly marketed foam balls make learning skills less threatening for some players.

"Over and Back": Have all class members stand shoulder to shoulder (hands held) with a ball between their ankles. The goal is to cooperatively jump across the entire field and back without losing more than five balls in the process.

Write a new **fight song** for your soccer team.

Redesign this field to permit higher scoring.

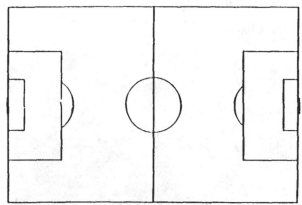

How much sweat can you produce in a day:
sitting all day in a cool room = (1 cup)
playing all day = (1 bucket)
running a 26-mile marathon = (2–3 buckets)

PHYSICAL EDUCATION CONTRACT

Name _Ian White, Joan Shigaki, Dion Williams_

Class _Team Sports - Putnam_

During the next ___2___ weeks, ~~I~~ *we* will work on accomplishing . . .

Performing 20 consecutive headers while in a circle.

I will need the following equipment . . .

One Nerf - one regulation

Teacher Approval _McElwan_ Date _10/27_

Progress—Week one _Good progress — Emphasize contacting the ball at the hairline._

Progress—Week two _26 legal hits. Almost a class record._

Progress—Week three _n/a_

Goal Accomplished ___X___ Not Accomplished _____

Teacher Comments:

Good team work.

Graded _____ Non-Graded ___✓___

ALL★STAR
MOTIVATOR

 ### "SOCCER GOLF"

Directions: Place nine traffic cones in a zigzag pattern (75 to 100 yards apart) across a large field. Distribute one ball to each player and divide players evenly among the cones. Players attempt to kick their ball to each cone in order with as few kicks (strokes) as possible. Count the number of kicks it takes to touch your ball to each cone. Low scores win.

Variations

- Alternate kicks with a partner.
- Try to kick oncoming balls away without losing your own.
- Time the event.

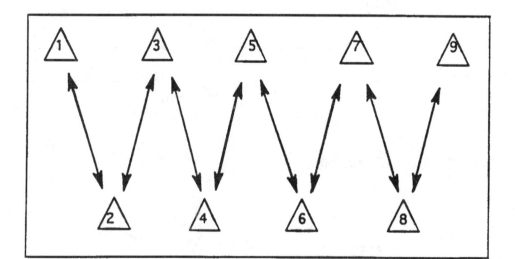

ALL STAR MOTIVATOR

"DANGEROUS CROSSING"

Goal: To cross the field or floor maintaining control of a ball five times in a row.

Directions: Distribute one ball per student. Place half the class on each end line. Select two guards to stand at mid-field/court. Following the start signal, players attempt to dribble their ball safely past the guards toward the opposite end line. Guards in the middle attempt to steal or kick away the balls of students as they cross the mid-line. Players maintaining control line up on the opposite side and await the next signal to cross. Students whose ball was stolen or touched become additional guards in the middle. **How many of you can make the dangerous crossing five times in a row?**

Variation: "Soccer Steal"

Directions: Students face from opposite end lines. Balls are distributed to one team. Following a signal to begin, students attempt to dribble their ball through the defense and across the opposite end line. Students who are successful repeat the crossings as the defense continues to grow. Switch teams after five crossings.

MOTIVATOR

 ## "MINUTE MASTERS"

#	Skill	Task	Level

Player

| 1 | Ball control | Keep a ball rolling in traffic with light taps (no stops) for one minute. |

All Star

| 2 | Passing | Exchange ten cooperative passes through two cones (3 feet apart) from a distance of 20 feet in one minute. |

MVP

| 3 | Juggling | Use any body part to keep a ball juggling off the ground for one minute. |

ALL☆STAR MOTIVATOR

 ## "NON-STOP SOCCER"

The objective of this activity is for each student to keep **two** balls rolling **at all times.** Distribute two tennis balls per student. Students find an open space and place a tennis ball by each foot. A container is placed next to the instructor at mid-court. Once the clock starts, students begin moving both balls (trying to keep them in close proximity). Once a ball stops, even momentarily, the instructor deposits it in the container. When ten balls are inside, the clock stops and the first record is established. Try to keep them going longer on each trial.

This drill reinforces keeping the ball close to your foot as well as concentration and coordination.

ALL★STAR MOTIVATOR

 ## "BONEHEAD SOCCER"

Directions: Most soccer players are familiar with legal body parts used to move and control the ball. The question is, how else can we educate them while utilizing these particular bones and joints? **Bonehead Soccer** teaches anatomy, while refining their skills. The teacher calls out the bone and students work on consecutive contacts (juggling or trapping) off that area. Toss the ball from the metacarpals and trap or spike off the:

- <u>Metatarsals</u>   Top of foot
- <u>Cranium</u>   Head
- <u>Femur</u>   Area between knee and hip
- <u>Clavicle</u>   Shoulder
- <u>Sternum</u>   Chest
- <u>Fibula</u>   Area just below knee
- <u>Patella</u>   Knee

*What bone areas were best for striking? Trapping?

ALL STAR MOTIVATOR

"FOUR-BALL SOCCER"

Soccer is one of those large-group games that can be dominated by a small number of players interfering with the skill development of the rest. An excellent modification to the traditional game is "Four-Ball Soccer." It activates an entire class and provides more opportunities to improve skills.

Rules: Four players from each team serve as goalies and remain in the goal area. All other players are allowed to move freely from one end of the playing field to the other. All players can use any body part *other than hands* to propel the ball. The game begins with two players from opposite teams kicking balls into their opponents' side of the field. As goals are scored, balls are returned to midfield and rekicked. Play is stopped on touched balls with a resulting free kick from the point of the infraction. Balls crossing side or end lines are moved to the out-of-bounds line and thrown in by an opposing player.

Credit: Janet Smith—*JOPERD*, March 1982.

ALL STAR MOTIVATOR

"HEADS UP"

Heads Up is a soccer/volleyball activity that encourages the soccer skill of heading. Following a serve, the receiving team is allowed three contacts on its side of the net. **One of those contacts must be off the head.** Points are awarded for the required as well as additional headers during the receiving sequence. A team that heads all three contacts scores five points. All other volleyball rules apply. Play a game to 25.

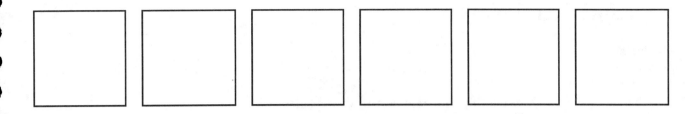

Softball

PRE-GAME PLAN

> "It's not the wrapping or the size of the package that counts—
> It's what is inside that's important."
> —*Dennis Iwami*

Recreational softball is growing in popularity with increasing participation in "mixed" play. Experiences in this chapter center around throwing, catching, hitting, and base-running skills. Traditional apparatus will be supplemented with a variety of alternative equipment.

HIGHLIGHTS

M	Work on catching on both the glove and non-glove sides of the body, play "One Step" and "Pickle."
T	Increase ball-tracking proficiency, play "Strike Out," and practice modified double plays.
W	New Hip-To-Be-Fit circuit, Agility Test.
Th	Practice swing-and-run technique, play "Fox Tail Baseball" and "Coneball."
F	Contracts.

BENEFITS

- Lifetime activity.
- Improve eye-hand coordination.
- Learn teamwork.

RESOURCES

Amateur Softball Assoc. (ASA)
2801 N.E. 50th
Oklahoma City, OK 73111

USSSA
3935 S. Crater Road
Petersburg, VA 23805

UNIT: SOFTBALL (LESSON 1)

Objectives:

- Increase pitching accuracy.
- Practice catching on the throwing and non-throwing sides.
- Practice base-running technique.

WARM-UP: "50"

Practice

INDIVIDUAL

- (Tennis balls) Practice throwing the ball off a wall. Make five catches when the ball is directly in front of you, five on your glove side, and five on your non-glove side. Repeat, increasing the velocity of your throws.
- Practice charging the ball as it comes off the wall.

PARTNERS

- Place two hoops 45 to 50 feet apart. Partners take turns pitching and catching back and forth. Catchers should kneel with their glove held inside the hoops. Who can throw three strikes first? Nine?
- Work on pitching toward the hoop with a high 10- to 12-foot arc.
- Work on flat pitches only.
- How fast can you pitch underhand and maintain accuracy?
- **"One Step":** Partners face each other. After each successful exchange (catch), players take one step back. See how far apart you and your partner can be before one of you misses. After a miss, both partners return to their starting positions.

GROUP

- **"Pickle":** In groups of three, mark off two bases 50 to 60 feet apart. Place one fielder at each base. The third person attempts to move from one base to another without being tagged. Once a player is touched, a different player becomes the runner. Who can steal the most bases? *Variation:* Play "Trickle" by adding a third base (triangle), one more ball, and one more runner.
- **"Hit the Cut Off":** Place lines of four players 25 yards apart. Following the signal to start, see which line can be the first to move the ball from the first player to the last player. *Option:* Have players run to the end of the opposite line following their throw.

Place students in lines of five or six. Jog a quarter-mile course passing a softball from the front of the line backwards. As the last person receives the ball, he or she runs to the front of the line and repeats the process. Can you jog a quarter mile with less than five misses? Three?

"Hand Baseball": *Rules:* Two players are needed for this game. A decision is then made as to who bats first. Each player puts one hand behind his or her back. On a signal, each player sticks out a hand with one to five fingers showing. Totals are then made for both players. Even numbers help the batter while odd numbers help the pitcher.

All runners must be forced to the next base. Runners may not advance on an out. On a double play, the batter plus the runner on the nearest base to home is out. A double or triple play with the bases empty means only one out. A triple play with one player on base means two outs.

Pitchers and batters switch positions after three outs.

Code:	Even		Odd	
	2 fingers—	walk	3 fingers—	out
	4 fingers—	single	5 fingers—	out
	6 fingers—	double	7 fingers—	double play
	8 fingers—	triple	9 fingers—	triple play
	10 fingers—	home run		

Source: Craig Cunningham, UCLA.

Invent a piece of equipment that would save the wear and tear on a catcher's knees.

What is included in baseball's Triple Crown?
Answer: **Batting Average, homeruns, and runs batted in (RBI's).**

UNIT: SOFTBALL (LESSON 2)

Objectives:

- Increase throwing accuracy.
- Improve catching proficiency utilizing softball and non-softball apparatus.

WARM-UP: THREE 10-SECOND SPEED JUMP-ROPE TRIALS

Practice

INDIVIDUAL

- Distribute one ROCKETBAL™ per student. Let the ball hang from your dominant thumb. Place the index finger and thumb of the opposite hand on the ball. Launch it straight up and catch it as it descends. Can you accomplish the following eye-hand coordination tasks?
  - a. Catch it with two hands.
  - b. Catch it in your right hand; left hand.
  - c. Catch the tail only. Without moving your feet.
  - d. Make three consecutive catches.
  - e. Make a full turn and catch. Add a jump.
  - f. Use the stop watch to time the maximum air time of your launch.

  *Rocketbals™ are available through Jack Johnson, 12724 SE 254th Place, Kent, WA 98031. For more information, call 206-631-4311.

PARTNERS

- **"Strike Out":** Students pitch at the 2′ x 2′ strike squares from 40 to 60 feet back. If three strikes occur before four balls, he or she moves clockwise to the next square (batter). How many strike-outs can you achieve in the time allotted? More than one player can pitch at a square.

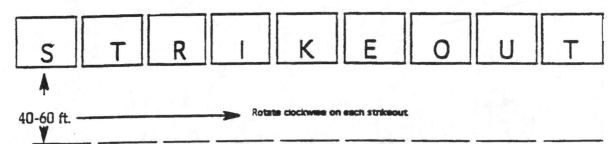

40-60 ft. ———————————————→ Rotate clockwise on each strikeout

GROUP

- **"Double Play":** Place players on bases in a triangular formation. Player #1 throws a ground ball to player #2 who fields and throws to #3. Player #3 tags the closest base and throws on to the last base in the triangle. Rotate bases after three turns.

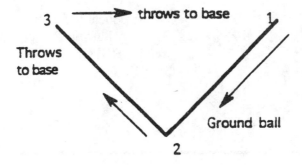

182

Partners with gloves and one ball face one another at midfield. Each time the ball is exchanged successfully, each player takes one step back. How far apart can you be before missing? When a ball is dropped, both players return to their starting positions. *Option:* Try this with ground balls.

Create a press release describing your debut as a pitcher for the Kansas City Royals.

Explain how a pitcher threw 31 pitches in one inning and only gave up one run.
Answer: **Numerous foul balls.**

"Describe the Big Picture": A small child sat in the centerfield bleachers at his first baseball game. His mind was full of fast-food snacks, the noise of the crowd, and the color of the field. *What didn't he see?* (Include) Regional economics, entertainment, etc.

What two softball players make up a battery?
Answer: **Pitcher and a Catcher.**

Wednesday
HIP-TO-BE-FIT FITNESS CIRCUIT

	FITNESS COMPONENTS	ACTIVITY	DESCRIPTION	RESOURCE
1	Endurance	STEP & TURN	Step, make a 1/2 turn, and step off the foldable mat. Repeat.	
2	Coordination	JUMP STICK	How many consecutive jumps can you make?	
3	Balance	BILLY BOARD	How many full turns can you make in 1 minute?	Billy Boards Inc. (206) 361-1614
4	Endurance	AEROBICS	Follow a commercial aerobics tape.	
5	Upper Arm Strength	PARTNER PULL UP	Can you do 10 or more?	
6	Arm Strength Flexibility	ROPE SWING (over foldable mat)	Can you clear the mat without touching it?	
7	Balance	BALANCE MASTER	How long can you keep rocking without letting the ends touch the ground?	Gopher 1-800-533-0446
8	Upper Arm Strength	INVERTED JUMP PULLS	How many times can you raise your feet above the bar?	Sportime 1-800-283-5700
9	Leg (Thigh) Strength	TOWEL RACE	Work your feet together and apart to race a partner across the gym.	
10	Upper Arm Strength	WIDE ARM PUSH UP	How far apart can you move the blocks and continue to do push-ups?	

WEEKLY TEST

UNIT: SOFTBALL (LESSON 3)

Objectives:

- Increase batting efficiency.
- Improve catching skills.
- Work on base-running techniques.

WARM-UP: LONG RUN FOR PLACE

Practice

- **"Swing and Sprint":** Set up lines three deep and a minimum of five yards apart. Have students assume appropriate batting stance, swing, drop the bat, sprint 30 yards down the field, and return on the outside to the batting line. Repeat five times.

PARTNERS

- <u>Foxtail</u> **"Straight Up Baseball":** Spin the Foxtail hard and throw it as high as you can, straight up. Your partner has to catch it as it comes down. If the catch is made on the top color, right next to the ball, he or she gets a homer. Otherwise, here's how it goes:

  Top seam . . . triple

  Middle color or bottom seam . . . double

  Bottom color . . . single

  A miss, of course, is an out. The same with "ball fouls" (when the ball hits your hand coming through, even though you end up hanging on to the tail). And in this game one out is all you get. Change sides every miss or ball foul.

GROUP

- **"Soft Toss":** Take turns hitting balls tossed slowly into the batter's target zone. Balls should be hit into a standing mat (inside) or cyclone fence (outside). Pitchers are stationed 10 feet away opposite the hitter's back foot.
- **"Pepper":** Pitchers face hitters 15 feet away. Batters practice hitting underhand pitches directly back to the pitcher on one or two bounces. How many consecutive hits can you return to the pitcher without a bounce?
- **"2 vs. 2 Coneball":**

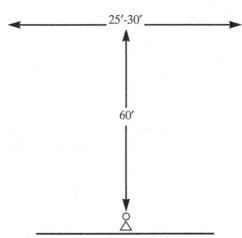

25'-30'

60'

Restraining line for waiting batters

TWO VS. TWO CONEBALL

Two vs. Two Coneball is a fast-paced, task oriented, lead-up activity that allows fundamental softball game skills to be taught in a relatively small area.

Rules for this activity are similar to those of regulation softball with the following exceptions:

- A batter is out following one clean strike or two foul calls.
- One out ends that team's half of an inning.
- There is only one base to run to.
- Players are required to run when changing from batting to fielding positions.
- Balls must be hit between two outer cones.

Nearly all other softball rules and strategies apply, e.g., force outs, covering bases, etc.

Arrange partners 15 to 20 feet apart. Practice jogging parallel across an unobstructed field, exchanging throws while on the run. When you can run the field without a miss, repeat at a sprint.

Where do you think these softball terms come from?

Bunt?

Shortstop?

Inning?

List three tips for learning to hit the ball the opposite way.

Possible answers:
- closed stance
- look for outside pitch
- let your hands lead the way
- aim the bat in the direction desired

Why is pitching underhand less stressful on the arm than an overhand delivery?

What does it mean to hit the cycle in softball and baseball? *Answer:* **Single, double, triple, and home-run.**

PHYSICAL EDUCATION CONTRACT

Name _Tam Hutchinson_

Class _Team Sports — 3rd Period_

During the next ___3___ weeks, I will work on accomplishing . . .

A better score on the softball wall test. I will also focus on catching fly balls on the run and keeping my head down on short hops.

I will need the following equipment . . .

Tennis ball, softball, glove.
A person to assist — throwing fly balls.

Teacher Approval _McEwan_ Date _5/27_

Progress—Week one _Improved upon catching on the run._

Progress—Week two _Still has trouble on short hops. Wall test time has improved by 4 points._

Progress—Week three _Improved in all areas._

Goal Accomplished ___X___ Not Accomplished _____

Teacher Comments:

Hope you make your summer team.
Keep practicing.

Graded _____ Non-Graded _✓_

ALL STAR
MOTIVATOR

 ### "QUICK HANDS"

The goal of this activity is to increase the ability to barehand a slow bouncing ball and throw accurately to a target.

Directions: Tape 2-foot squares on a wall (4 to 5 feet high) and a throwing line 20 feet back.

- Facing the wall, drop a tennis ball, barehand with throwing hand, pivot and try to hit the wall target. How fast can you catch and release?
- Next, stand sideways to the target, drop, catch, and throw.
- Can you execute this drill when catching off the second bounce?
- Take three steps back, toss the tennis ball ahead, **charge,** catch, and throw.
- How many rebounded balls can you hit inside the target square in 60 seconds?

ALL★STAR MOTIVATOR

☆ "TIMED TEAM THROW"

Directions: Place players at each of nine positions. The goal of the game is for the team to throw a ball from player to player in the correct order as quickly as possible. The pitcher initiates the timed sequence by throwing to the catcher. From there, the ball travels to third, to left field, to short, to centerfield, to second base, to right field, to first base, and on to home. As the ball is received by the catcher, all of the other eight players sprint home forming a single line behind the catcher. The last person to line up stops the clock. It's important for all players to stay in their designated zones. Emphasize quick but accurate throws.

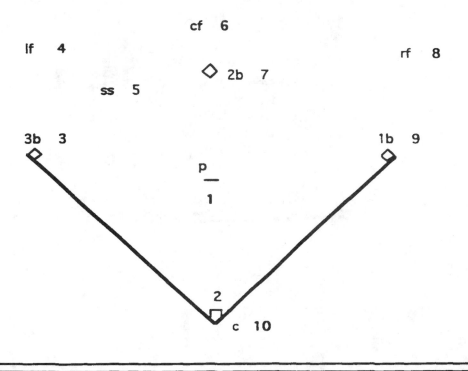

ALL STAR MOTIVATOR

"BATS-UP"

(*Coach*) "Your bat's too heavy." (*Player*) "No it's not—it's just right." (*Coach*) "Why are you striking out?" (*Player*) "I'm going for bad pitches."

If you have ever tried to convince players to try a lighter bat, here's a test that will often prove your point. Have the student grip the bat near the handle and hold it directly out in front (shoulder height) for one minute. If the player is able to do this with a straight arm and minimal shaking, then the bat is probably appropriate.

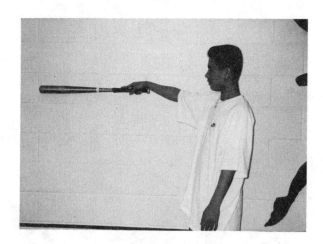

MOTIVATOR

 "GET INTO THE SWING"

Work on the following hitting tips as you practice each of the drills below:

T • Take a stance a bit wider than the shoulders.
  • Hands are in with bat held horizontal.
I • Both elbows are pointed down.
  • Hands on bat are loose until impact.
P • Swing inside out with a full arm extension.
  • Hit with weight off inside of back foot.
S • Wrists snap on impact.

Bat Behind

Kneeling One-Handed Swings

Broomstick/Plastic Golf Ball

ALL★STAR
MOTIVATOR

"COVER UP"

One method to improve catching skills is by exchanging a glove for a paddle. Circular pieces of wood (1/4″ to 3/8″ thickness) with a face a bit larger than a ping-pong paddle provide a tool for teaching players to use two hands when catching. Fasten a strip of inner tube or elastic on one side for your hand.

In partners, practice tossing a tennis ball back and forth using the throwing hand to **trap** (cover) incoming balls. Work on quick exchanges and increase the velocity as confidence grows. This is an excellent drill for infielders.

ALL★STAR
MOTIVATOR

"ACU-PITCH"

Groups of two to three number off. Pitcher #1 faces a hoop taped on a wall 45 to 60 feet back. The first pitcher throws at the target. If the ball hits inside, a strike is recorded and a second toss is given. This process continues until the ball hits outside the hoop. Once a player misses, the next player steps up. Who can throw the most consecutive strikes?

ALL★STAR
MOTIVATOR

 ### "HAND BASEBALL"

Rules: Two players are needed for this game. A decision is then made as to who bats first. The two students may sit or stand to play. Each player puts one hand behind his or her back. On a signal, each player sticks out a hand with one to five fingers showing. Totals are then made for both players. **Even numbers help the batter while odd numbers help the pitcher.**

All runners must be forced to the next base. Runners may not advance on an out. On a double play, the batter plus the runner on the nearest base to home is out. A double or triple play with the bases empty means only one out. A triple play with one player on base means two outs. Pitchers and batters switch positions after three outs.

Code:	Even		Odd	
	2 fingers—	walk	3 fingers—	out
	4 fingers—	single	5 fingers—	out
	6 fingers—	double	7 fingers—	double play
	8 fingers—	triple	9 fingers—	triple play
	10 fingers—	home run		

Source: Craig Cunningham, UCLA.

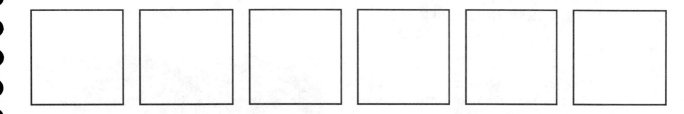

*S*oft Lacrosse

PRE-GAME PLAN

> "Success is not the result of spontaneous combustion.
> You must set yourself on fire."—*Reggie Leach*

Soft lacrosse is a modified lacrosse game utilizing a non-contact format and a soft stick head and ball. Activities in this unit focus on throwing, catching, scooping, and guarding.

HIGHLIGHTS

M	Practice throwing and catching with stationary and moving targets, play "Throw Out."
T	Increase throwing accuracy, play "Possession" and "Steal."
W	New Hip-To-Be-Fit circuit, Arm Strength Test.
Th	Complete Soft Lacrosse Task Card, play modified five-on-five game.
F	Contracts.

BENEFITS

- Aerobic activity.
- Improve eye-hand coordination.
- Increase speed and agility.
- Learn teamwork.

RESOURCES

NAGWS
AAHPERD
1900 Association Drive
Reston, VA 22091

CONTRIBUTORS

Gary Adrian
Islander Middle School
Mercer Island, WA

Judy Wilson
Overlake School
Redmond, WA

UNIT: SOFT LACROSSE (LESSON 1)

Objectives:

- Know that Soft Lacrosse is a non-contact game that promotes teamwork, eye-hand coordination, and conditioning.
- Understand that the proper grip for catching has the top hand near the neck, bottom at end. When throwing, top hand is at middle, bottom at end.
- Increase proficiency and the basic skills of throwing, catching, and scooping.
- To be able to scoop rolled balls.

WARM-UP: "50"

Practice

INDIVIDUAL

- Distribute tennis balls and sticks.
- Using the correct grip, practice throwing against a wall. How many can you catch in a row?
- How far back can you be and still catch the rebound (less than two bounces)?
- Find an open space and work on catching self-tossed balls. How high can you toss and continue to catch?

PARTNERS

- With a partner, begin throwing and catching in close proximity.
- Gradually move further apart.
- Throw exchanges on the ground to practice scooping.

GROUP

- Practice passing and moving in groups of three.
- Place one person in the middle for a game of keep away. Rotate after each interception, or 30 seconds.
- Can the three of you move across the gym or field in a weave (basketball) pattern?
- **"Throwout":** Divide the class into two equal teams by stick color and form two single-file lines. The instructor throws the ball out and the first player in each line competes for possession. Tosses are made in several directions so more players can participate at one time. Once students understand the drill, smaller groups with student leaders doing the throwing can organize in appropriately spaced areas. *Vary the game by having the players shoot on goal.*

Team 1 0 0 0 0 0 0 0	
	• Instructor
Team 2 X X X X X X X	

In groups of three, create an individual skill drill that is **performed to music.**

The difference between a **sprain** and a **strain** can be confusing. Usually, injuries to the joints are most often classified as sprains while injuries to the soft tissue between joints (muscles and tendons) are strains. List three strategies for decreasing these types of injuries.

What is the fastest method for moving a ball across the field? **(Long tosses or short quick ones.)** Guesstimate the results before trying both methods.

How many calories are there in one pound of body fat? *Answer:* **3,500.**

UNIT: SOFT LACROSSE (LESSON 2)

Objectives:

- Improve passing accuracy.
- Increase shooting proficiency.
- Learn the skill of cradling (stick in—basket up) while standing and running.

WARM-UP: THREE 10-SECOND SPEED JUMP-ROPE TRIALS

Practice

INDIVIDUAL

- Work on tossing upwards and turning before you catch.
- How far out in front can you toss and still catch?
- Work on catching the ball above your head and below your knees.

PARTNERS

- Throw and catch at different distances. Can you make five consecutive exchanges without the receiver moving his or her feet?
- **"Possession":** Combine two sets of partners. To score a point, a team must have three or more consecutive possessions and one completed pass. When scored upon, the defensive pair must do a previously agreed-upon exercise. This team then gains possession for the next series.

GROUP

- **"Steal":** Line students up behind four hoops as shown in the illustration. Place 12 to 13 balls in the center of the gym or field. On the "GO" signal, the first person in each line scoops a ball from the center and drops it in his/her hoop. Only one person is allowed to go from each line at a time. When all the balls are taken from the center, players may then run and scoop from the hoop with the most balls. Players may not guard collected balls. The winning team yells "STEAL" when it has five balls in its hoop.

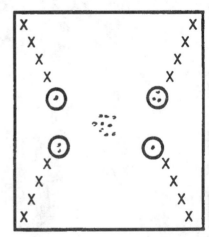

Practice a two vs. two passing game where team #1 attempts to complete five consecutive passes without a drop or interception. On the next series, work on ground pick-ups.

What steps would have to occur for the Native American game of lacrosse to become a full-fledged Olympic sport?

Create a target golf (lacrosse) game with a partner. Vary the length of the holes to promote passing accuracy.

What is the average speed of a sneeze? *Answer:* **68 mph.**

Wednesday
HIP-TO-BE-FIT FITNESS CIRCUIT

	FITNESS COMPONENTS	ACTIVITY	DESCRIPTION	RESOURCE
1	Balance Agility	TIRE JUMPS	Find three different ways to cross the line of tires without touching the ground.	
2	Coordination	TUBE SOX	Work on tossing high in the air and catching low to the ground.	
3	Power	MAT STACK	How many times can you get up and off in the time provided?	
4	Strength	CHAIR GYMNASTICS	Create 5 safe strength-building exercises on a straight-back chair.	
5	Flexibility	ARCH OVER	Practice handstands before the foam spotting aid and arch over.	SPORTIME 1-800-283-5700
6	Coordination	SHOE POPS	Alternate tossing and popping (with feet) the ball back to a partner.	
7	Upper Arm Strength	ONE ARM PUSH UP	Partners assume a push-up position (shoulder to shoulder). Place inside hands around partner's back and attempt to raise up.	
8	Coordination Strength	CORE exchange	Alternate rolling back and exchanging the carpet core using only your feet.	
9	Endurance	AEROBICS	Can you dance to the aerobics tape?	
10	Balance	ROPE WALK	Practice maintaining balance on the rope while moving forward and backward. Try this while dribbling a basketball.	

WEEKLY TEST

UNIT: SOFT LACROSSE (LESSON 3)

Objectives:

- Review and practice basic skills.
- Learn how to play a modified five-on-five game of Soft Lacrosse.
- Know the rules for basic lacrosse.

WARM-UP: AEROBICS (MUSIC)

Practice
Soft Lacrosse Task Card

		Yes	No
INDIVIDUAL	**Can You:**		
	• Run, scoop, throw, and catch the ball off the wall 5 out of 8 times?	_____	_____
	• Throw off the wall with your dominant hand and catch with your non-dominant?	_____	_____
	• Reverse this?	_____	_____
	• Hit a self-selected target 3 times in a row?	_____	_____
PARTNERS	**Can You:**		
	• Make 5 exchanges in 30 seconds (10 yards back)?	_____	_____
	• Pass and catch while moving across the gym/field?	_____	_____
	• Move across the gym/field without dropping the ball?	_____	_____
	• Repeat **decreasing** the number of passes?	_____	_____

GROUP

- **"Ultimate Lacrosse":** (Use this game as throwing and catching skills improve.)
- Rules are the same as "Ultimate Frisbee™."
- The game starts with a throw-off from the 20-yard line.
- The receiving team has possession and must complete a minimum of at least three passes before a goal attempt.
- A point is scored by completing a pass to a teammate who is in the end zone.
- Only two steps are allowed after the catch.
- The defensive team must give the player with the ball 5 yards' clearance to pass.
- A missed attempt on goal may be brought to the 10-yard line and played by the opposing team.
- Change ends and repeat throw-off after each goal.

Soft Lacrosse (the actual 5-on-5 game)

2 defenders:	Guard the goal
	May not cross the center line
	Play man-to-man defense
	Pass the ball over the center line to attackers
2 attackers:	Advance the ball (at least 2 passes)
	Shoot for goal
	May not cross the center line
1 rover:	Faces off to start the game and after a point
	Checks other rover, and may play anywhere on the field

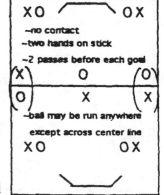

"On the Run": In groups of three to four, play a **non-stop** cooperative game moving the ball across the field without any stops on the way.

Research the history of lacrosse.
- Where did the game originate?
- How have the rules changed?
- In what areas of the country is it most popular?
- Is it an Olympic sport?

In groups of 6 to 12, create a game-related lacrosse drill in a circular formation that incorporates running, passing, and catching while one group moves clockwise and the other moves counterclockwise.

How much blood does the heart send through its valves with each heartbeat? *Answer:* **1/2 cup.**

PHYSICAL EDUCATION CONTRACT

Name _Gina Shames_

Class _1st Period Team Sports_

During the next _____1_____ weeks, I will work on accomplishing . . .

Improving my scooping, catching and throwing skills.

I will need the following equipment . . .

On stick — one ball (wall)

Teacher Approval _DMann_ Date _11/19_

Progress—Week one _You have made some improvement — Let's extend this goal into a two week one and add Jeremy to work with you_

Progress—Week two _Extend_

Progress—Week three _n/a_

Goal Accomplished ___✓___ Not Accomplished _____

Teacher Comments:

Extended to week two.

Graded _____ Non-Graded ___✓___

203

ALL★STAR
MOTIVATOR

"SOFT LACROSSE CIRCLE PASS"

Directions: Establish circles of five students evenly spaced about 20 feet apart. Following a signal to begin, #5 tosses to #1 who catches, returns the ball to the middle and sits down. This procedure continues until all players complete the cycle. The first team to sit wins the first period.

Try these other variations:

- Rotate all players through the middle position.
- Repeat with ground balls.
- Make two passes in a row.
- Beat your time.

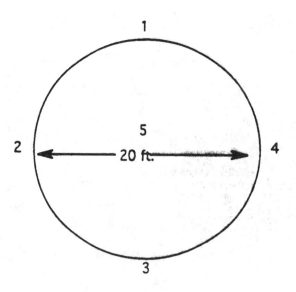

ALL STAR MOTIVATOR

"SOFT LACROSSE EXCHANGE"

Directions: Divide the class into four even teams. Outfit each team with a different colored vest. Place teams by color into four separate squares on a volleyball court. Assign *one* "permanent" player from each team on the court directly across the net. (See the illustration below.)

Distribute sticks to each student and give one ball for each colored team. Following a signal to begin, team members attempt to join their "permanent" player by catching his or her ball and returning it. A caught ball allows that player to EXCHANGE courts. Players may intercept other team balls to move across or stop others from doing the same. The first team to EXCHANGE their entire team wins.

yellow	(red)	green	(blue)
yellow	yellow	green	green
yellow	yellow	green	green

red	red	blue	blue
red	red	blue	blue
red	(yellow)	blue	(green)

ALL STAR MOTIVATOR

"ZIGZAG LACROSSE PASS (TIMED)"

Directions: Organize into groups of six and place players 15 to 20 feet apart in the pattern shown below. Following a signal to begin, player #1 passes to player #2 and so on down the line. If an error occurs, that player repeats the pass. When the ball reaches player #6, it is thrown (in the air) back to #1. As it is caught, the team yells **"ONE."** How many rotations can your team score?

Variations:
- Increase the distance.
- Change hands.

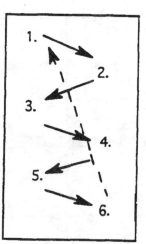

ALL★STAR MOTIVATOR

 ## "3-STEP WEAVE"

Goal: To correctly perform the weave described below while crossing a large field.

Directions: Place students in groups of three. Distribute sticks and one tennis ball to each group. Teams form near one end line. Following a signal to begin, teams attempt to cross the opposite end line passing in the formation shown below. Players perform the weave, passing after every three steps. *Tip:* Pass, move behind the receiver, circle, and prepare to catch again. How many teams are able to cross the field with no more than two misses? One miss? How fast can you cross?

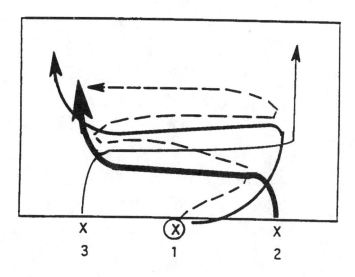

ALL STAR
MOTIVATOR

TIMED SCOOP IT UP

Directions: Teams face each other 10 yards apart at mid-field. A group of five hula hoops are placed between the two teams.

Following a signal to begin, one team throws the ball over the heads of the receiving team. That team has 10 seconds to collect and throw the balls toward the hoop targets. Thrown balls remaining inside the five hoops count as one point for that player's team. After each 10 second trial, teams change roles.

- Throwers -

30'

- Receivers -

ALL STAR MOTIVATOR

"PASS THE NITRO"

Directions: Fill 10 to 12 small balloons (tennis-ball size) with water. Next, form a large circle with students standing 10 feet apart. Number off "1," "2," around the circle. Following a signal to begin, #1s pass a colored balloon **counterclockwise** around the circle. Dropped or popped balloons are replaced and start over at the front of the line. #2s pass a different colored balloon **clockwise**, trying to beat the opponent's balloon back to the starting point.

   "Coop-Pass": Each player passes a balloon to the person on his/her right when the teacher calls **"pass."** Points are scored for each balloon surviving the rotation.

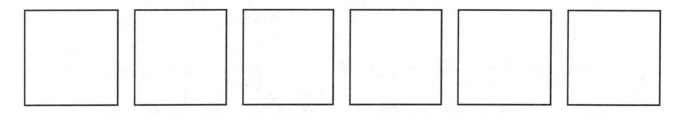

Soft Tennis

PRE-GAME PLAN

> "I hear . . . and I forget
> I see . . . and I remember
> I do . . . and I understand."

Soft tennis is similar to regular tennis with the following exceptions: (1) A high density foam ball is used, and (2) the game is played on a badminton-sized court. This unit focuses on groundstrokes, serves, and modified games.

HIGHLIGHTS

M   Increase forehand proficiency, work on volleying with a partner, play "Attack and Defend" and "One-Minute Tennis Madness."

T   Alternate forehand and backhand strokes, complete peer analysis of partner strokes, play, "Champs and Challengers," learn ball pick-up techniques, play "Four Square."

W   New Hip-To-Be-Fit circuit, Muscular End Test.

Th   Perform "Two-Minute Circuit," play "Add On" and "Around the World," practice "Spin to Win" techniques.

F   Contracts.

BENEFITS

- Eye-hand coordination.
- Lifetime activity.
- Sex equitable.
- Adaptable to a variety of spaces.

RESOURCES

U.S. Tennis Association
51 E. 42nd Street
New York, NY 10017

CONTRIBUTOR

Nancy Osborne
Pacific Northwest Section
USTA

UNIT: SOFT TENNIS (LESSON 1 WITH HIGH-DENSITY FOAM BALLS)

Objectives:

- Learn fundamental grips.
- Increase forehand groundstroke proficiency.
- Improve accuracy of forehand volley.

WARM-UP: "50"

Practice

INDIVIDUAL

- From the ready position, bring the racquet back, step toward target, drop racquet head, contact ball over front foot, and finish with a high follow-through. With your side to the target and hitting wrist *stiff,* work on rallying the ball off the wall for one minute (15 feet back).
- Next, set a personal one-minute record allowing one bounce between each hit.
- Tape hula hoops on the wall five feet off the floor.
- How many contacts inside the hoop can you make in one minute?
- Can you improve this score?

PARTNERS

- Select a partner and face each other with an open face racket (4 to 6 feet apart). Practice bumping the ball back and forth in the air—no bounces allowed. It may help you to merely "bump" or "tap" the ball without swinging.
- Can you volley six balls in a row?
- Take one giant step away from each other. Can you maintain a rally with increased distance between you and your partner?
- Can you bump the ball in a rainbow arc (ten feet)?
- Can you maintain control and increase the speed of the volley?
- Can you and your partner alternate volleys off the wall?

GROUP

- **"Attack and Defend":** In groups of four, place a "defender" on one side of the net and three "attackers" on the opposite. The first attacker in line starts the game with a friendly drop-hit to the defender on the other side of the net. The attacker rushes the net and attempts to volley the ball away from the defender. If the attacker successfully executes these two shots in a row, he or she moves to the other side of the net and becomes the new defender. If the defender wins the point, he stays on his side to take on the next attacker in line.

"Tandem Tennis": Arrange students in lines of four or more. How many successful cooperative wall hits is your group able to make allowing only one bounce between contacts? Players should rotate to their left following each return and move to the back of their line. Challenge another group to a collective score game.

Write a Haiku poem about tennis. Haiku is a 17-syllable form that describes a point of nature. Try the following format:

Sample: Back and forth they go,
Serving, slicing, and slamming,
Tennis at its best.

(Five syllables) _____

(Seven syllables) _____

(Five syllables) _____

In small groups, discover a way to propel a foam ball in such a way that it will stop and return to you. The ball may not contact a wall or be hit by any implement other than the floor itself.

What racket sport derives its name from a soft spongy ball? *Answer:* **Squash.**

UNIT: SOFT TENNIS (LESSON 2)

Objectives:

- Demonstrate the difference between forehand and backhand grips.
- Increase backhand proficiency.
- Combine both groundstrokes in a game situation.

WARM-UP: THREE 10-SECOND SPEED JUMP-ROPE TRIALS

Practice

INDIVIDUAL

- Starting with the forehand "shake hands" grip, turn your hand 1/4 inch so that the index knuckle is on the top level. Assume the "ready position." As you turn shoulders and bring racket head back low, change to the backhand grip. Practice shoulder and grip change on both sides.
- Facing the wall, with racket held flush against your body, practice "bumping" the ball against the wall using the new backhand grip. How many consecutive hits can you make?
- Move about six feet from the wall, turn your side to the target, criss-cross your tossing hand over the racket arm, and attempt a longer stroke pattern while rallying against the wall.
- Alternate forehands and backhands off the wall. How many groundstrokes in a row can you hit?

  CUES: a. stiff wrist, b. side to target, c. low to high swing pattern

PARTNERS

- Designate one partner as the "coach," the other as the "player." Coaches stand with backs against the wall, and first toss a ball to the forehand side of the player who hits back to the coach and returns to the ready position. Coaches then toss balls to the backhand side, noticing that players have changed their grips. Coaches give specific feedback, e.g., side to target, low to high swing, while making sure that players change grips each time. Toss ten, then change roles. As skills improve, coaches can lessen time between tosses, forcing players to recover more quickly. Coaches can increase distance of toss away from players, forcing them to move to the ball and recover to the ready position.

GROUP

- **"Champs and Challengers":** Students pair up with a doubles partner. Three to four doubles teams take turns spinning their rackets to determine which team will begin on the "champs" side of the net. (One doubles team at a time.) The object is for the challenger team to win two points in a row against the champs team, and assume the champs side of the net. Challenger teams always start the sequence with a friendly drop-hit serve. The champs side tries to accumulate ten points. Standard rules and court etiquette are emphasized at all times.

Place students in lines of six, shoulder to shoulder, three feet apart. Work on moving a ball, from one end of the line to the other, with each player contacting the ball *in order*. How many balls can you move across without a break in the sequence?

Check a newspaper for the set scores from either a high school, college, or professional tournament. Next, write a short story about the **imagined highlights.**

Figure out a way to place 10 tennis balls in three hoops so that there's an **odd** number of balls in each hoop.

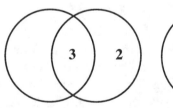

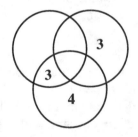

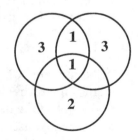

How much does your brain weigh? *Answer:* **3 lbs.**

214

Wednesday
HIP-TO-BE-FIT FITNESS CIRCUIT

	FITNESS COMPONENTS	ACTIVITY	DESCRIPTION	RESOURCE
1	Eye-Hand Coordination & Reaction Time	CATCH-BALL	Call a color, toss, and try to catch that color with one hand.	Sportime 1-800-283-5700
2	Eye-Foot Coordination	hacky sack	How many consecutive foot contacts can you perform?	Gopher 1-800-533-0446
3	Agility	ROCKET BAL	Shoot the ball off a wall, run, and catch. How many can you catch in one minute?	Rocketbal (206) 631-4311
4	Power	JUMP BALL	Drop a basketball (head high) and see how many times you can jump over before it stops bouncing.	
5	Upper Arm Strength	LAT PULL	Attach the circular inner tubes to the top of the door, kneel, and pull down.	Bicycle stores
6	Power	JUMP UP, ON, OVER	Work on jumping onto the two folded mats and jump off. Jump your age and rest.	
7	Coordination	BUKA BALL	How many consecutive contacts can you make in a row?	Gopher 1-800-533-0446
8	Balance	STILTS	Work on moving in all four directions.	Gopher 1-800-533-0446
9	Leg Strength	CHAIR-SAND LEG EXTENSION	From a sitting position, lift the sand-filled containers (sets of ten).	
10	Eye-Hand Coordination	HIT 'N STIK	Work on batting form, emphasizing a level swing.	Sportime 1-800-283-5700

WEEKLY TEST

UNIT: SOFT TENNIS (LESSON 3)

Objectives:

- Increase racket and ball control proficiency.
- Practice intermediate skills necessary for successful play.
- Improve on-court foot speed.

WARM-UP: LONG RUN FOR PLACE

Practice

INDIVIDUAL

- (Solo Tennis, Tennis Trainer, and Jocari are three examples of tennis balls with elastic strings anchored to a weighted base.) Students stand by the base, drop the ball, and play the return after one bounce. Students can alternate forehand and backhand strokes on each return.
- How many consecutive hits can you make?

PARTNERS

- **"Two-Minute Circuit":** (Assign two to three sets of partners per circuit).
- **"Tennis Hacky Sack":** Work on alternating hits in the air between two sets of partners. Players cannot hit the ball twice in a row. What is the best score your group can record?
- **"Smash":** Partner #1 hits the ball upward while #2 lets it bounce and smashes it into a foldable mat.
- **"Hoopster":** Practice short drop shots into hoops placed five to ten feet from the net. Score a point each time your ball touches inside a partner's hoop.
- **"Stationary Volleys":** Place a partner inside a hoop and work on cooperative exchanges. Score points for each contact hit while in the hoop.
- **"Target Serves":** Practice serving diagonally across the net to a retriever who is without a racket. Each time the serve is inside the designated area, that partner continues to serve and score points. After a miss, partners change roles.
- **"Step Back Volleys":** Partners face at the net and take a step back after each successful volley. Following a miss, partners return to the net and start over. How far back can the two of you go?

GROUP

- **"Add On":** Place six players on each side of the net. Following a "friendly serve," one player from each side vies for a legal point. Once a point is scored, the scoring team adds another player. The player losing the point goes to the end of the line and a new player enters the court. Play continues until one side has all six players on the court.
- **"Around the World":** Place three to six players on each side of the net. Player #1 from the right serving court hits the ball over the net, rotates to his/her right, and runs to the opposite side. The receiving player returns the ball, rotates to his/her right, and runs to the opposite side. How many consecutive "legal" hits can be made before a miss occurs?

"Step Back Volleys": Beginning from a distance of ten feet, partners volley back and forth stepping back following each **good** contact. Once a miss occurs, partners return to their starting positions and start over. How far apart can you be while continuing to volley?

Find a smooth wall at home. On your knees, practice volleying a **sponge** ball off the wall. How many consecutive volleys can you perform? Graph your best daily scores and return to your teacher.

	M	T	W	Th	F	Sat	Sun
+							
25							
20							
15							
10							
5							

Many players mentally visualize strokes. Find a comfortable place at home to relax and form a mental picture of your stroke from backswing to follow-through. Repeat the exercise frequently, focusing on any correction that needs to be made.

What do you think the average resting heart rate is:

    for a person? *Answer:* **60-80.**
    a canary? *Answer:* **500-800.**
    an elephant? *Answer:* **25-50.**

PHYSICAL EDUCATION CONTRACT

Name _Lannon Lorr_

Class _Merca_

During the next _____3_____ weeks, I will work on accomplishing . . .

Increasing service speed and accuracy in both service courts (Goal) Ten 1st serves in a row into desired service area.

I will need the following equipment . . .

Racquet, sponge ball, regular tennis ball — courts as available

Teacher Approval _Merca_ Date _4/28_

Progress—Week one _Thirteen consecutive good serves. Had a little trouble from the left side._

Progress—Week two _n/a_

Progress—Week three _n/a_

Goal Accomplished_____✓_____ Not Accomplished _____

Teacher Comments:

That was quick. How can we work on your ground scores ?

Graded _____ Non-Graded ___✓___

ALL STAR
MOTIVATOR

"ONE-MINUTE TENNIS MADNESS"

Directions: Organize students in groups of four and distribute racquets, balls, and one score card per team. Rotate through the nine-station circuit, attempting to accomplish listed tasks in less than one minute. When groups are successful, they draw an X over that space on the grid. When unsuccessful, draw a circle. How many teams can score three more "x's" in a row?

TIC-TAC-TOE SCORE CARD

Hit clockwise to each player (in order) three times in a row. **Circle Volleys**	All four players hit forehand strokes off a wall ten times in a row, allowing one bounce between strokes. **Forehands**	Score a collective team total of 100 backhands off the wall. **Backhands**
Hit ten consecutive team wall rebounds in a row. Hit and move to the end of the line. **Line Exchanges**	To mark an X, all four players must hit ten individual volleys in a row off a wall. **Wall Volleys**	Place a hula hoop 10 feet from a wall. Form a single line and attempt to lob balls off the wall into the hoop. Hit 3 inside to score an X. **Hoop Lobs**
Place a tennis ball between your heels. Jump, flip the ball upward, and catch. Teams must catch a **collective** total of 12 in 60 seconds. **Coordination**	Place racquets on the floor. Students **jump** over their racquets as many times as possible in one minute. A **collective** score of 400 scores an X. **Conditioning**	Line up five empty tennis cans one foot from a wall. Servers stand 20 feet back. Knock down all five to score an X. **Serving**

ALL STAR
MOTIVATOR

"PICK-UP"

Someone once said that 75% of tennis is picking up the ball. Try each of the different techniques pictured below and then invent one of your own. They may save your back.

Outside foot lift

Pull and scoop

Tap

Your idea here

ALL★STAR MOTIVATOR

 ## "FOUR SQUARE"

Option 1

In any racquet sport, running your opponent is an important strategy. The object of the **Four Square** drill described below is to hit the ball into each of your partner's four squares before he or she can contact each of yours. Play a game to ten, counting one point each time you score four squares first. Squares do not have to be hit in numerical order.

Option 2

Partners must hit the squares in numerical order.

3	4
1	2
2	1
4	3

"PROGRESSIVE TENNIS"

Once you successfully complete a task, move ahead to the next. Score one point for each task.

Name _____

Can You?

1. Hit a ball down five times in a row using first a forehand grip, then a backhand grip?

2. Play a ball off a wall five times in a row? Move to an imaginary line 20 feet back and repeat? _____

3. Roll your ball around the rim of your racket ten times in each direction? _____

4. Alternate hits off your racket five times on each side? _____

5. Volley the ball off a wall five times in a row? _____

6. Hit five backhand strokes off a wall five times in a row, allowing one bounce between contacts? _____

7. (Tape a hoop to a wall.) Hit five consecutive forehand volleys inside the hoop from 10 feet back? Backhand volleys? _____

8. (Select a space on the wall.) Hit your ball inside this space 7 out of 10 times from 20 feet back? _____

9. Starting 20 feet from the wall, take a step back each time you successfully hit the rebound? (After one bounce) How many of you can go five steps back? Eight? _____

10. Choose a partner and play a game to 20 points creating your own set of rules? _____

Final Score _____ /10

"SPIN TO WIN"

Directions: A slice is a stroke that produces underspin and sidespin. Learning to slice the ball is essential to becoming a complete player. Work on the following individual, partner, and small group drills, and watch your game improve.

Individual: Practice bumping self-tossed balls upward using both forehand and backhand grips. With the forehand grip (right handers), move the racket from right to left. To execute a backhand slice, the racket must move from left to right.

Partners: Partner #2 (20 feet away) tosses to #1's forehand side. Partner #1 executes a **spinning** one-bounce return. Alternate every ten returns. See if you can make the ball jump to one side, or stop momentarily.

Group: Form circles of three or four. Work on applying spin on each contact as you move the ball around the circle. How long can you keep the ball in the air with controlled spins?

"RACKET REPS (1,000)"

Directions: Improving sport skills requires constant repetition of game-related movement patterns. Fill in your beginning and completion dates once all the tennis balls in a column are filled in (one ball equals 100 strokes).

Beginning Date _____   Completion Date _____

SERVES   FOREHANDS   BACKHANDS

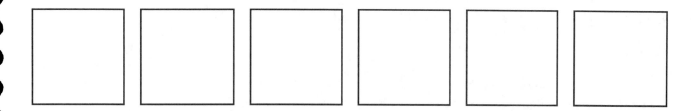

*S*treet and Line Dancing

PRE-GAME PLAN

> "There is no form of mental existence independent of a person's physical existence. To think otherwise is an illusion."
> —*A. Lowen ("Depression of the Human Body")*

For far too long rhythm and dance experiences have been limited to the experiences of the instructor. This unit provides instruction for some current, yet basic street and line dances that can be led by the instructor or students.

HIGHLIGHTS

M	Learn rhythmic stretches, practice "Step Stomp" dance with variations, try "Sport Shadow" exercises.
T	Increase cardiac fitness level by performing the "Running Man" and "Cowboy Boogie."
W	New Hip-To-Be-Fit circuit, Endurance Test.
Th	Perform "Four-Square Aerobics," learn "Happy Feet" and "Scissors" steps, create a new dance.
F	Contracts.

BENEFITS

- Means of creative expression.
- Sex equitable (social).
- Lifetime activity.
- Improve rhythmic skills.
- Aerobic activity.

CONTRIBUTOR

Christy Lane
LDI Productions
Spokane, WA

UNIT: STREET AND LINE DANCING (LESSON 1)

Objectives:

- Increase body awareness through rhythm.
- Improve overall level of fitness.
- Increase comfort when moving to music.
- Create self-expression through dance movements.

WARM-UP: "50"

Practice

INDIVIDUAL

- Now that the heart rate and body temperature are up, work on the following individual stretches. These stretches will decrease injury during dance, increase range of motion, and reduce soreness. Hold each stretch for at least 20 seconds.
- Using popular "Top 40" music (students can assist):
  1. Have students place hands behind their head—press head downward and hold.
  2. Slowly and gently, to music, tilt head forward.
  3. Control your neck as you lift your chin to ceiling.
  4. "Nod" your head half count, then up to tempo of music.
  5. Pretend you're a football player and "hit your shoulder forward."
  6. Slowly lean to the left and then to the right.
  7. Lift your rib cage and pretend someone "socked" you in the chest.
  8. Push your hips to the right and then push to the left. Bump with partner.

PARTNERS

- Partners stand side by side and "do the bump" with their hips. Partners change to back to back and "bump" each other with their hips. Partners learn to count music by "slap, slap, shake 5" with each other. As they count out loud (1, 2, 3, . . .) to music they slap each other's right hand, then left hand, grab right hands to create a handshake, bringing the hands up in the air and then down.

GROUP

- Divide the class into lines facing the music. Here are some basic moves that all ages can do. These same steps can be put together to make a variety of routines. Allow your students to create their own when they feel comfortable.

STEP-STOMP DANCE WITH VARIATIONS

Step right foot out.

"Stomp" the left foot together.

Step the left foot out.

"Stomp" the right foot together.

In groups of three or more, practice dancing and lip-syncing to a short mix of four songs (10 seconds) each. *Teacher:* Judge student performance on transition, synchronization, and energy.

Many of the dancers performing on "Top 40" videos have had classical training. Why might this enhance an aspiring dancer's chances of making it professionally?

Like an old game that stretches hands and feet
A heavy-set singer sets it to a beat.
Who am I? *Answer:* **Chubby Checker**—*The Twist.*
Create another dance riddle.

How many times does the average human heart beat in a day? *Answer:* **100,000.**

UNIT: STREET AND LINE DANCING (LESSON 2)

Objectives:

- Improve body awareness through rhythm and movement.
- Increase cardiac fitness level.
- Feel comfortable while moving to music.
- Create routines with dance steps learned.
- Increase range of motion.
- Perform a line dance to any set of music.

WARM-UP: THREE 10-SECOND SPEED JUMP-ROPE TRIALS

Practice

INDIVIDUAL

- Repeat the rhythm section in Lesson 1. Have one student call out a name of one of the dances learned in Lesson 1. Have another student demonstrate it. Repeat until all dances are demonstrated correctly.

PARTNERS

- Work together in partners to learn the **"Running Man"** dance. Check each other so both of you know the steps.

| Bring one foot up. | Step with lifted foot as you slide other foot back. | Lift back foot. | Lunge again. |

GROUP

- **"Cowboy Boogie":** Divide the class into rows or lines facing the instructor. Place hands on hips. This dance can be done to country or "Top 40" music.

PART I:	Grapevine to right	(4 counts)	(step right foot to the right, cross left foot behind, right foot to the right, step left foot together and scuff heel)
	Grapevine to left	(4 counts)	(same as above, going the other way)
PART II:	Walk forward	(2 counts)	(step right foot, scuff left heel forward)
	Walk forward	(2 counts)	(step left foot, scuff right heel forward)
	Walk backward 4 steps	(4 counts)	(right, left, right and lift left knee up)
PART III:	Put left foot down and lean forward	(2 counts)	(rocking motion)
	Lean backward	(2 counts)	
	Forward, back, forward	(1 count each)	
	Pick up right foot and scuff 1/4 turn to face left.		
PART IV:	Dance repeats from the beginning, facing the new left direction.		

COOPERATIVE

Create a partner contact sequence to "Top 40" music. At no time during the dance can the two of you lose contact.

INTERDISCIPLINARY

In order to pace yourself when engaging in any aerobic exercise program, it's important to be able to compute your **personal target heart rate.** Using the formulas below, figure both your minimum and maximum heart rate.

MINIMUM TARGET HEART RATE		MAXIMUM TARGET HEART RATE	
Beginning number	220	Beginning number	220
Subtract your age	_____	Subtract your age	_____
Subtotal	_____	Subtotal	_____
Subtract resting pulse	_____	Subtract resting pulse	_____
Subtotal	_____	Subtotal	_____
Multiply by .60	_____	Multiply by .80	_____
Subtotal	_____	Subtotal	_____
Add resting pulse	_____	Add resting pulse	_____
Minimum Target HR=	_____	**Maximum Target HR=**	_____

Critical Thinking

UCLA brain researcher Arnold Schiebel states, "Anything that's intellectually challenging can probably serve as a kind of stimulus for **dendritic** growth, which means it adds to the computational reserves in your brain."
How can dance add to these reserves?
Possible answers:
- requires thinking
- choreographing rhythm patterns
- synchronizing dance combinations with music
- creating new moves and combinations

Source: *Life* magazine, July 1994

TRIVIA

Name three organs of which you have two. *Answer:* **Lungs, kidneys, ears, and eyes.**

Wednesday
HIP-TO-BE-FIT FITNESS CIRCUIT

	FITNESS COMPONENTS	ACTIVITY	DESCRIPTION	RESOURCE
1	Upper Arm Strength	MAT STAND	Practice handstands onto and off a foldable mat.	
2	Power	TIE TOUCH	Hang neck ties or strips of tape from the sides and bottom of a backboard. How many can you touch?	
3	Coordination	FINGER TIP EXCHANGE	Place one beanbag in the palm of your dominant hand and a second between your index and your middle finger. Toss both and reverse their positions as you catch.	
4	Upper Arm Strength	KAYAKING	Place bicycle hand grips on the ends of 36-inch dowels (1-inch thick). Sit cross-legged on a scooter and race your partner in traditional kayak style.	
5	Speed	BEAT THE BALL	Partner #1 rolls the ball across the floor while #2 attempts to beat it to a designated location. Repeat 3 times before changing roles.	
6	Upper Arm Strength	CRUTCH SWING	Stand side by side, balance, swing legs back, hip forward. Who can travel to a finish line in the **least** number of steps?	
7	Coordination	PARTNER JUGGLE	Stand shoulder to shoulder. Practice exchanging two tennis balls. When the first peaks, throw the second. Try three. The person with two starts first.	
8	Leg Strength	HAMSTRING HELPER	Partner #1 lies on stomach. Partner #2 places fingers on #1's heels and applies slight pressure as #1 curls forward.	
9	Endurance	TEN	Place bowling balls 25 to 30 feet away. Partners roll toward their pin. Misses force that partner to touch a front and back wall. Strikes allow that partner to roll again. Who can knock down 10 pins first?	
10	Upper Arm Strength	PULL DOWN	Attach bicycle inner tube strips high enough for adequate tension. Partners kneel and pull the tubes downward. How many can you do?	

WEEKLY TEST

UNIT: STREET AND LINE DANCING (LESSON 3)

Objectives:

- Perform a line dance to any set music.
- Increase aerobic activity using a line dance workout.
- Incorporate sequences into student's movement memory.
- Lead a warmup to music.

WARM-UP: LONG RUN FOR PLACE

Practice

INDIVIDUAL

- **"Four-Square Aerobics":** Using current "Top 40" music, have the first person in line #1 come to the front and lead the class in exercises or dance steps, staying with the music. The second student in line runs a lap around the room and takes over as leader when reaching the front. Repeat with six to eight different leaders. Encourage students in line to try their best to stay with each leader.

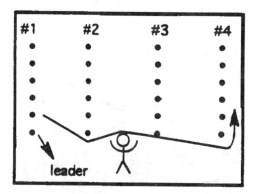

PARTNERS

- Perform rhythm section with partners facing each other. Repeat "slap, slap, shake 5." Work together to learn **"Happy Feet"** and **"Scissors."**

Happy Feet

Scissors

Toes point out as you "slap water in your face."   Toes go in. Repeat other side.   Kick one foot out.   Bring it together. Repeat with other leg.

GROUP

- **"Freestyle":** Review routine from Lesson 1. Add "Happy Feet" and "Scissors" to the end of the routine. After many repetitions, review the "Cowboy Boogie" and add it to the end of the entire routine. Divide students into two groups. Have each group perform for the other. Encourage the audience to be very responsive with their applause. Have one student introduce the group: ". . . and now, ladies and gentlemen, we proudly present, Group #2!" Work on performance skills such as smiles, eye contact, and "selling the routine" with energy. At the end of the routine, give the students 32 counts to improvise (strut their stuff). Strike a pose at the end. You might want to video the results.

"Service Learning": In small groups teach a new street or line dance to a group of senior citizens, scouts, church group, etc. Report your experience to your instructor. *Instructor:* A video illustrating the students' efforts can be given extra credit.

Americans as a whole eat too much fat. This practice often results in weight-management problems and the risk for heart disease. The Western Dairy Council suggests that 30% or less of your daily caloric intake come from fat. Professional dancers closely monitor their daily fat intake. For the next week (Monday–Sunday) calculate your fat intake and see if you are able to stay within these recommended guidelines. **Fat budgets for teenagers (depending on weight and gender) usually range between 80–115 grams per day.**

Weekly total: _____ grams.

"Attitude Is Everything": Attitudes toward dance are often difficult to change. What are some strategies for assuring active involvement by ALL class members when participating in either street or line dancing?

Possible discussion topics may include:

- choice of music
- self-consciousness
- dance modifications
- student helpers
- put-downs

How far does the average man walk a day? *Answer:* **7 miles.** Women? **10 miles.** *Source:* American College of Foot and Ankle Surgeons.

PHYSICAL EDUCATION CONTRACT

Name _Kaylan Turner_

Class _Putnam – Dance_

During the next ___2___ weeks, I will work on accomplishing . . .

Work with Crystal and Clay on creating and performing an original Hip-Hop line dance.

I will need the following equipment . . .

Boom Box – Tape and adequate space.

Teacher Approval _Bull Putman_ Date _3/26_

Progress—Week one _Haven't had adequate practice time due to assembly. Encouraged to work outside of school._

Progress—Week two _Performed for class – Good teamwork._

Progress—Week three _____

Goal Accomplished ___X___ Not Accomplished _____

Teacher Comments:

I'm impressed. You spent a lot of time outside of school. It was obvious.

Graded _Ⓐ ✓_ Non-Graded _____

233

ALL★STAR MOTIVATOR

 ## "SPORT SHADOWS"

Tired of those old aerobic tapes? Have you stepped your last step? Shaken your hands in the air until you just don't care? Put the following sport moves to music and re-energize your exercise routines.

SPORT	MOVEMENTS
BOXING	**Match** the leader's footwork, jabs, counters, and hooks.
FOOTBALL	**Duplicate** the leader's ball-carrying moves forward, backward, and side to side.
BASKETBALL	**Mimic** the leader's dribbling, jump shots, rebounds, and pivots.
SOFTBALL	**Follow** the leader's fielding, throwing, and swinging actions.
KARATE	**Copy** the leader's chops, kicks, jumps, and punches.
VOLLEYBALL	**Simulate** the leader's sets, bumps, serves, digs, and rolls.
TENNIS	**Shadow** the leader's forehands, backhands, serves, and volleys.

REMEMBER—EACH SPORT MOVE MUST STAY WITH THE BEAT OF THE MUSIC.

ALL★STAR MOTIVATOR

"HIP, FIT, AND STREET LEGIT"

HIP, FIT & Street Legit

And to celebrate this feat has choreographed a dance that's sweet and has the beat!

CONGRATS TO _____

Instructor _____
Date _____

ALL★STAR

MOTIVATOR

"TOWEL DANCES FOR THE DECADES"

Directions: Arrange students in groups of 5 or 6. Distribute one bath towel to each student. Assign a specific decade to each group. Teams have 15 minutes to choreograph their routines. Following this preparation, sharing takes place.

1960 _____

1970 _____

1980 _____

1990 _____

"CREATE-A-DANCE"

Directions: Students work in groups of 4 to 6. The group selects a style for their creation. The dance may not exceed 32 counts and must be presented in the formation indicated.

COUNTS	FORMATION	STYLE
32	Line	Country
32	Circle	Folk
32	Line	Hip Hop
32	Circle	Locomotor
32	Line	Fifties
32	Partners	Ballroom
32	Choice	Choice

*If used for a presentation, music and dress should be related to the era and style. Groups may be further motivated through the use of videotape and inter-class sharing.

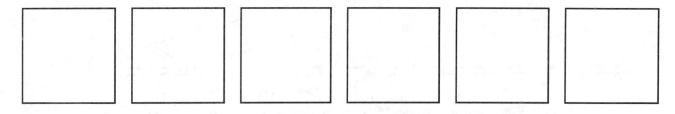

*T*able Tennis

PRE-GAME PLAN

> "Coming together is a beginning . . .
> keeping together is progress . . .
> working together is success."

Table tennis is an international sport. For physical education programs it's easy to learn and cost effective. The activities in this unit center around hitting accuracy and group motivational drills.

HIGHLIGHTS

M   Experiment with different grips while working on hitting accuracy and volleying consistency. Play modified games of "Hoopla," "End Zone," and "Blow Ball."

T   Improve ball-placement skills, play "Long Pong," attempt to reach ten perfect "TWT" rounds in "Tables with Talent."

W   New Hip-To-Be-Fit circuit, Flexibility Test.

Th   Alter serving speeds and *extend* hitting distance from table. Play "Around the World."

F   Contracts.

BENEFITS

- Increase eye-hand coordination, reaction time.
- Sex equitable.
- Lifetime activity.

RESOURCES

U.S. Table Tennis Association
210 Saturn Drive, North Star
Newark, DE 19711

UNIT: TABLE TENNIS (LESSON 1)

Objectives:

- Practice with two standard grips.
- Learn basic stroke patterns.
- Improve placement proficiency.
- Know that table tennis requires fast reactions.

WARM-UP: "50"

Practice

INDIVIDUAL

- Using a "shake hands" grip, kneel down 3 to 5 feet from a wall and practice pushing the rebounds directly back to the wall. Work on hitting the ball at the *top* of the bounce.
- Alternate forehand and backhand strokes.
- Are you able to hit 25 good returns without a miss? 50?
- Try the last task using a *pen holder* grip.

PARTNERS

- Set up half the tables as shown in illustration #1 and the other half as shown in #2.
- Who can score ten points first?
- **"Hoopla":** Points are scored only when balls land inside an opponent's hoop.
- **"End Zone":** Points are scored only when your ball lands inside the taped end zone.

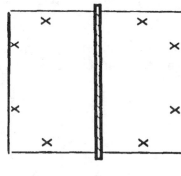

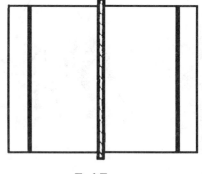

Blow Ball   Hoopla   End Zone

GROUP

- **"Blow Ball":** Remove nets and place students as shown in the illustration. Each student is responsible for defending his or her eighth of the table. Points are scored when balls are blown over a player's edge. Each player begins with a ball. Use of hands is not allowed.

"Two at a Time": Work on keeping **two** balls going between partners at a time.

The average 150-lb. person will burn around 250 calories (one Snickers™ bar) per hour when playing table tennis. About how many calories is this each minute?

Source: *Fitness for Life,* **Corbin and Lindsey, Scott Foresman, 1979**

As you rally with a partner, practice applying underspin and topspin on your returns. Why is it easier to produce spin from an outside-in stroke than from an inside-out?

What color of shirts do table tennis players wear in high-level competition? *Answer:* **Black.**

UNIT: TABLE TENNIS (LESSON 2)

Objectives:

- Learn to apply spin.
- Improve ball placement accuracy.
- Apply basic skills and rules to modified games.

WARM-UP: THREE 10-SECOND SPEED JUMP-ROPE TRIALS

Practice

INDIVIDUAL

- Find a clear wall space and work on applying spin by contacting the **bottom** of the ball in a right-to-left motion (right-handers). When imparted correctly, the ball should change directions after the bounce.
- Are you able to spin it in the opposite direction (left to right)?

PARTNERS

- **"Ping-Pong Patterns":** With eight players per table (one ball per pair), work on continuous rallies with the partner directly across from you.
- Which pair can perform the longest rally?
- Play one minute before rotating one position to your right.
- See how many wins you can accumulate in four rotations.
- Play a diagonal game to eleven points. (1 vs. 5) (2 vs. 6) (3 vs. 7) (4 vs. 8).

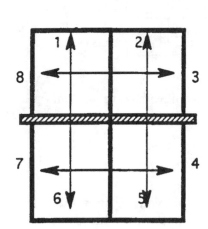

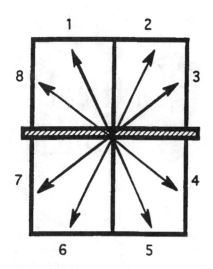

"Cooperative Five-Step": Play a cooperative five-step back game. Begin with a friendly serve. After each good return, that player takes a step back from the table. This rally continues until a player either misses or completes the five-step goal.

The form shown illustrates an example of a **single elimination** tournament for 32 players. How would you implement a **double elimination** tournament?

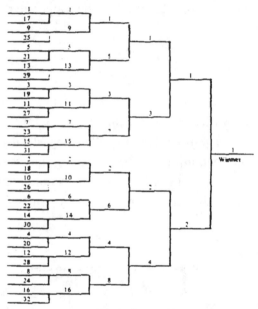

Why must players serve with an open (flat) palm?

You can hold your brain in the palm of your hand, but a computer with the same number of "bits" would be 100 stories tall and cover the State of Texas. **Source:** *The Three Pound Universe* (Kagel, Arnold, Inc.)

Wednesday
HIP-TO-BE-FIT FITNESS CIRCUIT

	FITNESS COMPONENTS	ACTIVITY	DESCRIPTION	RESOURCE
1	Flexibility	PRONE TRUNK LIFT	#1 places hands on back of neck, lifts chin, and holds for 3 seconds. #2 measures height of chin.	*Fitness for Life* by Corbin and Lindsey, Scott Foresman, 1979
2	Endurance	PERIMETER JOG	How many nonstop laps can you complete?	
3	Upper Arm Strength	SCOOTER VAULT	Sitting on the scooter (back to wall), push off with hand and lay back pushing the scooter out.	
4	Muscular Endurance	MEDICINE BALL EXCHANGE	Sit facing and exchange the ball on each alternating sit-up.	
5	Power	hoop jump	Take turns jumping outside to inside at different heights.	
6	Upper Arm Strength	SMILE OFF	Face each other on a bar or ring. Who can hang the longest?	
7	Arm Strength and Coordination	WHEEL CHAIR RACE	Who can wheel through the cone course first?	
8	Upper Arm Strength	WALL WALK	From a push-up position, slowly walk your feet up the wall. To dismount, turn sideways.	
9	Upper Arm Strength	MEDICINE BALL PUSH	Partners lie facing on stomachs and attempt to push the ball past their opponent.	
10	Coordination	LOLO BALL ROPE SKIP	How many jumps can you accomplish?	Sportime 1-800-283-5700

WEEKLY TEST

UNIT: TABLE TENNIS (LESSON 3)

Objectives:

- Improve paddle-control skills.
- Increase hitting distance and accuracy.
- Change serving speeds.

WARM-UP: LONG RUN FOR PLACE

Practice

INDIVIDUAL

- Distribute a ball and paddle to each student. Find a clear space and hold the paddle at belt level (face parallel to the ground).
- Can you drop the ball and maintain a low controlled bounce by gently moving your hand upward on impact?
- Can you alternate paddle sides after each hit?
- Is anyone able to incorporate the rim and handle (as a point of contact) into the sequence?

PARTNERS

"Can You and a Partner":
- Apply backspin so that the ball stops and moves slightly backward toward the server? (*Hint:* Hit the ball downward and turn the paddle face upward as it strikes the ball.)
- Perform three low (fast) and three (high) bouncing serves in a row?
- Keep two balls going at a time?
- Practice exchanging lobs a minimum of six feet high?
- Make a full turn between hits? Touch the floor? Perform two jumping jacks?
- Exchange ten drop shots that land within a foot of the net?
- Take a step back after each successful exchange?

GROUP

- **"Around the World":** Player #1 hits into the right service court (player #2) and moves to his or her right to the opposite side. Player #2 returns to player #3 and moves to the opposite side. Play continues until a point is scored. How many consecutive hits can the four of you accumulate?

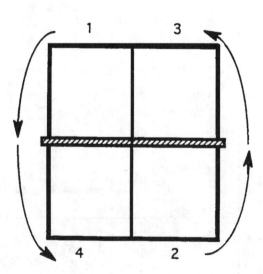

"OPPOS(hits)": Place two players on each side of the net. Begin by serving from the right side of the table (diagonally) to the opposite right service area. The receiving player returns it down the line. Players receiving the ball from one player return it to another player. Continue this, seeing how many **collective** hits your foursome can score. How fast can you move the ball?

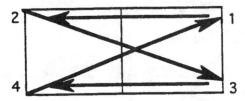

International rules state that the table tennis racquet can be any size, weight or shape. Design a new racquet that will improve your play.

With four students per table, create five different geometric hitting patterns. **Sample** rectangle

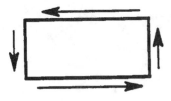

How many years of an average life is spent eating? *Answer:* **6 years.**

PHYSICAL EDUCATION CONTRACT

Name _Terry Archer_

Class _Indiv. Spts. 3rd_

During the next ___2___ weeks, I will work on accomplishing . . .

Improving skills in order to finish in top five of class table tennis tournament. I will practice at home each night.

I will need the following equipment . . .

Table, racquet, ball, partner

Teacher Approval _McEwan_ Date _6/1_

Progress—Week one _Practiced in class and at home. Serve becoming proficient. Needs to hit corners._

Progress—Week two _Finish tournament in fourth place. Lost to Julie in semi-finals._

Progress—Week three _n/a_

Goal Accomplished ___X___ Not Accomplished _____

Teacher Comments:

The practice at home helped.

Graded _____ Non-Graded _✓_

ALL★STAR MOTIVATOR

 ## "SPEED LIMIT"

The faster two partners can perform a "friendly" cooperative rally, the higher their level of skill.

Directions: From a ready position (body not touching the table), begin a timed rally for 60 seconds. This activity is a *collective speed test* which means that all *good* hits count as a point. After an error occurs, the rally continues counting from the last legal hit.

90+	Outstanding
76–89	Good
60–75	Average

Variation: Take one big step back from the table and try to equal or improve your score.

ALL★STAR
MOTIVATOR

 ### "INFINITE PONG"

Directions: Playing either singles or doubles, concentrate on continuous rallies that set partners up for easy returns rather than scoring points. Start with a "friendly" serve and see which group can establish the longest errorless rally.

Variations:

- Allow each group three minutes at a table before rotating to play another similarly skilled team. Record your best mark in chalk on the table top.
- Add "Around the World" with players rotating to their right after each successful return.
- Alternate hits with a doubles partner.

ALL★STAR
MOTIVATOR

"LONG PONG"

Place traffic cones 10 to 15 feet from the end of each table. The goal for each player is to touch his/her own cone while not allowing opponents to touch theirs. A misplay by an opponent results in one point. A touched cone results in three. Games are played to 21 points. This variation teaches quickness and hitting accuracy. A cooperative version calls for players to touch their cone between hits.

ALL★STAR MOTIVATOR

 ## "PLUS OR MINUS"

"Plus or Minus" is an integrated activity calling for quick thinking and strategic hitting skills.

Directions: Chalk a – on the left service area and a + on the right side of the table. Each player begins with five points. The object of this drill is to hit the ball to a specific side (normally the opponent's backhand). When the ball lands in a player's – side, he or she subtracts one point from the current total. A ball landing on the + side adds a point to that player's total. Each + or – score is **vocalized by the receiving player.** Whoever has the highest total after three minutes wins.

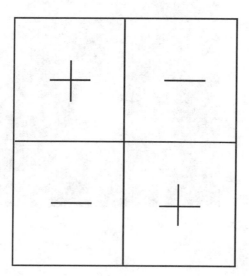

ALL★STAR MOTIVATOR

☆ "TWT (TABLES WITH TALENT)"

Players are arranged as shown in the illustration. The object is for each player to hit directly to the next numbered player. A successful round (eight successive hits) results in one point for that team. Cooperation and skill lead to high scores. When an error occurs, the ball returns to the #1 position. When a table's players total ten perfect rounds, they sit down. The first table to sit wins.

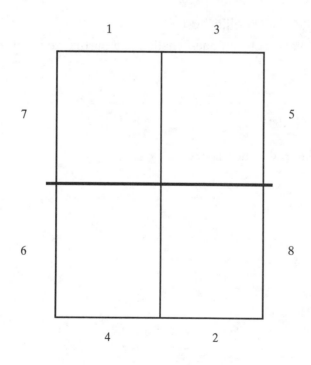

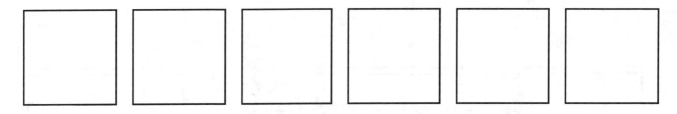

*T*rack and Field

PRE-GAME PLAN

"If It's to Be—It's Up to Me."

Track and field activities can be divided into running, jumping, and throwing events. Secondary instructors often find it difficult to motivate students in these areas. This unit will assist teachers in this endeavor.

HIGHLIGHTS

M   Learn proper running form, mix running with other motor skills, predict running times, play "Accel Decel."

T   Transfer jumping techniques to other sports, work on hurdling and high jumping skills, play "Live Wire."

W   New Hip-To-Be-Fit circuit, Agility Test.

Th   Practice modified shot-put techniques, challenge a partner to a put for distance contest.

F   Contracts.

BENEFITS

- Increase cardiovascular endurance, speed.
- Lifetime activity.

UNIT: TRACK AND FIELD—"RUNNING" (LESSON 1)

Objectives:

- Know basic running techniques.
- Improve running form.
- Experience fun when running.

WARM-UP: "50"

Practice (Teacher cues).

INDIVIDUAL

- **"Arm Action":** thumbs up—hands and shoulders relaxed—weight on balls of feet—run relaxed—maintain stride length—as speed increases so does forward lean.
- **"Section Running":** (Place reminder signs on traffic cones along the designated course).
- Practice the following skills while completing a quarter-mile course.

First 50 yards	_____	run knees high
Second section	_____	jog
Third section	_____	sprint
Fourth section	_____	jog backwards
Fifth section	_____	split leaps
Sixth section	_____	bounds—one leg to the other
Seventh section	_____	sprint
Eighth section	_____	side straddle
Ninth section	_____	finish with long strides

PARTNERS

- **"Prediction":** Join with a partner for a game of "Prediction." Write down the time (minutes and/or seconds) you predict it will take for both of you to *cross together* a designated finish line 100 to 440 yards away. Since you must cross the line together, if one of you speeds up or slows down, the other must do the same. Work together to produce the best non-walking time possible.

```
               Prediction Card
Names _____
100 yd. dash
    predicted time _____
    actual time _____
440 yd. dash
    predicted time _____
    actual time _____
```

GROUP

- **"Turbo Tube Run Down":** How many side wall touches can your team make before the water moves from the top to the bottom bottle?
- **"Baton Passing":** Working in groups of four, practice exchanges with palms up and palms down in 20- to 50-yard intervals. Work on exchanging from a jog before progressing to a sprint.

COOPERATIVE

"**Synchro Sections**": Divide into groups of three to five and synchronize group movements as you move through the following five stations:

   a. Hop 10 times on the same foot.

   b. Jog backwards from one cone to another (30 yards).

   c. Perform 10 hurdle steps.

   d. Sprint 3/4 speed for 50 yards.

   e. Run and complete a long jump from a mutual start line.

Create a cooperative transition movement between sections.

INTERDISCIPLINARY

Using the following formula, translate Joe's time in the 100-yard dash to miles per hour.

Example: 100-yard dash = 11.0 seconds
X = Number of yards   # of sec. in 1 hour X # of yds.
Y = Number of seconds # of yds. in 1 mile X their time

Then $\dfrac{3600x}{1760y}$ = mph $\dfrac{3600 \times 100}{1760 \times 11} = \dfrac{360000}{18360}$

Ans. = 18.6 mph

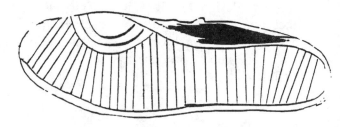

Be a creative **soul** by designing a creative **sole** on this typical tennis shoe. Your product should: permit the user to jump higher, provide increased traction, and wear longer.

Critical Thinking

TRIVIA

If a high jumper could jump as high as a flea, he or she would be able to leap almost as high as the Empire State Building. (*Men's Health,* Jan./Feb. 1994)

UNIT: TRACK AND FIELD—"JUMPING" (LESSON 2)

Objectives:

- Learn a variety of jumping techniques.
- Improve jumping proficiency.
- Transfer jumping techniques to related activities.

WARM-UP: THREE 10-SECOND SPEED JUMP-ROPE TRIALS

Practice

- How far can you jump forward off two feet? Mark your starting line (toes) and ending line (heels). Practice five standing long jumps and record your best effort in chalk.
- With a running start see how many more inches you can add to your score when taking off on or behind the first chalk line.
- How high can you be over the two marks?
- **"Hop, Step, & Jump":** Mark a new take-off line. Practice sprinting a short distance, HOP from the take-off point, STEP, and JUMP. (Try it from a standing start before implementing the running.)
- Work on an even cadence.
- **"Peer Hurdles":** Take turns sprinting and jumping over regular or makeshift hurdles (boxes, PVC pipe, hoops, or jump ropes stuffed in traffic cones). Watch each other, emphasizing the following cues:
  - Pick your natural lead leg
  - Arms close to body
  - Body erect, knees high
  - Lead arm is opposite lead leg
  - Toes up as leg clears hurdle

- **"High Jump":** (SAFETY) Proper mat protection, jumping techniques, and predetermined traffic patterns are essential in maintaining a safe learning environment. Because of the larger class numbers participating, emphasis will be on the straddle as opposed to the "flop."
- Working in groups of three, jumpers select height of rope and rotate after three attempts.
- With 7 to 10 steps back, use a straight-on approach (20–45°), plant-off foot closer to the bar, vigorously kick trail leg toward bar, clear the bar face down landing on the back. Who can jump the highest?

INDIVIDUAL

255

COOPERATIVE

"Pass Back": In groups of five or more, begin jogging single file around a track or field. Practice passing a tennis ball overhead to each student in line. When the ball reaches the last person, he or she sprints with the ball to the front and repeats the process. How many laps can you complete without a miss?

Draw a cartoon depicting some element of the sport of track that illustrates a typical hurdle in life.

INTERDISCIPLINARY

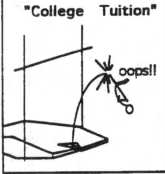

Sample

Your idea

Critical Thinking

"Prediction": Working in partners, write down your **guesstimate** of both you and your partner's 440 times. Add these together, run the quarter, and see how close these scores are to your **actual** time.

How many peanuts are needed to make a 12-oz. jar of peanut butter? *Answer:* **548.**

TRIVIA

Wednesday
HIP-TO-BE-FIT FITNESS CIRCUIT

	FITNESS COMPONENTS	ACTIVITY	DESCRIPTION	RESOURCE
1	Strength & Balance	SHOULDER WRESTLE	Facing in a kneeling position (mat), students place both hands behind their back and touch shoulders. Try to move each other out of balance.	
2	Upper Arm Strength	WAND WRESTLE	Players face with hands gripped alternately on the wand. Each player attempts to touch his or her end of the wand to the floor.	
3	Eye-Hand Coordination	EDGIES	See how many times in a row you can strike a tennis ball off the **edge** of your racquet.	
4	Upper Arm Strength	CHAIR DIPS	Place each heel on a different chair. Place your hands on the third chair. Practice lowering and raising as many times as possible.	
5	Balance & Leg Strength	BACK UP	Players stand back to back (elbows locked). Following the start signal, each player tries to back the other up past a designated line.	
6	Speed & Agility	FLAG TAG	Designate a zone from side wall to side wall, 20 feet wide. Place partners at opposite walls and take turns running past the partner on defense.	
7	Speed & Flexibility	HOCKEY HURDLES	Place hockey sticks on top of the traffic cones and practice running and jumping the hurdles spread 15 feet apart.	Flaghouse 1-800-221-5185
8	Upper Arm Strength	CHAIR BACK PUSH UPS	Partner #1 sits backwards on a chair and counts partner #2's push-ups on the back of the chair.	
9	Coordination	VOLLEY BIRD	Use your open palm to strike the volley bird upwards. Challenge your partner to a game of consecutive contacts.	Flaghouse 1-800-221-5185
10	Upper Arm Strength	PIN DOWN PUSH UP	Place 6 to 10 plastic bowling pins or 2-liter soda bottles 30 feet away. Partner #1 rolls a basketball or rubber bowling ball at the pins. #2 does push-ups for each pin knocked down.	

WEEKLY TEST

UNIT: TRACK AND FIELD—"SHOT PUT" (LESSON 3)

Objectives:

- Practice safe throwing procedures.
- Evaluate performance of others.
- Perform standing and **glide** delivery patterns.

WARM-UP: LONG RUN FOR PLACE

Practice

INDIVIDUAL

- Distribute one tennis or softball to each student.
- Find a clear space, face a wall (ten feet back), and place the ball **low** in your palm.
- Try putting the ball with fingers together and apart.
- What release works best? Remember, you can't throw the ball.
- How far can you put the ball when feet are stationary? Work on exploding from the legs.
- Next, hold the ball near your ear (palm up) and practice the delivery pictured below.
- Draw an imaginary circle with your eyes. *Right-handers:* Place your right foot in the middle of the circle and left at the front. With knees slightly bent, use your entire body as you drive forward, shifting weight from right to left foot. *Teacher:* After several attempts, ask students what increases throwing proficiency—legs or upper body? **Answer** Legs.

PARTNERS

- Challenge a partner to a put-for-distance contest. Select a starting line and take one big step back. Turn your back to the intended target, pivot, and release.
- Who can put the farthest after three attempts? Remember to mark the spot where the ball first impacts the ground.
- On the next round of three throws, evaluate each other on the following:
  a. **Hips are low.**
  b. **Back is to direction of target.**
  c. **Use entire body on release.**

GROUP

- In teams of three to five, take turns putting the ball across a football or soccer field. What team can cover the distance with the fewest number of throws? Remember, the second thrower puts from the first point of impact—not where it stops rolling.

"Combine": Select groups of three and challenge another threesome to a combined standing long-jump effort. Jumper #1 begins from the designated starting point. Jumper #2 places his or her toes where the heels of the first jumper lands and performs the next jump. This process continues with jumper #3. Upon completion, the combined distance is measured.

"Closing the Gap": Some researchers estimate that women track athletes will catch up to the men in the marathon as early as 1998. Check *The Guinness Book of World Records* for the endurance scores for men and women in 1972 and 1993 and see if this might happen.

Pre-race rituals are quite common among elite track athletes. Some visualize crossing the finish line, while others find different ways to relax. If you were preparing for an Olympic event, what preparations would you make?

How many consecutive misses eliminate a high jumper in track? *Answer:* **Three.**

PHYSICAL EDUCATION CONTRACT

Name _Debbie Tulson_

Class _Individual Sports (3rd)_

During the next _____3_____ weeks, I will work on accomplishing . . .

Cutting 10 seconds off my quarter mile score which is currently 1:33

I will need the following equipment . . .

Track / Timer

Teacher Approval _Mary Cates_ Date _5/15_

Progress—Week one _Dropped Score 1:27_

Progress—Week two _Score down 1:23_

Progress—Week three _New P.R. 1:19 Great!!_

Goal Accomplished _____X_____ Not Accomplished _____

Teacher Comments:

_These are the dividends for hard work.
Nice Going!_

Graded _____ Non-Graded _✓_

Jog-A-Thon

Need money for your program and you don't have a lot of time to plan for a fundraiser? Consider the Jog-A-Thon. **Here's what you need:**

- **A theme or reason for the pledge run, e.g., "Dash for Cash."**
- A student pledge package that includes rules of the event, a pledge sheet, a lap score card, and a list of prizes for the students collecting the most pledges.
- A running area (track or large field).
- Volunteer runners (students) willing to gather pledges and run laps the day of the event.
- **Physical education students can run during class. Those not enrolled in P.E. may run during lunch as well as before and after school.**
- A formula for pledges and laps completed.
- Juice or fruit for the runners.
- Incentives for students to solicit.

Sample

Most money	Most Pledges
First prize $25	First prize $25
Second prize $20	Second prize $20
Third prize $15	Third prize $15
Fourth prize $10	Fourth prize $10
Fifth prize $5	Fifth prize $5

Class prize—Sundae party for highest amount collected. It is not uncommon to collect thousands of dollars after a single day!

- -

_____ Jog-A-Thon

My name is _____ and I'm running in the _____ Jog-A-Thon.

I am planning to run _____ laps. You may pledge any amount you wish for each lap I complete,

or make a flat donation. You can make your check payable to _____. Checks

are preferred to cash. Thank you for helping.

Sponsor	Amount per Lap	Total Pledged	Total Collected	Sponsor's Initials

Laps verified by: _____ Total amount collected: _____

ALL★STAR MOTIVATOR

 ## "LANE CHANGE"

Bored with running? Try this. Utilizing a 6- or 8-lane quarter-mile track, place an even number of students behind each lane. Following a signal to begin, students jog when in **even** lanes and walk the **odd**-numbered lanes. As laps are completed, students rotate to their right (8 moves to 1). The goal is for students to complete the two miles in a given amount of time, e.g., twenty minutes. Record individual times and allow further trials to improve scores.

WALK	RUN	WALK	RUN	WALK	RUN	WALK	RUN
1	2	3	4	5	6	7	8

"ACCEL-DECEL"

The following acceleration-deceleration track activity is printed on a 5″ x 8″ tagboard card and serves as a great warm-up activity that can be accomplished either in the gym (circular traffic pattern) or on an outside track. The teacher announces the number of trials and the student begins running. Seconds are counted on a "one thousand one" basis.

TRIAL	SPRINT	JOG	WALK	REPETITIONS
1	2 sec.	3 sec.	4 sec.	3
2	3 sec.	4 sec.	5 sec.	4
3	4 sec.	5 sec.	6 sec.	5
4	5 sec.	6 sec.	7 sec.	6
5	6 sec.	7 sec.	8 sec.	7

ALL STAR MOTIVATOR

"ODD OLYMPICS"

Directions: Rotate through the following circuit and record the best of two tries.

ODD OLYMPICS SCORE CARD

EVENT	BEST SCORE
Hoop throw for distance	_____
50-yard box hurdles (Time)	_____
100-yard backward dash	_____
Broomstick throw for distance	_____
Standing backward long jump	_____
Backward overhead medicine ball throw	_____

ALL★STAR
MOTIVATOR

"SPEED UP"

Sports Radar:

Did you ever wonder how many miles per hour you can run? Olympic sprinter Carl Lewis is said to run nearly 26 miles per hour. The sports radar gun indicates how many mph you can run and is a great motivator for increasing speed. It can also assess throwing speed.

Speed Chute:

The speed chute was developed by a track coach in the former Soviet Union. The chute is lightweight, attaches to a waist belt, and fills up to produce drag as the runner increases speed. Students like the feeling generated when the wind fills up the chute. Many professional athletes use the speed chute to increase their speed.

MOTIVATOR

"LIVE WIRE"

Challenge students to see how many laps they can accumulate by running and jumping the circle of 8 to 10 **long** (turning) jump ropes. Jumpers **touching** a rope take the place of one of the turners at that rope. Once students become more skilled, have them perform a jump in the middle of each rope encountered. All ropes should be turning in the same direction (toward the jumpers).

ALL★STAR MOTIVATOR

"FLEX 'N' EFFEX"

"Check Your Flex": Slowly lean over (knees locked) and try to touch your toes. Hold this position and slowly count to five. Remember how close your fingers were to, or on, the floor. Next, bend your knees (see the photo) and hold this position for 45 seconds. Remember to keep both heels on the floor. Once again, straighten up and repeat the first test. Try this before the V-Sit and Reach test.

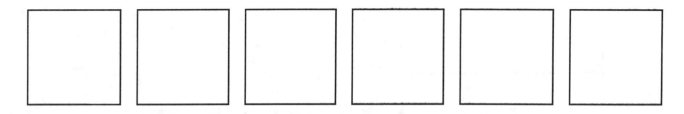

*T*umbling

PRE-GAME PLAN

> "Losers visualize the penalties of failure; winners visualize
> the rewards of success."—*Dr. Rob Gilbert*

The ability to handle one's body in a variety of situations is a prerequisite for success in all sports. This tumbling unit can help provide this success by presenting a variety of motivational physical challenges.

HIGHLIGHTS

M   Practice beginning *flight* activities, participate in a variety of cooperative learning experiences, play "Dominoes."

T   Work on increasing body control while moving in and out of balance, construct group pyramids, complete "Home Gymnastics" motivator.

W   New Hip-To-Be-Fit circuit, Arm Strength Test.

Th Set a personal record in the "Alternative Olympics," work on counter balances and "Trios," take the "Beam Master" challenge.

F   Contracts.

BENEFITS

- Increases balance, power, strength, flexibility, and muscular endurance.
- Sex equitable.
- Performance possibilities.
- Individualized.

RESOURCES

U.S. Gymnastics Federation
P.O. Box 7686
Fort Worth, TX 76111

UNIT: TUMBLING/GYMNASTICS (LESSON 1)

Objectives:

- Control body before, during, and after flight.
- Increase upper arm strength, power, flexibility, and balance.
- Cooperate with a partner and small group.

WARM-UP: "50"

Practice

INDIVIDUAL

- **"Flight Circuit":** Work on controlling your body during short- and long-term flight.

"Can You":

- Vault over low Swedish Box to crash pad?
- Jump off springboard (pikes—straddles—tucks) into a hula hoop?
- Jump into a handstand? Can you do three in a row?
- Perform a smooth swinging dismount from the end of the parallel bars?
- Skin the cat off two climbing ropes?
- Face a partner, bend, jump and attempt a 360° turn? Who can perform the most rotations on a single jump?
- Touch your toes when dismounting the balance beam?
- Jump from jogger to jogger while maintaining balance?
- Perform a (spotted) walkover or back handspring off the incline mat?
- Do a front handspring off a rolled mat? Flat mat?

PARTNERS

- Work on three different ways to lift your partner into the air.
- Find a way to lift each other alternately (one lift after another).

UNIT: TUMBLING/GYMNASTICS (LESSON 1) (cont'd)

GROUP

"Cooperatives":

- **"Alpha Beam":** Arrange your team on the beam by height. Once in place, rearrange in alphabetical order (first names). If a team member steps off, he or she mounts from the opposite end of the beam.
- **"Ropamid":** Create a pyramid off the floor using the climbing ropes.
- **"Inverted Shapes":** Using a long piece of elastic, form the following shapes while inverted.

Alpha Beam

Ropamids

Inverted Shapes

Find a way to perform a **cooperative** cartwheel, roll, or balance.

Research the history of gymnastics and find out what countries currently hold Olympic titles in both the men's and women's categories.

Construct a floor exercise routine and diagram it in the box. Your exercise must cover each corner and should include rolls, changes of direction, levels, balances, and flight.

The body's more than 600 muscles account for 40% of its weight.

UNIT: TUMBLING/GYMNASTICS (LESSON 2)

Objectives:

- Control body while in and out of balance.
- Increase strength, balance, and flexibility.
- Cooperate in small groups.
- Create sequences from traditional skills.

WARM-UP: THREE 10-SECOND SPEED JUMP-ROPE TRIALS

Practice

INDIVIDUAL

How many of the following **sequences** can you do?

• Handstand, roll out, back roll.	Yes _____ No _____
• Cartwheel, round-off, back roll extension.	Yes _____ No _____
• Swedish fall, leg circles, tripod to headstand, push to handstand, roll out.	Yes _____ No _____

PARTNERS

- **"On and Off Balance":**

Standing Push-ups

Partners face, fall forward, and push back to a standing (balanced) position. Each time a successful counter balance and recovery is made, partners step further apart. How far apart can the two of you be?

Squat Thrust

Partners face in a catcher's position (2–3 feet apart). Each partner attempts to push (palm to palm) or fake the other out of balance. Play a game to ten points.

272

UNIT: TUMBLING/GYMNASTICS (LESSON 2) (cont'd)

Walking Handstand

Partner #1 kicks into a handstand by placing his or her hands on #2's feet. Try walking from this position.

- **"Pyramids":** Construct a six-person pyramid with two of the participants performing handstands.
- Create a six-person pyramid with the top person inverted.
- Create a six-person pyramid that moves.

Create a ten-person pyramid (4, 3, 2, and 1). Can you remove person #6 without toppling the formation? Can someone in level 1 switch places with someone in level 3?

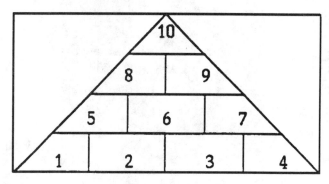

Research the history of gymnastic apparatus. Where did the prototypes for the pommel horse, parallel bars, side horse, and beam originate?

Create a three-person balance where two students are off the floor.

What is the heart made of? *Answer:* **Mostly muscular tissue.**

Wednesday
HIP-TO-BE-FIT FITNESS CIRCUIT

	FITNESS COMPONENTS	ACTIVITY	DESCRIPTION	RESOURCE
1	Power	backward JUMP	Challenge your partner to a backward jump for distance contest.	
2	Coordination	HAIRLINE HEADERS	See how many times you can contact a ball just below the hairline of the forehead.	
3	Upper Arm Strength	SWING AND FLICK	Place a basketball between your ankles, swing out on the bar, and release the ball. How far can you throw the ball?	
4	Reaction Time	QUICKNESS RULES	Partner #1 holds a ruler on the 12-inch mark. #2 places the thumb and index finger (without touching) next to the 0 mark. Partner #1 drops and #2 squeezes to catch.	
5	Balance Strength	BODY ROLLS	How many balances can you perform on the Body Roll tubes?	Hungarian Foreign Trade Co., Budapest
6	Upper Arm Strength	LOW ROW	Sit cross-legged on a scooter and challenge a partner to a side wall to side wall "low row (hands only)" contest.	
7	Balance	BLIND SCALE	Close your eyes and count the number of seconds you can maintain balance while in a front scale position.	
8	Speed	Hustle Shots	Make 3 free throws in a row. Run, retrieve your ball, and return to the foul line after each shot.	
9	Arm & Abdominal Strength	LONGEST LEVER	Face each other from opposite ends of the parallel bar. See who can hold their legs up longer.	
10	Endurance	SIDE TO SIDE SPRINT	Face your partner from the opposite side wall. Following the start signal, see who can touch more walls in the time allotted.	

WEEKLY TEST

UNIT: TUMBLING/GYMNASTICS (LESSON 3)

Objectives:

- Learn safety techniques for constructing pyramids.
- Work cooperatively in small groups.
- Explore counter-balancing possibilities.
- Experiment with non-traditional gymnastics.

WARM-UP: LONG RUN FOR PLACE

Practice

INDIVIDUAL

- **"Alternative Olympics":** Rotate through the five stations below and record your own personal best.
  - a. Pull-ups on still rings.   (best)_____#
  - b. Swing forward off bar for distance.   (best)_____ft.
  - c. Handstand inside hoop.   (best)_____sec.
  - d. Dual rope hang for time.   (best)_____sec.
  - e. Consecutive rope skips on beam.   (best)_____#

PARTNERS

- Work on the following **"Counter Balances."**

"Bottoms Up"

"Twin Towers"

PARTNERS

"Knee Stand"

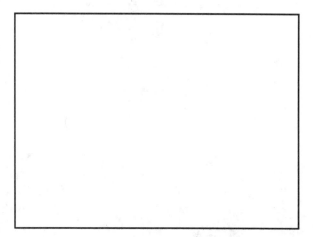

Invent Your Own

GROUP

- **"Trios":** How many of the following trios can your threesome perform? Remember to mount and dismount safely.

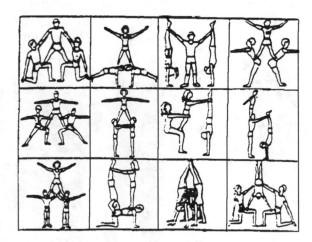

COOPERATIVE

Create a matching routine that incorporates a jump, a turn, and a roll.

INTERDISCIPLINARY

A National Safety Council report cited that the four major venues for accidents (home, work, auto, public) cost the nation more than $173 billion in 1991. List two preventive strategies for the sport of **gymnastics** that will reduce the risk of an accident.

1._____

2._____

The activity pictured is called "Bottoms Up." Find a partner of equal size and try this stunt. If you are unable to perform it, watch those who can. List five things that made them successful.

Critical Thinking

Does your stomach shrink when you reduce food intake? *Answer:* **No. Your stomach expands and contracts in relation to the food you put into it.**

TRIVIA

PHYSICAL EDUCATION CONTRACT

Name *Sue Jimirez*

Class *Individual Sports — (Davis)*

During the next _____ 2 _____ weeks, I will work on accomplishing . . .

An unassisted back handspring

I will need the following equipment . . .

Mat & Spotter.

Teacher Approval _C. Davis_ Date _12/2_

Progress—Week one _You need to work at home on your hand-stands. You are still bending too much in the handstand phase._

Progress—Week two _Able to perform on 6" crash pad w/o touching head. In another week you should accomplish._

Progress—Week three _____

Goal Accomplished _____ Not Accomplished _X (close)_

Teacher Comments:

Let's extend this one more week.

Graded _____ Non-Graded _✓_

ALL STAR
MOTIVATOR

 ### "DOMINOES"

Have you ever observed lines of dominoes? When arranged in rows, they will fall in order one after another. In the sport of tumbling there is a movement called a Swedish Fall. Performers stand at attention, arms at the side, fall forward, and at the last second catch themselves in a push-<u>UP</u> position.

Directions: Place students in groups of three to five in front of a line of mats. Practice falling in order within your small groups. When you have mastered the domino effect, join together with another group. As groups continue to grow, challenge each other to a domino (alternating fall) contest.

ALL STAR MOTIVATOR

 "HOME GYMNASTICS"

Men's and women's Olympic gymnastics include the following events: rings, floor exercise, even/uneven bars, vault, pommel horse, high bar, and beam. Survey your home and determine how you might duplicate skills from these events using inexpensive or readily available fixtures.

SAMPLES

EVENTS:
High bar
Parallel bars
Floor exercise
Pommel horse
Beam

MODIFICATIONS:
Door jam pull-up bar
Dips off three chairs
Rug
Chair (lever)
2″ x 4″ board (cartwheel)

- -

YOUR IDEAS:

Rings _____

Floor Exercise _____

Bars _____

etc.

281

ALL★STAR
MOTIVATOR

"THANKS FOR YOUR SUPPORT"

Find three ways to:

- Support a partner in a handstand.

- Lift a partner into a balance.

ALL★STAR
MOTIVATOR

 ## "BEAM MASTER"

Directions: To become the master of the beam, students must accomplish each of the following stunts while moving the length of the beam:
   a. Walk across forward with one turn.
   b. Walk across backward.
   c. Walk halfway, touch a knee, and walk off.
   d. Elevate both feet above the head.
   e. Bounce a ball along the top.
   f. Step through a partner-held hoop.
   g. Jump rope five times on top.
   h. Walk across with eyes closed.

ALL STAR MOTIVATOR

 ## "WEEKEND GYMNASTIC CHALLENGES"

Directions: The following challenges are presented to students during their last scheduled class of the week and evaluated upon their return. Testing may be conducted in squad lines or by an honor system. The entire process of presenting and evaluating the skill should require no more than two minutes of class time. Results may be used for squad points, extra credit, individual grades, or just for fun. All stunts can be performed safely at home. A good time to practice is during television commercials.

Nose to Knee Stretch

Head Touch to Floor

Stand—Lower to Squat—
Balance for 10 Seconds

Cossack Kicks or Bear
Dance (4 times)

Jump Your Toe

Shoot Through

Unassisted Back Bends

2 Wall Push-ups—
Touch Head to Floor

Jump the Broom Stick

Leg Circles

5 Second (L) Lever

Knee Jump to Feet

Swedish Fall Push-Up
Clap

Kip-up

5 Second Handstand
Unassisted

284

ALL★STAR
MOTIVATOR

"GYMNASTIC WALL SPRINGS"

In tumbling and gymnastics, shoulder strength is essential to produce spring. Try this drill using a wall or stairs.

- Face a wall three feet back.
- Practice falling forward, catching yourself by bending both arms just before your head and chest touch the surface.
- Push yourself back to a balanced position.
- How quickly can you spring back to a stand?
- Repeat, moving your feet back slightly each time.

Variations:

- Try from tiptoes.
- Try with arms extended upward.

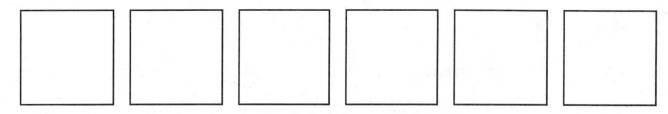

*V*olleyball

PRE-GAME PLAN

"Win without boasting, lose without excuse."

Volleyball is an excellent means of teaching cooperation. An inherent problem with the in-school game is that it's too often played with large groups, jeopardizing skill acquisition by weaker players. The majority of work in this section will focus on individual and small-group drills.

HIGHLIGHTS

M   Improve serving form and accuracy, play "Switch," participate in "Volleyball Variations."

T   Work on passing and blocking techniques, play "Three Strikes and You're Out" and "Gar**BAG**e Volleyball."

W   New Hip-To-Be-Fit circuit, Muscular End Test.

Th   Learn teamwork, play "Four-Square Volleyball," and set a "3-Ball Keep It Up" record.

F   Contracts.

BENEFITS

- Increases power and eye-hand coordination.
- Lifetime activity.
- Sex equitable.
- Teaches cooperation.

RESOURCES

U.S. Volleyball Association
1730 East Boulder Street
Colorado Springs, CO 80909

CONTRIBUTOR

Laura Sue Doty
Volleyball Coach
Roosevelt High School
Seattle School District

UNIT: VOLLEYBALL (LESSON 1)

Objectives:

- Know and practice under- and overhand serving techniques.
- Increase serving form and accuracy.
- Work on deep-serving consistency.

WARM-UP:

Practice

INDIVIDUAL

- Find a clear wall space, move 10 to 15 steps back and practice serving both under- and overhand above an imaginary or taped line 8 to 10 feet high. Try to serve so the ball comes right back to you.
- Can you toss the ball, jump, and overhand serve to the same area?
- Divide the class in half. With one team serving and one retrieving, servers work on moving from level one to level three. All scoring serves must land within the designated area 10 feet from the back line. Allow each side two to three minutes of serving time.

Level one (1 of 5)
Level two (3 of 5)
Level three (4 of 5)

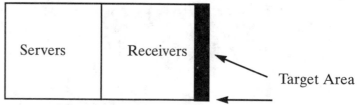

Target Area

PARTNERS

- Divide the class in half. Distribute one ball to each pair. Start at the ten-foot line on opposite sides of the net. Serve back and forth. As students' success increases, take one step back each time you can receive the ball without moving your feet. Return to the start line each time you have to move.

GROUP

- **"Switch":** Play a regulation game with one exception. Each time a player performs a legal serve, he or she moves to the other side and remains there until six (same) team members have moved across. When this occurs, a new game begins.

"SET-shots": Select a partner and position your-selves on opposite sides of a basketball goal. Alternate sets toward the hoop. How many baskets can the two of you make in one minute?

Write a one-page position paper to your local school board promoting the benefits of varsity **coed** volleyball.

Create an **"all active"** volleyball drill that moves to the beat of a Mother Goose rhyme. Yes, you have to say the rhyme as you perform the drill.

In a lifetime, your heart might pump 77 million gal-lons of blood. That would fill all the tanks in the New England Aquarium 150 times. —American Heart Association

UNIT: VOLLEYBALL (LESSON 2)

Objectives:

- Improve individual blocking technique.
- Increase passing proficiency.
- Practice cooperation and teamwork.

WARM-UP:

Practice

INDIVIDUAL

- **"Block Jumps":** Stand sideways to the wall, bend, and jump upwards, marking the top of your jump with chalk or a piece of tape. Next, face the wall and do ten continuous block jumps using good technique (palms forward, feet shoulder-width apart, knees flexed). Upon the extension of arms, thumbs should be pointing up, fingers **spread and stiff** ready to flex on ball contact. How many jumps out of ten can you touch at or above your original mark?

PARTNERS

- **"Three Strikes and You're Out":** The object in this activity is not to strike out, and to be one of the last set of partners left standing. If you make three mistakes, you're out and you and your partner must sit down. Use any combination of skills with good technique.

  For example:
  1. Player #1—passes—player #2—passes (Repeat)
  2. Player #1—passes—player #2—passes—player #1—sets—player #2—sets (Repeat)
  3. Player #1—passes—player #2—sets—player #1—hits—player #2—passes—player #1—sets

  Repeat game several times.

GROUP

- **"3's Pepper":** Players A and C dig and hit while player B (middle) sets. The setter must be ready to hustle to the ball if the dig is passed poorly. Player A tosses to B who sets back to A who (bumps, sets, or hits) to C who passes to B who sets back to C who (bumps, sets, or hits) back to A. Beginners may want to stay with single skills.

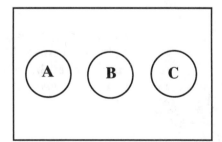

"On Your Backs": Form circles of four to five. Lie on your backs (feet toward center) and practice consecutive passes, trying not to let the ball get away from your circle. What's the highest number of successive hits your group can attain? Allow groups to start with a beachball or oversized ball first.

Timing is crucial when spiking the ball. What happens when you hit the ball during its **ascent** (under)? *Answer:* Most often the ball will carry out of bounds.

What usually occurs when hitting the ball too late or on top? *Answer:* Balls that are hit on top usually result in a net ball or missed hit.

Devise an **offensive** strategy for your volleyball team that utilizes the strengths of each individual player.

At age 65, who has more bone mass, men or women? *Answer:* **Men have 91% of original bone mass while the average woman has only 74%. Source:** *Berkeley Wellness Letter*, July, 1993.

Wednesday
HIP-TO-BE-FIT FITNESS CIRCUIT

	FITNESS COMPONENTS	ACTIVITY	DESCRIPTION	RESOURCE
1	Balance	LOG ROLL	How far can you move the log down the mat?	Carpet stores
2	Arm Strength & Flexibility	HAND STAND ARCH OVER	Perform a handstand on a soft mat and slowly let your legs fall forward ending in an arch.	
3	Flexibility	MAT V SIT AND REACH	In a sitting position, legs 12 to 18 inches apart, knees locked, how far forward can you reach?	
4	Balance	BELLY BUMPER	Who can remain on the mat the longest?	Gopher 1-800-533-0446
5	Leg Strength	WALL BALL ROLL	Work on moving the ball up and down the wall using only your feet.	
6	Balance	ROPE SCOOTER SWING	Stand on the scooter and hold the rope tight as your partner provides the push.	
7	Leg & Stomach Strength	BALLOON JUGGLE	Lying on your back and using just your feet, keep the balloon from touching the ground.	
8	Upper Arm & Stomach Strength	BOTTOMS UP	Sit facing, raise legs— push together lifting bottoms off the floor.	Cowtails and Cobras I & II Adventure Press P.O. Box 157 Hamilton, MA 01936
9	Upper Arm & Stomach Strength	BALL LEG ROLL	Sit facing, place ball in one partner's lap and work on moving the ball from one lap to the other.	On the Ball Benchmark Press 701 Congressional Blvd. Carmel, IN 46032
10	Flexibility	JUMP THE STICK	Practice jumping or stepping over the stick.	

WEEKLY TEST

UNIT: VOLLEYBALL (LESSON 3)

Objectives:

- Concentrate on performing three hits per side.
- Improve timing for blocking.
- Learn proper rolling techniques.
- Increase individual competencies.
- Emphasize the concept of teamwork.

WARM-UP:

Practice

INDIVIDUAL

- **"Recovery Rolls":** Lie on your back with arms extended perpendicular. Bring feet over shoulders to the left or right of midline while turning the head in the opposite direction. Return feet back to the floor and try the other side. Practice this motion rocking back and forth; when comfortable, continue momentum by driving down with upper arms and roll over.
- How many safe recovery rolls can you perform in 30 seconds?
- **"Keep It Going":** (one minute) Using a particular skill (bump or set), try to keep the ball in play, minimizing the number of mistakes.
  SCALE
  0–1 mistakes = excellent
  2–4 mistakes = good
  5–6 mistakes = work on ball control

PARTNERS

- **"High Fives":** Form two lines on opposite sides of the net. Place pieces of colored tape at the top of the nets every ten feet. Partners pair automatically from both lines as they jog parallel from the first to the last net. Each time partners come to a piece of tape, they jump and give each other high fives.

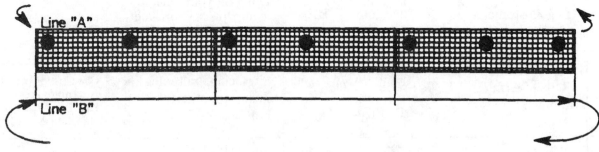

GROUP

- **"Four-Square Blanket Volleyball":** Practice moving a volleyball counterclockwise from court to court. Cooperate or compete for points.

"Coop Spikes": Working in groups of three, player #1 stands on a chair or bench adjacent to the net with a ball held as shown in the photo. Player #2 jumps and spikes the ball over the net. Player #3 receives the spike and all players rotate.

Tape a line ten feet from the opposite baseline and serve 15 balls toward that zone. What was your best percentage after three trials?

Predict the number of seconds it will take for you and a partner to set **ten** balls back and forth over a net. Write down your estimated number of seconds and follow with your actual score.

Prediction _____ (sec.) Actual _____

What are four ways to keep your blood pressure down?
- Keep weight down.
- Don't eat too much salt.
- Exercise.
- Don't smoke or drink alcohol.

PHYSICAL EDUCATION CONTRACT

Name _Mark Degraw_

Class _Team Spts. 2nd_

During the next _2_ weeks, I will work on accomplishing . . .

Improving my ability to spike the ball.

I will need the following equipment . . .

Net, ball, partner to assist.

Teacher Approval _OJ Fun_ Date _11/14_

Progress—Week one _Worked on plyometrics, hitting off partners hand (on chair). Took power jump test 29 inches_

Progress—Week two _Practiced blocking techniques — ran a mile increased power jump (standing) by one inch. 30"_

Progress—Week three _n/a_

Goal Accomplished _X_ Not Accomplished _____

Teacher Comments:

You hard work paid off. Congrats . . .

Graded _____ Non-Graded _✓_

ALL★STAR MOTIVATOR

"GARBAGE VOLLEYBALL"

Directions: Partners grasp opposite ends of a large plastic garbage bag and attempt to catch and throw regulation volleyballs over a net or elastic rope. Cooperating with another set of partners:

PRACTICE:

- exchanging over the net or rope.
- exchanging two balls at a time.
- performing five exchanges without moving your feet.
- exchanging ten in a row without the ball hitting the floor.

PLAY A GAME TO FIVE POINTS:

- Points are scored only when serves are delivered backwards.
- Receivers make a 360° turn prior to each catch.
- Catches are made with receivers kneeling or sitting down.

ALL★STAR MOTIVATOR

"TIC-TAC-TOE VOLLEYBALL"

Directions: This drill emphasizes serving accuracy. Select teams of nine. Player #1 from side "A" serves the ball into side "B"s court. The player catching the ball serves back and—if that serve is good—sits down. Balls not caught in a zone also result in that player sitting. This process continues until one team can sit three in a row on the opposite team. If a ball is caught by a sitting player, this frees him or her and that player returns to a playing position. Accuracy counts in this "Serve and Sit" game.

1	2	3
4	5	6
7	8	9

Side A

Side B

"VOLLEYBALL

After students have completed basic individual skills and drills, some time can be devoted to the following group variations.

GAME	DIRECTIONS
• **Single Skill Volleyball**	Once a skill is selected, e.g., bumping, the ball can only be returned by that particular skill.
• **Sit Down Volleyball**	This variation is played on either knees or seats. Balls may only bounce once before contact is made. A maximum of three hits per side is allowed.
• **Blanket Volleyball**	In this variation use the same rules as "Four-Square Volleyball" (Lesson 3). The difference here is that the ball is caught and tossed from a blanket.
• **Blind Volleyball**	Drape a sheet or parachute over the net. This game calls for quick reflexes, as students can't see the ball until the last second.

ALL★STAR
MOTIVATOR

"3-BALL (KEEP IT UP) RECORDS"

Directions: Spread class members evenly about the gym. The instructor begins by tossing or serving a regular or oversized volleyball into the air. A second and third ball follow shortly thereafter. Students attempt to keep each ball in the air with **legal hits.** Once a ball touches the floor, the instructor pulls it out of play. Time starts when the first ball is sent into play and ends when the last touches the ground. Try this once each day, recording and comparing classes' best scores.

ASA Mercer Middle School—Seattle School District, WA

ALL★STAR
MOTIVATOR

"POWER BALLOON VOLLEYBALL"

Directions: This activity emphasizes the **serve, bump, set,** and **spike** sequence as well as the alternating hit rule. The slow-motion action of the balloons allows students to refine techniques.

Arrange partners on opposite sides of a standing foldable mat (four per mat). One partner (right side) initiates play by executing an under- or overhand serve over the mat. Receiving partners "vocalize" the sequence of *bump, set, spike.* Points are scored when a balloon is not hit in the proper sequence or hits the floor. Boundary lines can be marked in chalk or existing lines can be used.

ALL★STAR MOTIVATOR

"3 VS. 3 BOO-BOO VOLLEYBALL"

Place teams #1 and #2 on opposite sides of the net. Additional (waiting) teams line up behind the end line of team #2. The teacher and/or students stand near one end of the net with the game, plus one extra, ball. On the "go" signal, the instructor tosses a ball to team #1. Team #1 gets three hits to send it over. Play continues until one team "Boo-Boo's." If it's team #2, they rotate back behind the waiting teams and a new team rotates in. Winners always stay on (or rotate to) court one. The teacher can control the pace of the game by tossing in a second ball at any time.

```
┌─────────────┬─────────────┐   T   T
│ Court #1    │ Court #2    │   E   E
│             │         X   │   A   A
│  O          │             │   M   M
│             │     X       │
│         O   │          X  │   #   #
│  O          │             │   3   ④
└─────────────┴─────────────┘
```

By: Jan McNeely & Don Wills
South Whidbey School District
Langley, WA

300

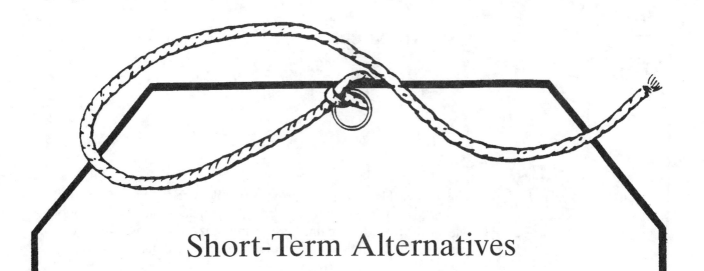

Short-Term Alternatives

"And where it is for one, mightn't be for another."
—Splash Mountain—Disneyland

The following short-term options provide opportunities for students to explore new movement patterns and expend their personal skills inventory. The options included here are but a few of the alternative activities being taught in public and private schools throughout the world. For students to realize the full benefits from these activities, it is imperative that the instructor present those selected with the same energy and respect given to the traditional sports menu.

"No longer are there four seasons (football, basketball, baseball, track)."

UNIT: ADULT CPR

The goal of this course is to provide people with the knowledge and skill necessary in an emergency to call for help, to help keep someone alive, to reduce pain, and to minimize the consequences of injury or sudden illness until professional medical help arrives.

Adult CPR participant manuals, adult "manikins" (1 per 3 students), TV, videocassette player, community CPR video, adult CPR exams.

Classroom or gymnasium

Day One: 50 minutes

Introduction to the Course: 10 minutes
Responding to an Emergency: 40 minutes
       Deciding to Act/Recognizing an Emergency
       Taking Action

Day Two: 55 minutes

Checking an Unconscious Victim: 20 minutes
Checking the Conscious Victim: 10 minutes
Prevention: 10 minutes
Breathing Emergencies
       Helping a Conscious Choking Victim: 15 minutes

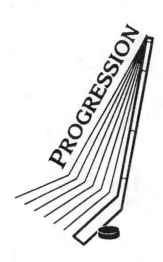

Day Three: 55 minutes

Rescue Breathing: 30 minutes
Helping the Unconscious Choking Victim: 25 minutes

Day Four: 55 minutes

Recognizing a Heart Attack: 10 minutes
Adult CPR: 30 minutes
Preventing Cardiovascular Disease: 15 minutes

Day Five: 25–50 minutes

Adult CPR Examination: 25 minutes
Exam Grading/Discussion: 25 minutes (optional)

Adult CPR participant manual and instructor manual, equipment and supplies available through local American Red Cross units.

Other ARC Courses: Standard First Aid; Infant and Child CPR; Community CPR; and Community First Aid and Safety.

UNIT: DOUBLE DUTCH

Double Dutch has undergone radical changes in the past ten years. It has moved from predominately fast jumping and fancy turning to an international sport featuring show-stopping rhythmics and high-level acrobatics.

Two 12- to 16-foot beaded, sash cord, or licorice (plastic) ropes.

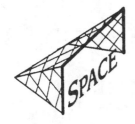

Gymnasium, asphalt, or flat carpet.

TIPS FOR SUCCESSFUL JUMPING

- Enter from the turner's side just as the back rope (furthest from you) touches the ground.
- Jump close to the ground, on the balls of your feet.
- Relax and stay in the center of the ropes (lowest point).
- Perfect stunts outside the ropes before attempting them inside. Use the cue: **"One-Two-Ready-Go."**

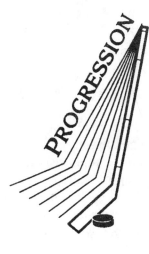

TIPS FOR SUCCESSFUL TURNING

- Shake hands with the ropes.
- Turn alternately from nose to waist. Do not bring your hands past the midline of your body.
- Turners should focus their attention on the jumper's movements, speeding, stalling, or slowing the ropes according to the stunt being performed.

LEVELS

The following skills are categorized by levels, each increasing in difficulty. Careful preparation must be made before using ropes during tumbling or other potentially dangerous stunts. It is good practice to work on skills both on and off mats prior to executing them inside the ropes. At times it is advantageous to use a single rope before adding a second rope. In addition, mats may be placed under the ropes before moving to a hard surface. When skills have been mastered, the jumper is ready to perform inside the ropes.

LEVEL ONE	LEVEL TWO	LEVEL THREE
Jump in place	Jog in place	High knee jog
Two-foot 360°	One-foot 360°	Partner turns
Touch the floor	Squat jump	Low dance moves
Jump rope inside	Double unders	Partner rope skills
Bounce a ball	Partner passes	Bounce through legs
Beanbag toss/catch	Juggle 3 beanbags	Rings or clubs
Push-up	Partner push-ups	Push-up between partner's legs

Round-off or front-handspring out to in:
- Enter when back rope touches ground.
- Pick up hands quickly.

Round-off or front-handspring inside:
- Face outward and throw stunt when front rope touches ground.
- Turners move with jumper.

Round-off or front-handspring with partner from out to in:
- Synchronize entry on "One-Two-Ready-Go."
- Enter when back rope touches the ground.

Back-handspring out:
- Turn your back outward.
- Throw back-handspring when rope closer to jumper's back touches ground.
- Move rope away from jumper.

Back-handspring inside:
- Turn your back outward.
- Throw back-handspring when rope closest to jumper's back touches the ground.
- Move with jumper.

Back-handsprings out with a partner:
- Turn backs outward.
- Synchronize exit on "One-Two-Ready-Go."
- Throw back-handsprings when the rope closest to backs touches the floor.
- Move ropes away from jumpers.

UNIT: KORFBALL

Korfball is the only team sport that requires coeducational play by the rules of the game. The game allows for a true gender-integrated curriculum. Additionally, korfball places significant emphasis on motor movement mastery of flow and timing, and sport skill development of ambidexterity. These, along with game skills such as passing, cutting, and shooting, create a highly articulate sense of team play. Finally, the game is physically exerting and thus works well towards class health-related goals.

Korf standards: 2 steel base plates, 2 posts, 2 extension pieces, 2 brackets. These may be constructed by shop classes or substituted by using floor-positioned volleyball or badminton standards.

    Imported wicker baskets: These may be substituted by using plastic laundry buckets.

    Korfball balls: These may be substituted by using standard soccer balls.

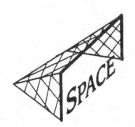

Gymnasium, asphalt play area, or grass field large enough to accommodate long-distance shooting. A field also allows for the 3-zone modification listed below.

PROGRESSION

A. BALL HANDLING (in pairs)
    Stationary Strong Hand
    Stationary Weak Hand
    Stationary Alternating Hands
B. CUTTING
    Pattern Cuts
    Option Cuts
    Ball Handling with Slide
    Ball Handling with Cuts
C. SHOOTING
    Figure-6 Technique
    Stationary Set Shot
    Cutting Set Shot
    Penalty Shot
    Running-In Shot

D. OFFENSE
    3-Person Post and Set
    3-Person Post and Running In
    3-Person Post Set Fake and
        Running In
E. DEFENSE
    Guarding Technique
    Shadowing
    Rebounding
    Counter-Attack Passing
F. STRATEGY
    4-Person Post Unattended
    4-Person Post Shadowed
    Game Modifications

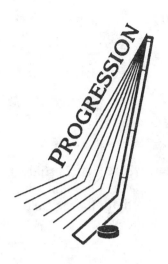

MODIFICATIONS

- **"Reaction Shot":** Drill the game half-court with a designated shooter who must react with a set shot or a running-in shot according to the actions of the instructor. This enables the designated player to feel the movement of a defender rather than predetermine the shooting option.

- **"Numbered Shot":** Play the half-court game with a shadow defense. Require only one pass to get the ball to a shooter. Advance and require two passes; then three . . . and so on. This enables the players to look ahead and think strategically and use all teammates in the passing plan.

- **"Bumper Korf":** Allow one point for a ball that hits the korf, two points for a ball that scores a korf. This creates more shot attempts and encourages weaker players.

- **"Buddy Korf":** Require a cross-gender assist prior to any shot. This nurtures the use of female players by male players and begins to establish the pairing notions of the game.

- **"3-Zone Korf":** Create a middle zone between the two offensive ends. This allows for free-wheeling play in the center zone and involves many additional players.

Dr. Dan Tripps, Seattle Pacific University, Former National Team Coach. Equipment and teaching materials may be ordered by contacting:

United States Korfball Federation
1636 South Florence Place
Tulsa, OK 74104
TEL.: 918-742-0354.

UNIT: OMNIKIN BALL (MODIFIED)

Omnikin Ball is a hit-run-and-trap team game where EACH student is as important as the other. Developed in Canada, Omnikin players experience a fast-paced, cooperative, aerobic activity that is challenging—and fun. The rule format is simple and students can play with little preparation.

One 3′ or 4′ diameter Omnikin ball. The Omnikin ball is light and durable. Its wide valve ensures easy inflation and deflation.

Gymnasium or grassy area.

Lead-up Activities:
1. Lie on backs in lines of five or six. Try to move the ball down the line with slight taps from fingers and toes.
2. Toss and catch with hands only. Toss and catch with backs only.
3. "Quick Trap": Toss out and time each group for the quickest trap.
4. "Down the Line": Have two lines facing. Practice moving the ball down the line without touching the floor.

Modified Rules:
- Designate a color for each team.
- Three or four teams consisting of 4 to 5 players form a square around the serving team.

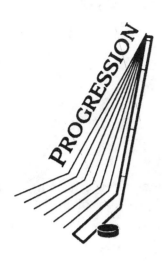

- All players from the serving team freeze the ball. Prior to the serve, the server calls **"Omnikin"** and one of the colors of a different receiving team, e.g., **"Omnikin Blue."** The ball is then hit with an upward trajectory, and the Blue team must freeze it with all players in contact within five seconds. The ball must travel a minimum of twelve feet and has to be trapped by the receiving team before it hits the ground.

Scoring:
- One point is awarded <u>each</u> team not involved in the error.
- Each side of the square around the serving team should have at least one player from each color.
- Strike balls into areas that are difficult to reach.
- Servers fake the direction in which they are going to hit.
- Use any body part to stop or trap the ball.

UNIT: ORIENTEERING

Orienteering provides physical conditioning, endurance training, and the life skills of map reading, navigation, and problem solving.

- Maps for individuals or small groups.
- Control markers.
- Hole punchers or stamps.
- Note-keeping supplies (watch, paper, pencil, etc.).

*Compasses are used by serious orienteers but are optional for P.E. classes.

Simple orienteering exercises can be held in a classroom, but more interesting ones require a larger area. The grounds of normal-sized elementary schools are often adequate. The campus of a larger school or college can provide more interesting challenges. Whatever area is used, it needs to be mapped and the map needs to be reasonably accurate and legible.

- Maps
- Map Reading
- Following the Map

Most orienteering maps are of forested areas and are quite detailed. Maps used for major competitions are typically produced as follows: Aerial photos are obtained, usually from a state department of natural resources but occasionally from special flights. These are used to construct a photogrammetric base map, an expensive process requiring the use of a stereo plotter. This base map shows everything that can be identified on the aerial photos that might be of interest to the orienteer (roads, trails, fences, boulders, buildings, clearings, lakes, streams, hills, and ridges). This information is then checked in the field. Any changes

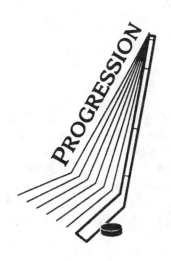

or additions are then made to the base map. The final map is then drawn and printed.

The symbols used are standard throughout the world, making it possible for orienteers from one country to read an orienteering map in another country without too much difficulty. These symbols are printed using five colors of ink: black for buildings, roads, trails, and fences and rock features; blue for water; brown for topographic information; green for thick vegetation; and yellow for clearings. Forested areas that are easy to travel through are shown as white on the map.

A simple map of a school yard can be drawn in black and white. Usually, an engineering or landscaping map of the school grounds can be redrawn for orienteering use. A clearly drawn pencil sketch can be used, or even photocopies of the school's floor plan.

Control Markers

Control Markers used in major events are usually made of cloth, and are three one-foot squares sewn together to fashion a prism. Each of the squares is of two colors, divided diagonally with the upper square white and the lower square orange. For low-budget events, a marker can be two dimensional—a square sheet of plywood or cardboard will do. Smaller sizes can be used for playgounds and classrooms.

A variety of hole punchers or stamps provide proof that runners have located a marker. Many physical educators have students run in teams, decoding clues at various check points around campus.

Mike Schuh
P.O. 17005
Seattle, WA 98107
(206) 783-3960

United States Orienteering Federation
P.O. 1444
Forest Park, GA 30051

UNIT: RACEWALKING

Most students are accustomed to running in physical education and the thought of walking—especially with the techniques discussed here—often takes a selling job by the teacher. When practiced regularly, the benefits are numerous. Racewalking or power walking will improve upper and lower body muscle tone, burn calories and fat, and develop cardiovascular fitness, all without the risks of injury associated with jogging. A skilled racewalker is just as fast as most trained runners. The world record for the mile is around 5-1/2 minutes.

- Comfortable, lightweight tennis shoes with adequate support and stability as well as low heel height with a flexible rubber outsole.
- Loose-fitting shorts.

Running tracks, sidewalks, or other flat safe areas.

Racewalking technique is really similar to regular walking technique, just speeded up and refined. Good posture is essential for good race-walking technique and should be a goal of every walking-for-fitness program. In particular, strive for:
- Shoulders back with head erect.
- Rib cage and lower abdomen flat.
- Lower back relaxed, with a minimum of "sway."
- All motion forward-and-back, with a minimum of sideways deviation, in shoulders, hips, knees, and feet.

These elements of good posture should be emphasized at all times:
- Arms bent at a 90-degree angle or better at the elbow. Hands swing back no further than the end of the buttocks, nor higher than the midline of the chest in front. Hands come to some spot in the mid-chest area.
- Arms swing forward and backward along the waistband, trunk, or buttocks.

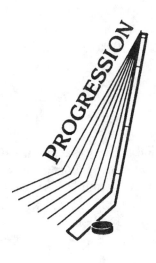

- Body remains in upright position. No falling behind hips with trunk or buttocks.
- Hips rotate forward and down.
- Knees are straightened, with relaxed quadriceps.
- Feet are angled up high on landing, rolled right up on the toes in pushing off (string ankle flexion).
- Feet land in straight line as hips turn with the stride.
- Push off with the second and third toes, right over the top of the foot.

A basic program of racewalking for fitness should include three to four half-hour sessions of fast-speed racewalking, using proper technique, per week.

Technique Productions, 4831 N.E. 44th, Seattle, WA 98105

Brown Shoe Company, Naturalizer Division, 8300 Maryland Avenue, P.O. Box 354, St. Louis, MO 63166

UNIT: ROLLER SKATING

Roller skating is a popular physical and social activity. Secondary students in the Seattle Public Schools rated it as their favorite physical education unit. Roller skating can increase your dynamic balance and coordination. Skating is not restricted by physical size, overall strength, or past athletic experience. It has numerous lifetime benefits.

Quality roller skates are the only skates that should be purchased. Buy from companies with good reputations. Whether you select in-line, precision, or free ball-bearing wheels, additional spare parts and tools should be purchased. At least one staff member should be trained to repair the equipment correctly. Some school districts require a safety workshop for staff before teaching the unit.

Wood or linoleum floors.

Once you have obtained and laced the correct-sized skates and the traffic pattern (counterclockwise) has been established, the following progression can be initiated. All skills can be taught first by walking (stepping through it).

- **"T-Stop Position":** The right foot is pointed forward with the left against heel of the right foot. Weight is on the back foot.

- **"Falling":** Relax, landing on large body parts (buttocks), recover by bringing hands in, cross leg, push to a stand. Always be aware of traffic.

- **"Scissors (Sculling)":** Knees slightly bent, put pressure on the inside edges pushing skates apart. Pressure on the outside edges brings them back together. Repeat this sequence.

- **"Stopping (T-Stop)":** When skating forward the non-skating foot drags sideways against the forward foot. The weight shifts gradually to the back foot as forward motion slows.

- **"Push and Glide":** Start from a T-position, push off one foot, lift trail leg, and repeat with opposite foot. Try to extend your glide.

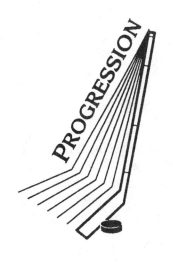

- **"Turns (180-three turn)":** Trace a "3" on the floor. These turns are accomplished on one foot.
- **"Backward":** Begin from a wall. Bring knees together, push off with inside edges—knees separate and heels come together. Practice without a wall push. Weight is over toes. Next work on backward stroking.
- **"Partners":** Synchronize your push and glide strokes. Try to use different hand positions. Skate in threes.
- **"Scale (Arabesque, front spiral)":** Practice skating on one foot with the trail leg parallel to the floor. The body forms a T-shape.
- **"Crossover":** The crossover helps change direction and gain speed. Simply cross the front foot over the back. Practice when skating in both directions and backward.
- **"Level Changes":** Each time you cross the mid-court line, lower your body position. Extend arms forward, feet together, bend knees to a squat position. Can you extend one foot forward (Shoot the Duck)?

OTHER MOTOR SKILLS WITH EQUIPMENT

- balance a beanbag on your head
- skate around a hula hoop
- manipulate a tennis ball with a hockey stick
- juggle
- dribble a ball
- pick up objects

GAMES

- **"Catch the Flag":** Divide the class in half and form two single lines at opposite ends of the floor. Students create a chain (hands on hips). A flag is carried in the back pocket of the last person in each line. On the signal, lines begin skating in a counterclockwise direction attempting to secure the other team's flag. The action stops when the flag is captured or one or more skaters break the chain. Only line leaders can *Catch the Flag.*

Roller Skating Rink Operators Association, P.O. Box 81846, Lincoln, NE 68501.

Complete Book of Roller Skating, Victoria Phillips, Workman Publishing, NY, 1979.

Roller Skating Fundamentals and Techniques, Sharon Kay Stoll, Leisure Press, NY, 1983.

Alternative Sports and Games, Turner and Turner, Ginn Press, 1989. Needham Heights, MA, 02194.

RESOURCES

UNIT: ROWING

Rowing is a challenging sport, both mentally and physically. It offers an opportunity for students to learn a sport where few have past experience, there are no individual "stars," and each person can be a contributing member of a team. It is a low injury, low stress sport. Physical size and gender are not factors for success. Rowing is an excellent activity for developing cardiovascular fitness.

Competitive sweep rowing is practiced in a long racing shell and each person controls one 12-foot oar. An 8-oared shell 60 feet long has places for eight rowers and one person (coxswain) who steers. Boats come in various sizes and styles with the smallest being a single scull (18 feet to 27 feet) with one-person sculling utilizing two 9-foot long oars. The rower sits on a sliding seat that rolls on tracks.

An initial obstacle to overcome is access to the specialized equipment. You can often arrange to participate in an existing rowing program that can be found in many communities. Older used rowing equipment can be purchased from collegiate rowing programs that regularly update their inventory of boats. Additional safety equipment, including vest-style lifejackets, is essential.

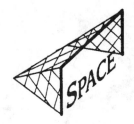

Lakes, canals, rivers, and other waterways with some protection from high wind and weather exposure.

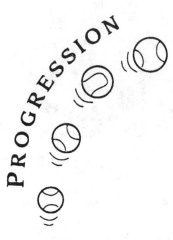

Rowing is slow moving and structured at the beginning level. The care and handling of the specialized equipment, water safety education, and basic stretching are included in the first session. Rowing skills can be introduced on land using rowing machines.

- Upright posture, balance, breathing, and hand position on oar handle.
- Rowing cycle includes the careful placement of the oar blade into the water, the level pulling of the oar handle (similar to pulling across a table top), applying downward pressure to the handle of the oar to release it from the water, "feathering" to change the angle of the blade, and the level return of the oar handle back to the beginning.
- When the blade first enters the water, the legs quickly apply pressure. The back and shoulders join in and the final pull is with the arms.

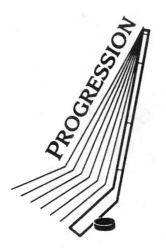

Shell

- The mental concentration focuses on balance, practicing the skill, and achieving precision teamwork of duplicated motions. The challenge increases as the boat gains more speed and racing techniques are introduced.
- Practice drills isolating a technique.

RESOURCES

U.S. Rowing West Regional Office, 811 First Avenue, Suite 264, Seattle, WA 98104; (206) 625-9003.

Kathy Whitman, Aquatics Director, Seattle Department of Parks and Recreation.

UNIT

UNIT: SKATEBOARDING

BENEFITS

Skateboarding is an activity that develops and refines dynamic balance and weight distribution skills. Continued practice also increases eye-foot coordination and offers unlimited opportunities for creativity and recreation.

EQUIPMENT

- skateboards
- shoes with "friction" soles
- wrist guards
- knee pads
- helmets

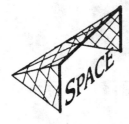

SPACE

Any smooth flat area without pedestrian or vehicular traffic areas should be dry and free of debris.

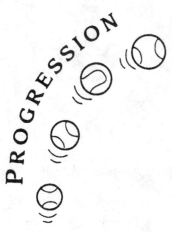

PROGRESSION

- Select the **lead** foot. This is usually the dominant foot and is placed in the middle of the board to maximize stability as the **back** foot pushes off.
- Bend the knees, keep the head up, arms out for balance, relax.
- Balance: Keep your shoulders over your hips and hips over ankles.
- Falling is part of the learning process. Learning to fall correctly can decrease the risk of injury. Use your safety equipment and roll onto the body's naturally padded parts.
- As the student becomes more proficient, he or she can experiment with the board foot placed over the front and back wheels.
- Once the student can push and glide forward, practice should focus on turning. Turning a skateboard is to either the toe side or the heel side. Pressing down on toes will turn the skateboard to the toe side. Pressing down on heels will turn the board to the heel side.

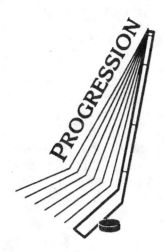

Beginning Tricks:

- **"Wheelie":** Balance on back wheels as long as possible. Start with short distances. To increase distance, keep arms forward.
- **"Nose Wheelie":** Same as above, but do it off the front foot moving forward.
- **"Tick Tacks":** This trick is a sequence of fast kick turns left and right.
- Add kick turn circles.

Steve Coutcher
Gravity Sports
Renton, WA 98058
(206) 255-1874

In cooperative challenge activities, students compete to *complete*, not to defeat. Stronger students assist those not so highly skilled. Goal-setting centers around cooperation and successful completion of a task. Students work in groups of five or six, thus allowing all to be active.

- 3 balance beams or taped lines
- balloon
- climbing ropes
- trolley (2″ x 6″ board) with counter-sunk holes for ropes
- blanket, sheet, or tablecloth
- Three 4-foot long 2″ x 4″ boards
- 3 rubber car tires
- One 16-foot beaded or sash cord rope

Gymnasium

STATIONS

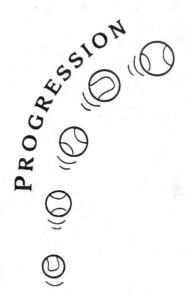

- **"Rope Pyramid":** Students construct a pyramid off the floor.
- **"Birthday Beam":** Students move onto a balance beam, lining up by height. Once the group has mounted, students rearrange themselves by the month they were born. Students stepping off remount at one end.
- **"Trolley":** Students stand on the boards, pull up on the ropes, and synchronize steps either forward or backward.
- **"Blanket Basketball":** Students hold a sheet, blanket, or tablecloth. Place a basketball in the middle and attempt to send the ball through the hoop.
- **"Fizzle":** Group circles the designated inflator. The student inflates a balloon the size of a melon, holds it high above his or her head, releases it, and the group attempts to catch it before it hits the ground.

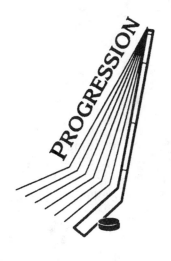

- **"Bridge":** Students attempt to move across the floor using four car tires and the three 4-foot long 2″ x 4″ boards. Students touching the ground must start over.

- **"Four Corners":** Place a high beam over a low beam. Students attempt to touch all four corners without falling off. A point is awarded when all four corners are touched.

- **"Wall Ball Push":** Students lie on backs (shoulder to shoulder) with feet up and against the wall. A medicine ball is passed along the wall using feet only. If the ball touches the ground, it must be returned to the starting point. Points are scored if the ball reaches the end of the line.

- **"Hoop Pass":** The group forms a line with hands held. The line leader picks up a hoop, steps through, and passes it down the line. A point is scored each time the hoop reaches the end. Only one hoop may be picked up at a time. (Remember, the hand chain cannot be broken.)

- **"Jump Together":** Two turners for the remainder of the group. The jumpers stand in the middle (hands held). A point is scored for every three consecutive jumps.

Trolley

Bridge

RESOURCES

Alternative Sports and Games, Turner and Turner, Ginn Press, Needham Heights, MA, 1989.

PROJECT ADVENTURE, P.O. Box 157, Hamilton, Maine 01936

UNIT: TEAM HANDBALL

Team Handball is an exciting and challenging game that combines the skills, rules, and strategies of basketball, soccer, and hockey. It involves running, dribbling, jumping, passing, throwing, catching, and goal tending. Originating in Europe, team handball has been an Olympic event since 1972.

The official game ball looks like a small soccer ball. Six- to eight-inch playground balls, volleyballs, nerf™ soccer balls, etc., may be substituted. Ball size will vary depending on the age and skill of a particular class. A regulation goal is two to three meters wide. Modified goals may consist of volleyball standards or traffic cones.

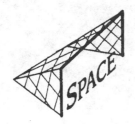

Gymnasium, concrete, or grassy area. A basketball court can easily be modified for team handball. Penalty shots may be taken from either the foul line or the end of the key.

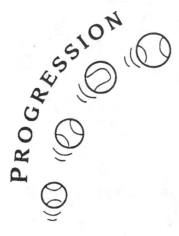

Playing Skills (Dribbling)

Find a space on the floor where you have enough room to bounce your ball without interference. Begin dribbling about the room and listen for my signal (clap). Upon hearing the signal, change the direction of your dribble. Next, roll the ball out in front of you and see how quickly you can pick it up and get it bouncing. Experiment with ways to dribble the ball under your legs and behind your back. Change hands and try again.

Designate an area approximately 10 feet square. Find a partner. One partner tries to dribble the ball within the area. The other partner tries to steal the ball away without fouling. Every 15–20 seconds a freeze signal will be given. At that time partners change positions.

Playing Skills (Passing)

Face a wall. Standing eight to ten feet away, pick an imaginary target. Using the following passes, see how many times you can hit this target out of ten tries.

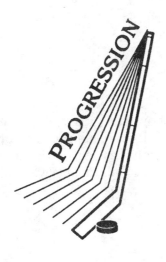

- Two-hand chest pass
- One-hand shoulder pass (add a jump)
- Two-hand overhead pass
- Hook pass
- Chest bounce pass

Which pass did you have the most success with?

Game Rules (Simplified)

The object of the game is to move toward the opposite goal by passing, striking, dribbling, or throwing. A regulation team consists of six court players and one goalie. Court players cover the entire court. Once a player receives the ball, he or she may take three steps, dribble (as many times as desired), take three more steps, pass or shoot within three seconds. Only the goalie may kick the ball. Minimal contact is allowed. The court is marked with a penalty, free-throw line, and a goal area. The goal area is for the goalie only; court players are not allowed in this space. One point is awarded for a goal. Violations and penalties are similar to basketball. A free throw is taken from the point of the violation, and the defense must remain three yards away from the player taking the free throw. A penalty throw is taken from the basketball foul line. Penalty throws are awarded when a player is fouled while in the process of shooting.

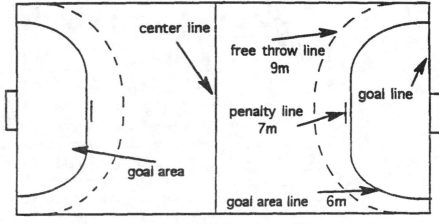

Side Line

"Team Handball," from *Physical Education and Sport for the Secondary Student*, M. Cavanaugh, AAHPERD, 1983.

H. Michaelson, Bethel School District, Spanaway, WA 98387.

UNIT: UNICYCLING

This sport offers a perfect opportunity for boys and girls to enter an activity where past experience, strength, and height are not essential for success. Unicycling is a unisex activity that promotes goal setting and determination. By following a sequential progression, students will find that their progress is accelerated.

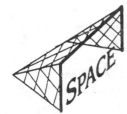

16″-, 20″-, or 24″-wheel unicycles (range in price from $80–$150).

Unicycling requires little space, and skills can be taught effectively inside or out.

- Place the wheel against the wall.
- Pedals are parallel (1/2 rotation).
- Rider rolls cycle forward, tips seat back, places seat between legs, puts pressure on back pedal to push the rider to an upright position.
- **Spotters** stand on each side with hands (palms up) lightly supporting rider's **outstretched** hands. (Rider's hands are palms down.)
- Once the rider is upright, the majority of his or her weight is distributed **to the seat.** Only light pressure is exerted on the pedals. From this position the rider begins to pedal forward with the spotters at each side. As soon as spotters feel the rider push down on hands, they **STOP** and vocalize **"HEAVY ON THE SEAT."** When pressure eases, the spotters begin moving forward again.
- When the rider can move across the floor with light pressure on the pedals, he or she may eliminate one spotter, and eventually ride unassisted.
- Ride unassisted—straight line.
- Turn left and right.
- Rock/idle.
- Ride a circle-eight pattern.
- Ride with a partner (hands held).
- Ride with one partner moving backwards.
- Ride backwards.
- Walk the wheel (feet on tire).

Stomach

Footsie

Walk the Wheel

Juggling

Seat in Front

Star

RESOURCES

Alternative Sports and Games, Turner and Turner, Ginn Press, Needham Heights, MA, 1989.
Unicycle Society of America, P.O. Box 40534, Redford, Michigan 48240.
One Wheel Jammin (A comprehensive Unicycle Video) Chuk-em Ent. (McEwan-Turner). 11080 Arroyo Beach Pl. S.W. Seattle, WA 98146

UNIT: WATER AEROBICS

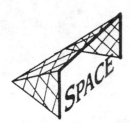

Participants in water aerobics experience a physical challenge and a low impact workout that can easily be modified to fit the needs of nearly every population. Water offers buoyancy and natural resistance, allowing students great toning for upper and lower body muscle groups. Cardiovascular fitness and flexibility also increase with these workouts.

Bathing suit or aerobic wear. Shoes/aqua socks are optional, but will protect feet. Wave Webs/gloves are also optional, but help with upper body toning and **feel** of water. Other optional equipment includes: kick boards, hand buoys, Frisbees™, balls, jugs, tubing.

Swimming pool 3–4.5 feet (5 feet) for a shallow-water class. Temperature 83°–85°.

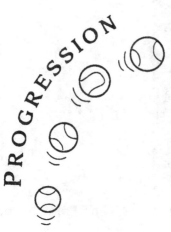

Classes should follow a format similar to the one below.

ACTIVITY	PURPOSE
Thermal Warm-up (5 min.)	• To lubricate joints.
	• Move O_2 to working muscles.
	• To warm body up because of temperature change.
Pre-stretch (3–5 min.)	• Prevent injury.
	• 10-second stretch for major muscles used in workout to come.
Cardiovascular Warm-up (5 min.)	• Gradually increase O_2 demands on heart.
Aerobic Phase (20 min. minimum)	• Exercise in target zone for increased fitness, fat burning, and wellness.
Aerobic Cool Down (3–5 min.)	• Gradually bring heart rate down.
Toning/Strengthening (optional)	
Flexibility (5–10 min.)	• Return body to normal state.
	• Prevent injury.
	• Relaxation.

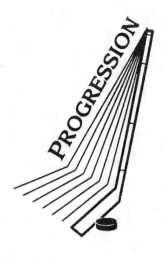

PROGRESSION

SAFETY:

- Proper form and movement execution.
- Encourage proper body alignment and work to promote muscular balance.
- Heels always need to settle to floor with each step.
- Have students find proper water depth for balance and control.

WORKOUTS:

Workouts should progress from simple to complex.
- In-place movements vs. travelling.
- Small movements vs. large movements.
- Bent lines vs. straight (not locked).
- One speed vs. a mix of slow/fast speeds.
- Neutral positions vs. force and power (plyometric).

Use basic motor skills in fun and challenging combinations (music optional).

Basic Jogging	Variations	
	• Extra high knees	Moving forward and back
	• Heels kick to butt	Touch heels with opposite hand in front and behind
Jumping Jacks	• Bounce 2 times out/2 times in	Jumping jack with a front kick
	• Crossing jacks	2 slow, 4 fast
	• Tilt upper body side to side	Travel any direction

These are really half jacks because arms stay under the water.

Scissors	• Slow/big	Tuck (use a center bounce)
	• Fast/small	With feet off floor
Bounces	• Ski with center bounce	
	• Tuck knees to chest while hands reach under thighs	
	• Twist	
	• Side to side and front to back (do one leg at a time)	
	• Bounce in a square	
Sport Moves	Example: Karate kicks, golf, tennis, baseball swings, soccer kicks, football drills, ballet leaps, volleyball/basketball shooting or blocking	
Water Walking	Examples: • Side stepping • Grape vines • Stork Walk • Disco • Swing • Step drag • March • Step touch	

RESOURCES

Aqua Exercise Association books and videos: (813) 486-8720
Janet Wilson, Seattle Parks and Recreation

UNIT: YO-YO

Yo-yo develops eye-hand coordination, enhances catching skills, improves motor skills, teaches sequencing, promotes individual accomplishments, and challenges each student to the level of his or her own ability.

Yo-yos (for the benefit of student and coach, a modular yo-yo that comes apart for easy knot removal)

Optional—"Vid-e-yo" (instructional video)

12 to 15 square feet per student

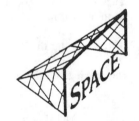

With the exception of the gravity pull, a yo-yo is always thrown over the end of the fingers, in the direction the back of the hand is facing. This is very similar to the way a Frisbee™ is thrown. The string should be attached to the middle finger, with a slip knot, between the first and second knuckles. The string must come from the finger to the top of the yo-yo; otherwise, the yo-yo will not roll off the end of the fingers properly.

Beginning Tricks

1. **Gravity Pull** (push—pull—wait—catch)
2. **Dribble** (multiple gravity pulls)
3. **Power Throw** (throw—turn—catch)
4. **Forward Pass** (drop—swing—catch) This is NOT a throw! The yo-yo is released behind you at the start of the swing. Swing is from waist high behind to chest high in front.

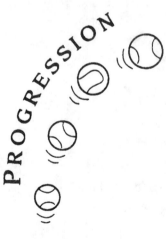

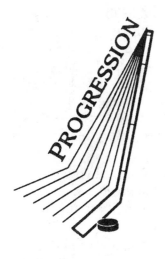

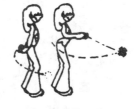

Power Throw   Forward Pass   Outside Loop

5. **Outside Loop** (drop—swing—push [or whip]) The early release is very important! The yo-yo goes down, out, returns, and makes a loop around the outside of the arm.

6. **Hop the Fence** (throw—stop—hop—pull) Start with elbow high and do a good Power Throw but don't turn your hand over. The yo-yo will come up and hop over your hand by itself. Then pull to get it to return to your hand.

7. **Inside Loop** (drop—swing—come here, go away) This is exactly the same as the Outside Loop except that the yo-yo goes past the arm on the inside of the wrist.

Spinning Tricks

1. **Sleeper** Making sure that the string is in neutral (let it hang until it stops spinning) and that there are no knots inside, start with the elbow held high, throw the yo-yo in the same manner as in the Power Throw but keep the hand relaxed. The yo-yo should "Sleep" at the bottom of the string. Turn you hand over and give a sharp jerk and the yo-yo should return to your hand.

2. **Walk the Dog** Throw a good Sleeper and gently lower the yo-yo to the floor. The yo-yo will "walk" away from you. (Hint: Don't allow any slack in the string or the yo-yo will jump back into your hand.)

3. **The Creeper** Start with Walk the Dog and carefully lower your hand to the floor as the yo-yo "walks" out. Give a jerk and the yo-yo will "creep" back to your hand. (A much easier version is to swing the "sleeping" yo-yo out in front of you and put your hand and the yo-yo on the floor at the same time, give a jerk and the yo-yo will return.)

4. **Around the Corner** Throw a fast spinner, then move the hand up and bring the yo-yo around the elbow so that the yo-yo is behind the arm. Keeping the elbow high so the string hangs over the arm, lower the hand to the string and give it a quick tug. The yo-yo will climb the string right over the arm and drop in front of the body where it can be pulled back to the hand in the same manner as the gravity pull.

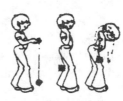
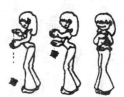

Walk the Dog   Around the Corner   Rock the Baby

329

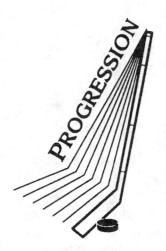

5. **Rock the Baby** Practice making the cradle without the yo-yo spinning. Hold both hands up in front of your face with the palms toward you, the yo-yo hand on the inside. The yo-yo hand moves over the opposite hand and then down, almost to the yo-yo. Grasp the string just above the yo-yo and then lower the opposite hand (which should have a triangle of string around it) so the yo-yo can swing through the triangle. When making the cradle is easy, try it with the yo-yo "sleeping." The idea is to "rock your baby" and then drop everything so the yo-yo will snap back into your hand.

6. **Skin the Cat** Start with the Sleeper. Put the first finger of your opposite hand on the inside of the string and push the yo-yo out and up. When the yo-yo snaps back toward your hand, whip it around in an inside loop.

7. **Flying Saucer** Start this trick with the "making a muscle" position. Throw the yo-yo down diagonally across your body in a very crooked Sleeper. Catch the string about six inches above the yo-yo with the thumb of the opposite hand, lift it shoulder high, and let it go to return to your hand.

Skin the Cat   The Flying Saucer

Mr. Pro-Yo, Dale Oliver
7439 Northwood Drive
San Francisco, CA 94080

PART TWO

ESTABLISHING AN ENVIRONMENT FOR SUCCESS

Part II of this resource provides a variety of tips, techniques, and statistics to help you in planning, delivery, and evaluation of your physical education program. These include:

- PARTICIPATION OF HIGH SCHOOL STUDENTS IN SCHOOL PHYSICAL EDUCATION
- Y.P.E. IS IMPORTANT
- SUCCESS-ORIENTED PHYSICAL EDUCATION
- PROBLEMS AND SOLUTIONS IN PHYSICAL EDUCATION
- COEDUCATIONAL CLASSES
- LESSON PURPOSE
- INAPPROPRIATE ACTIVITIES
- GAMES AND DRILLS THAT RATE AN "E"
- SAFETY ISSUES
- LEARNING COMPASSION
- UNIT DURATION
- LEARNING STYLES
- TECHNIQUES FOR SELECTING PARTNERS AND GROUPS
- MAINSTREAMING
- PUBLIC RELATIONS
- MOTIVATION
- STUDENT TESTIMONIALS
- P.E. RECORDS DAY SAMPLE POSTER
- PHYSICAL EDUCATION BILL OF RIGHTS
- SAMPLE PHYSICAL EDUCATION BENCHMARKS
- STUDENT EVALUATION
- PROGRAM EVALUATION

PARTICIPATION OF HIGH SCHOOL STUDENTS IN SCHOOL PHYSICAL EDUCATION

The following highlights are from the September 6, 1991 MMWR titled "Participation of High School Students in School Physical Education—United States, 1990" and are based on findings from the 1990 Youth Risk Behavior Survey conducted by CDC. The survey involved a nationally representative sample of 11,631 students in grades 9–12.

Health Outcomes

- Regular physical activity increases a person's ability to perform daily activities with greater vigor and may reduce the risk for specific health problems, including coronary heart disease, hypertension, noninsulin-dependent diabetes mellitus, colon cancer, and depression, as well as lower all-cause death rates.

- High school physical education (PE) classes provide an opportunity to ensure a minimal, regular amount of desirable physical activity and help establish physical activity patterns that may extend into adulthood.

Quantity of Physical Education

- Of students in grades 9–12, approximately half (52%) (males 56%; females 48%) reported that they were enrolled in PE classes.

- Only 22% of students (males 24%; females 19%) reported attending PE classes daily.

- Daily attendance in PE classes decreased substantially from 9th through 12th grade (9th grade, 34%; 10th grade, 26%; 11th grade, 15%; and 12th grade, 11%).

- Enrollment in PE may have decreased from a total of 65% in 1984 to 52% in 1990 based on a comparison of findings in this report with results from the 1984 National Children and Youth Fitness Study.

Quality of Physical Education

- Of students who attended PE class during the two weeks preceding the survey, about one-third (33%) reported exercising 20 minutes or more in PE class three to five times per week.

- Almost one-fourth (23%) of students attending PE class (males 19%; females 28%) reported not exercising 20 minutes or more during any PE class during the two weeks preceding the survey.

Y.P.E. IS IMPORTANT

REGULAR PARTICIPATION in **quality** physical education programs will:

- Prepare students with skills for future leisure pursuits through exposures to various individual, team, and alternative activities.

- Formulate activity patterns that can extend into adulthood.

- "Reduce risk for specific health problems including: coronary heart disease, hypertension, colon cancer, and depression, as well as lower all-cause death rates." (CDC 1990 Youth Risk Behavior Survey).

- Increase cardiovascular efficiency.

- Improve one's physical literacy.

- Develop students' sense of security with their own body.

- Improve overall mental health.

- Reduce stress and increase energy-enriching quality of life.

- Produce a positive effect on structural growth. (G.M. Elliot, CAPHER, 1970).

- Contribute to academic progress by boosting self-esteem.

- Provide students with a better understanding of the **why** behind movement.

- Improve understanding of health-related fitness concepts.

- Teach safety techniques, reducing accidents outside of school.

- Provide an outlet for creativity and self-expression.

- Increase awareness of physical opportunities within the community.

- Decrease anger, fatigue, and confusion. (*International Society of Sport Psychology*, Vol. 20, No. 10).

SUCCESS-ORIENTED PHYSICAL EDUCATION

Emphasizes:

A = All Students Active

> "Teachers who engage students in a maximum amount of skill-learning time by designing movement tasks at appropriate levels of difficulty promote learning because engaged time at a high rate of success is a strong predictor of motor skill achievement."
> —B. Howe and J. Jackson

C = Creativity

> "Through carefully constructed movement experiences the child's creative potential and capabilities are encouraged by allowing more self-discovery."
> —K. R. Barrett

T = Teaching Lifetime Fitness

> "Why do we have to wait until adulthood to learn some hard and expensive lessons about health-related fitness, nutrition, and lifestyle behaviors? The fact is we shouldn't."
> —Smith & Cestao

I = Integration

> "Cognitive learning is integral to the development of a physically educated person. Every movement is based on cognition. Therefore, it is necessary to teach concepts and principles that relate to skill acquisition and performance. It is also important that students understand the reasons for, benefits of, and ways to properly engage in healthy lifestyles. Incorporating cognitive content into lessons significantly increases the possibility of producing life-long movers."
> —H. M. Heitman

V = Victimless Delivery Systems

> "The reflective teacher assesses the ecology of the teaching environment to define the variables that will determine the most effective physical education program for a particular situation. Then the teacher plans the teaching process that will be most effective."
> —G. Graham, S. A. Hale and M. Parker

E = Equitable Experiences

> "The government will no longer tolerate and this nation can no longer justify inequities in the manner in which both sexes are treated."
> —Charles Bucher

PROBLEMS AND SOLUTIONS IN PHYSICAL EDUCATION

IT'S CLEAR THAT:

- Curriculum offerings are often limited to a few traditional sports.

- Instructors rarely venture outside of their instructional comfort zone.

- Students lack opportunities to map out their own personal movement pursuits.
- The majority of **PR** efforts are based on the successes of elementary programs.
- Beating an opponent remains an important teaching strategy.

- Physical educators are still being viewed as athletic trainers.
- Staff is more apt to attend coaching workshops than professional inservice.

- Instructional strategies focus heavily on the **actual** regulation game.
- Dress codes are difficult to maintain.

- Many schools have a high number of P.E. waiver requests.
- Class scheduling does not always allow ample set-up time.

WE NEED TO:

- Survey students to determine preferences. Eliminate monotonous single sport offerings and introduce a greater number of lifetime and alternative sport menus.

- Assign each staff member a minimum of one new activity per quarter, ultimately improving self-confidence and one's personal skills inventory.

- Establish student contracts for goals they want to accomplish.

- Many positive efforts occur between grades 6 and 12. Tell everyone who will listen.

- Stress cooperation and sportsmanship as well as competition. Establish an environment for success.

- Become a "personal trainer" for each and every student.

- Join and attend local, state, and national heath and P.E. workshops. If inservice is lacking, create some.

- Modify equipment, rules, and spaces to allow all students to succeed.

- Have a schoolwide design contest for required uniforms. If it's stylish, they will wear it.

- Make our courses more interesting, challenging, inclusive, and user-friendly.

- Improve communication between the schedule makers and P.E. staff.

CO-EDUCATIONAL CLASSES

"Enough Said—It's Coed"

> It's not the girls or boys,
> the size of the space, or number of toys,
> It's an attitude that's implied,
> not the body type, but the climate inside,
> It is high expectations for all that's sought,
> not the content, but how it's taught."

Tips for Success

- High expectations for all
- Eliminate stereotypes
- Pair by comparable ability
- Individualize skills
- Utilize short-term units to assure variety
- Assure equality
- Chart progress
- Establish an atmosphere for success
- Minimize talk—maximize activity
- Encourage practice outside of class
- Teach by prescription rather than by tradition
- Emphasize cooperation over competition
- Set an atmosphere for learning, not just recreation
- Utilize a variety of delivery systems
- Evaluate through cognitive and affective skills, as well as physical
- Modify rules to accelerate performance
- Be creative—think of different ways to present content
- Allow for varied abilities by using problem-solving phraseology
- Reinforce appropriate behaviors
- Teach to noncomfort as well as comfort zones
- Balance individual, dual, and team sport offerings
- Teach something new
- Smile upon entering the gym

LESSON PURPOSE

Each lesson should have **purpose.** If each of the elements below is present, student achievement will increase. How many of the items listed are in your lesson plans?

P ersonalize the lesson to each student's needs.

U tilize a variety of delivery systems.

R elate activities taught to the world of the student.

P romote problem-solving and higher level thinking skills.

O bserve positive efforts and celebrate those efforts with the entire class.

S et up safe, sequential, developmentally appropriate learning experiences.

E xpect the best . . . **"No one rises from low expectations."**

INAPPROPRIATE ACTIVITIES

In 1992, COPEC (Council on Physical Education for Children), completed a position paper entitled **"Developmentally Appropriate Physical Education for Children."** The 16 paraphrased components below are excellent examples of <u>**inappropriate activities.**</u>

<u>**Curriculum:**</u> Offering curriculums consisting primarily of large group games.

<u>**Cognitive Development:**</u> Students fail to receive opportunities to integrate their physical education experience with other classroom experiences.

<u>**Affective Development:**</u> Teachers ignore opportunities to help students understand the emotions they feel as a result of participation in physical activity.

<u>**Fitness Testing:**</u> Students complete a battery of physical fitness tests without understanding why they are performing the tests, or the implications of the results as they apply to their future health and well-being.
*   Students complete fitness testing without adequate conditioning.
*   Physical fitness activities are used as a punishment.
*   Students are graded on a single test.

<u>**Active Participation:**</u> Activity time is limited due to waiting in line for turns.
*   Students are organized in large groups, where getting a turn is based on individual competitiveness or aggressive behavior.
*   Students are eliminated with no chance to re-enter the activity.

<u>**Games:**</u> Games are taught with no obvious goal or purpose.

Forming Teams: Teams are formed by designated "captains" who publicly select one child at a time, thereby exposing lower-skilled students to peer ridicule.

- Teams put boys against girls, emphasizing gender differences rather than cooperation.

Gender-Directed Activities: Girls are encouraged to participate only in activities that stress traditionally feminine roles, whereas boys are encouraged to participate in aggressive physical activities.

Competition: Students are required to participate in activities that label them as either winners or losers.

Equipment: An insufficient amount of equipment is available for the number of students in a class (for example, one ball for every four students).

GAMES AND DRILLS THAT RATE AN (E)

Games and drills rate an "E" that:

- Eliminate students who need it most.

- Embarrass students in front of peers.

- Exclude students with long waiting periods.

- Endanger students through the employment of unsafe equipment, space, or techniques.

- Encumber with too many rules.

- Emphasize winning at all costs.

- Encourage single-sex groupings.

- Enforce feelings of superiority among selected students.

- Employ practices nonrelated to program goals.

SAFETY ISSUES

Due to a number of different factors, physical education has earned the reputation of being one of the most hazardous subjects in the curriculum. The activities themselves are not dangerous; it's the conditions, use of equipment, and space that cause the accidents. Potential sources of accidents in physical education include unsafe facilities, defective equipment, transportation, failure to provide proper instruction, improper supervision, hazardous conditions, inappropriate activities, and failure to warn. At your next meeting, read aloud the following questions and mark the appropriate column.

Questions	Answers	
	Yes	No
1. Is your instructional staff certified in physical education?		
2. Are activities taught through safe, sequential progressions?		
3. Is program supervision adequate in locker rooms, gyms, and outdoor fields?		
4. Is the student/teacher ratio in line with "academic" classes?		
5. Are emergency procedures posted and practiced?		
6. Are students warned of potential risks **before** participation?		
7. Is appropriate protective equipment utilized?		
8. Are traffic patterns for drills and games carefully defined?		
9. Is inservice required for staff prior to units of high risk, e.g., roller skating?		
10. Are outdoor facilities checked for hazards prior to use?		
11. Do activities **off** school grounds require parental permission?		
12. Is participation limited for students who continually disregard the rules?		
13. Is there an atmosphere of safe play?		
14. Are selected activities age-appropriate for the participants?		
15. Are physically demanding exercises balanced with less active activities?		
16. Are students of comparable size matched when engaged in contact-based activities?		
17. Are medical restrictions for identified students carefully followed?		
18. Is broken equipment removed or secured?		
19. Are safeguards, e.g., mats, placed in potentially hazardous areas?		
20. Do volunteer drivers have appropriate liability insurance?		

LEARNING COMPASSION

Most physical educators have been blessed with the ability to excel in a variety of activities. They have rarely experienced the tears of ridicule, the embarrassment of being picked last, or the frustration involved with learning a simple basic skill.

Consequently, some instructors find it difficult to empathize with students demonstrating less-than-perfect form and ability. This lack of patience and understanding jeopardizes growth and ultimately affects the school's program as a whole.

All students are unique. They learn to walk, talk, catch, and throw at different speeds. **Success-oriented physical education** caters to **all** students.

UNIT DURATION

Physical educators have divergent views on the number and length of activity units. One solution could be another question. What are we preparing our students for? If it is Division I basketball, we are most likely in the wrong profession. If our overall goal is physically literate adults with a library of physical skills and the desire to keep moving, two- and three-week units appear to be the intelligent choice. Mix different daily warmups with selected concluding activities and student interest will increase.

LEARNING STYLES

Students learn to walk, talk, read, throw, and catch at different rates and in different ways. Each person has a predominant learning style (feeling, watching, and doing); this is the method by which you learn best.

Some students learn best by relying on tactile clues (feeling). Others are aided by visual stimuli. Observing someone demonstrate the skill accentuates this group's learning readiness. The third and smallest group of students learn by doing. This population includes a high percentage of pupils normally classified as "high risk." The kinetic learner will often become impatient with the instructor's lectures and demonstrations and is most successful when physical movement and repetitions are involved.

The secret for maximizing the potential of the greatest number of pupils is by *tailoring the instruction of each performer.* While most can benefit from each of these styles, continued instruction with a single style may exclude or hamper a large number of students having a preference for the other two. The subsequent frustrations can lead to discipline problems and interest gaps. A *success-oriented physical education* lesson borrows bits from all three.

Source: Janet Nelson, *New York Times Magazine,* 4/26/93.

TECHNIQUES FOR SELECTING PARTNERS AND GROUPS

One of the daily activities that physical educators past and present have to deal with is the selection of students on teams. It's a process that can either expedite the activity process, or it can be a process that belittles students and becomes a risk factor for future involvement. The techniques listed below are quick and nonthreatening. The instructor reserves the right to switch one or more students to equalize any group. When these techniques are implemented, many of the competitive concerns are alleviated.

- Instructor equitably pre-selects teams.
- Clothing colors or colored strips of paper.
- Birthdays (months), birthdays (odd and even days).
- Alphabetical (first or last names).
- Sizes of tennis shoes.
- Squads or roll groups.
- Freeze game (positions on the floor).
- Draw cards from deck (odd and even, or suits).
- Find a partner of equal size and ability and face that person at mid-court.
  This is perhaps the best of all techniques. You can divide the partners facing into two equal teams, or divide half the sets of partners.

MAINSTREAMING

More and more students previously enrolled in adaptive physical education are being assigned to regular education classes.

Public Law 94-142, implemented in 1975, required specially designed instruction for all students with disabilities and emphasized normalized experiences. Each student has a comprehensive IEP (Individualized Education Program), which serves as a road map for future learning, leisure, and lifetime learning.

Instructors unaccustomed to the abilities and behaviors of special-needs students often feel unprepared to work with these physically challenged youngsters and question whether *their* classroom is the most appropriate placement (least restrictive environment).

Adapted PE consulting teachers are frequently available to school staff for review of needs and strategies for working with these students. Perhaps the best solution is establishing a cooperative climate that emphasizes positive growth, individualized skills, peer tutoring, and a celebration of differences. All students, regardless of physical or academic status, deserve QUALITY physical education.

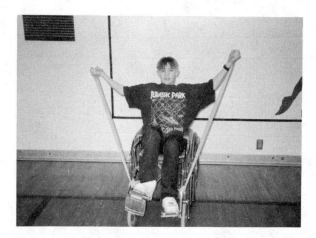

PUBLIC RELATIONS

Physical Education Isn't the Only Thing, But It Sure Beats What's Second

Regardless of the mistakes our profession has to live down, there are many promising trends. Physical education in the United States is changing for the better. As evidenced by the accompanying articles, there is support for its value and its existence within the basic education framework.

As advocates for change we cannot be content with a winning margin of 27% or being ranked the sixth priority on a list of basics. The only way for our professional stock to rise is through continuous quality programming. Our product is and always will be the students we teach. These same students grow up to be teachers, school board members, and legislators. Their past experiences remain in their memory banks forever—and when cuts are made, they are usually based on those past experiences.

Administrators Place Physical Education in the Basics

In the survey, the investigators asked the school administrators the following question: "If your budget were drastically reduced and you were told to teach only the basics, what courses would you teach?" Sixth on the administrators' list of basics was lifetime sports. Rounding out the top ten in rank order, the following subjects were listed: life science and American history; state history; civics; and earth science. A total of 85 courses were recorded in the survey.

Parents Rank PE Number One Subject in Dearborn, Michigan

For the second consecutive year, Dearborn, Michigan parents ranked physical education the number one required subject in their secondary schools. When given the opportunity to rate the curriculum in their schools on an A, B, C, D, and Fail scale, 83 percent of the parents surveyed indicated that the physical education program was either excellent or good. These same parents ranked the other required classes in the same manner: Mathematics, 75 percent; English, 74 percent; Science, 72 percent; and Social Studies, 70 percent.

Students Favor Physical Education

Earlier this year Scholastic Magazine, Inc., reported on its nationwide poll of 29,000 secondary school students in which it asked the question, "Which one of the following is your favorite course in school?" The courses listed included: Business; English; Fine arts/Performing Arts; Foreign Languages; Home Economics; Mathematics; Occupational/Career Training; Physical Education; Science; and Social Studies.

Physical education was by far the favorite course among the respondents. The poll shows that 27 percent chose physical education, with mathematics being the runner-up, but it had a distance vote of 16 percent.

Public Supports Physical Education in Gallup Poll

Based on the results of the eleventh annual Gallup Poll of the Public's Attitudes Toward the Public Schools, physical education and athletics are perceived as a positive aspect of the high school curriculum. The national totals show that 76% of the public ranks physical education as an essential subject.

Source: *Directions AAHPRD;* Council of City and County Directors. Vol. 7 No. 1. Fall 1979.

PROMOTE

To advance, raise to a more important rank, contribute to the progress or growth of, to sell or popularize, to advocate."

Imagine how powerful the field of physical education would become if all of its practitioners considered the practice of **program promotion** on the same level as grading, daily planning, coaching, and the infamous uniform checks.

Promotional activities must go beyond the yearly open-house experience and demonstrate more clearly the *why* behind the school program. They also must involve enrolled and non-enrolled students, staff, and the entire community.

Successful **P.R.** programs might include:

- "Jump Rope for Heart" events
- Lunchtime aerobic sessions
- School newspaper articles
- Students-of-the-Month awards
- Family activity nights
- Jog-a-thons and similar fundraisers
- Field days using outside volunteers
- Fitness and health fairs
- P.E. demonstration groups
- P.E. clubs
- Access for after-hour workouts
- Modern technology demonstrations (e.g., heart monitoring, body fat computers, etc.)

MOTIVATION

P.E. Records Day

Seattle's Physical Education Records Day is one school district's vehicle for motivating students to practice and excel in a variety of traditional and nontraditional physical skills.

The one-day three-hour event draws school champions from 80–100 schools. Competing in twelve different events, students attempt to establish personal and district records. The spring event welcomes over 1,000 competitors. New record holders appear on an annual Records Day poster which is displayed in every gym, locker room, and weight room in the district.

"Motivation is a force that leads individuals to ultimate achievement." (Kirkendall, Gruber, Johnson, 1987).

STUDENT TESTIMONIALS

6th	**Tammy Oreiro**	"This P.E. class gave me the confidence to do anything."
7th	**Krista Regan**	"Some kids don't play sports or other activities outside of school. P.E. should be offered for more than half the year."
8th	**Jill Kimball**	"This program, more than any other, has helped build my endurance and skills for all kinds of sports."
9th	**Kimura Taylor**	"We just learned and learned every day. . . . I felt so successful!"
10th	**Cesar Magat**	"The unicycling and double dutch were the best."
11th	**Hong Gu**	"The alternative skills prepared me for varsity sports. They kept me fit."
12th	**Kyle Leonard**	"I have so many positive memories from your class. . . . It was too much fun."
Graduate	**Cheryl Parks**	"As a child I always looked up to my P.E. teacher because I thought she was the neatest person I knew. I was determined to be just like her." (***new P.E. teacher***)

Best of Seattle '94

Seattle Schools
The Seattle Public Schools

DOUBLE DUTCH CHALLENGE XII & P.E. RECORDS DAY 1994

SPECIAL TEAM AWARDS

SPIRIT:
African Amer. Acad.

TOP DANCE:
Graham Hill

BEST DRESSED:
Graham Hill

SHOW TEAM:
Sanislo

TOP MOVE, ELEM.:
Sanislo

TOP MOVE, SEC.:
Denny

10-SECOND SPEED

PRIMARY

Jenny Chhim
Sanislo
64

INTERMEDIATE

Bridgett Massart
Maple
62 (Tie)

Christopher Quach
Sanislo
62 (Tie)

SECONDARY

Azizah Abdul
Graham Hill
62 (Tie)

Bridgett Massart
Franklin
60

CONSECUTIVE DOUBLE UNDERS

PRIMARY
Christopher Quach
Sanislo
210

INTERMEDIATE

Christopher Quach
Sanislo
403

SECONDARY
Hong Gu
Chief Sealth
304

OVERHAND PULLUPS

PRIMARY

Julie Fromm
Schmitz Park
31

INTERMEDIATE

Roberto Chavez
Sanislo
52

SECONDARY
Daniel Comito
Summit K-12
32

POWER JUMP

ELEMENTARY

Alex Allred
AE II
23.5 Inches

SECONDARY
Andrew Reed
Mercer
34 Inches

CONSECUTIVE FREE THROWS

PRIMARY

Derek Byrne
Alki
9

INTERMEDIATE

Rusty Lewis
Schmitz Park
15

SECONDARY

Nick Thorburn
Madison
22 (Tie)

Yoset Zerai
South Shore
22 (Tie)

FREESTYLE DOUBLE DUTCH

PRIMARY / ORIGINALITY

1st: Sanislo Scats
2nd: Orca   3rd: Dearborn Park

INTERMEDIATE / ORIGINALITY

1st: Sanislo Scats
2nd: Cooper   3rd: Graham Hill

SECONDARY / ORIGINALITY

1st: Denny Pioneers
2nd: Chief Sealth   3rd: Whitman

PRIMARY / SKILL AND EXECUTION

1st: Sanislo Scats
2nd: Orca   3rd: Dearborn Park

INTERMEDIATE / SKILL AND EXECUTION

1st: Sanislo Scats
2nd: Cooper   3rd: Graham Hill

SECONDARY / SKILL AND EXECUTION
1st: Denny Pioneers
2nd: Chief Sealth   3rd: Whitman

30-SECOND FREESTYLE JUGGLING

ELEMENTARY

Kao Hinh Saeteurn
Hawthorne

SECONDARY
Chris Francisco
Whitman

HOOP HANDSTANDS

PRIMARY
Jesse Williams
Schmitz Park
2:44

INTERMEDIATE
Jessica Trulson
Sanislo
2:28

SECONDARY
Summer Clemens
Hamilton
1:34

UNICYCLE
"Walk The Wheel"

Michael Warner
Denny
894 Feet

TABLE TENNIS
SECONDARY SINGLES
Jay Zeng
Hale
2nd: Ballard
3rd: South Shore

PICKLE-BALL
 SECONDARY / DOUBLES

Li Ang (Wen) Deng
Hale

Li Ang (Dong) Deng
Hale

2nd: Ingraham   3rd: Hamilton

ACCU-PITCH

ELEMENTARY

Alex Dunlop
Hawthorne
2 (Tie)

Jhomar Crouch
Bagley
2 (Tie)

Kenneth Martin
Whitworth
2 (Tie)

SECONDARY

Matt Turner
Rainier Beach
3 (Tie)

Michael Warner
Denny
3 (Tie)

Bunkeat Khung
South Shore
3 (Tie)

NEW FOR 1995:
SOCCER JUGGLING

1995 DOUBLE DUTCH CHALLENGE XIII & P.E. RECORDS DAY: MAY 11, 1995
For further information contact Bud Turner at 298-7985. Come and set a personal or District record!

346

PHYSICAL EDUCATION BILL OF RIGHTS

by Michael Marchs

In the Gymnasium I Have the Right to:

1. Participate in all activities for my age level.
2. Participate in all activities without getting hurt.
3. Participate without having my feelings hurt and people bothering me.
4. Participate in a safe environment with safe equipment.
5. Participate with all races and nationalities.
6. Progress at my own pace.
7. Learn.
8. Not have people talk about my progress.
9. Lose and not be teased.
10. Succeed and fail.
11. Be treated the same as others.
12. Work in my own personal space.
13. Speak when called on without interruption.
14. Ask questions and be listened to.
15. Have a 45-minute period.
16. Get a second chance.
17. Be friendly and kind and expect the same in return.
18. Work cooperatively.
19. Be physically educated.
20. Learn about fitness and how to take care of my body.
21. Learn what kind of exercises are good and what kind are not good.
22. Fair play in all activities.
23. Enjoy all activities.
24. Have fun.

NASPE News, **Winter 1993**

NASPE PHYSICAL EDUCATION OUTCOMES PROJECT

Examples of Benchmarks—Sixth Grade

As a result of participating in a quality physical education program, it is reasonable to expect that the student will be able to:

HAS	6	1. Throw a variety of objects demonstrating both accuracy and distance (e.g., Frisbees™, deck tennis rings, footballs).
HAS	6	2. Continuously strike a ball to a wall, or a partner, with a paddle using forehand and backhand strokes.
HAS	6	3. Consistently strike a ball, using a golf club or a hockey stick, so that it travels in an intended direction and height.
HAS	6	4. Design and perform gymnastics and dance sequences that combine traveling, rolling, balancing, and weight transfer into smooth, flowing sequences with intentional changes in direction, speed, and flow.
HAS	6	5. Hand dribble and foot dribble while preventing an opponent from stealing the ball.
HAS	6	6. In a small group keep an object continuously in the air without catching it (e.g., ball, foot bag).
HAS	6	7. Consistently throw and catch a ball while guarded by opponents.
HAS	6	8. Design and play small-group games that involve cooperating with others to keep an object away from opponents (basic offensive and defensive strategy) (e.g., by throwing, kicking, and/or dribbling a ball).
HAS	6	9. Design and refine a routine, combining various jump-rope movements to music, so that it can be repeated without error.
HAS	6	10. Leap, roll, balance, transfer weight, bat, volley, hand and foot dribble, and strike a ball with a paddle, using mature motor patterns.
HAS	6	11. Demonstrate proficiency in front, back, and side swimming strokes.
HAS	6	12. Participate in vigorous activity for a sustained period of time while maintaining a target heart rate.
IS	6	13. Recover from vigorous physical activity in an appropriate length of time.
IS	6	14. Monitor heart rate before, during, and after activity.
IS	6	15. Correctly demonstrate activities designed to improve and maintain muscular strength and endurance, flexibility, and cardio-respiratory functioning.
DOES	6	16. Participate in games, sports, dance, and outdoor pursuits, both in and outside of school, based on individual interests and capabilities.
KNOWS	6	17. Recognize that idealized images of the human body and performance, as presented by the media, may not be appropriate to imitate.
KNOWS	6	18. Recognize that time and effort are prerequisites for skill improvement and fitness benefits.
KNOWS	6	19. Recognize the role of games, sports, and dance in getting to know and understand others of like and different cultures.
KNOWS	6	20. Identify opportunities in the school and community for regular participation in physical activity.
KNOWS	6	21. Identify principles of training and conditioning for physical activity.
KNOWS	6	22. Identify proper warm-up, conditioning, and cool-down techniques and the reasons for using them.
KNOWS	6	23. Identify benefits resulting from participation in different forms of physical activities.
KNOWS	6	24. Detect, analyze, and correct errors in personal movement patterns.
KNOWS	6	25. Describe ways to use the body and movement activities to communicate ideas and feelings.
VALUES	6	26. Accept and respect the decisions made by game officials, whether they are students, teachers, or officials outside of school.
VALUES	6	27. Seek out, participate with, and show respect for persons of like and different skill levels.
VALUES	6	28. Choose to exercise at home for personal enjoyment and benefit.

NASPE PHYSICAL EDUCATION OUTCOMES PROJECT

Examples of Benchmarks—Eighth Grade

As a result of participating in a quality physical education program, it is reasonable to expect that the student will be able to:

HAS	8	1. Explore introductory outdoor pursuit skills (e.g., backpacking, rock climbing, hiking, canoeing, cycling, ropes courses).
HAS	8	2. Combine skills competently to participate in modified versions of team and individual sports.
HAS	8	3. Perform a variety of simple folk, country, and creative dances.
HAS	8	4. Use basic offensive and defensive strategies while playing a modified version of a sport.
HAS	8	5. Practice in ways that are appropriate for learning new skills or sports on his or her own.
IS	8	6. Correctly demonstrate various weight-training techniques.
IS	8	7. Sustain an aerobic activity, maintaining a target heart rate, to achieve cardiovascular benefits.
IS	8	8. Improve and maintain appropriate body composition.
IS	8	9. Participate in an individualized fitness program.
DOES	8	10. Identify and follow rules while playing sports and games.
KNOWS	8	11. Recognize the effects of substance abuse on personal health and performance in physical activity.
KNOWS	8	12. List long-term physiological, psychological, and cultural benefits that may result from regular participation in physical activity.
KNOWS	8	13. Describe principles of training and conditioning for specific physical activities.
KNOWS	8	14. Describe personal and group conduct, including ethical behavior, appropriate for engaging in physical activity.
KNOWS	8	15. Analyze and categorize activities and exercise according to potential fitness benefits.
KNOWS	8	16. Analyze offensive and defensive strategies in games and sports.
KNOWS	8	17. Evaluate the roles of exercise and other factors in weight control.
VALUES	8	18. Feel satisfaction on days when engaging in physical activity.
VALUES	8	19. Enjoy the aesthetic and creative aspects of performance.
VALUES	8	20. Respect physical and performance limitations of self and others.
VALUES	8	21. Desire to improve physical ability and performance.

NASPE PHYSICAL EDUCATION OUTCOMES PROJECT

Examples of Benchmarks—Tenth Grade

As a result of participating in a quality physical education program, it is reasonable to expect that the student will be able to:

HAS	10	1. Demonstrate basic competence in physical activities selected from each of the following categories: aquatics; self-defense; dance; individual, dual, and team activities and sports; and outdoor pursuits.
HAS	10	2. Perform a variety of dance (folk, country, social, and creative) with fluency and in time to accompaniment.
IS	10	3. Assess personal fitness status in terms of cardiovascular endurance, muscular strength and endurance, flexibility, and body composition.
IS	10	4. Design and implement a personal fitness program that relates to total wellness.
DOES	10	5. Participate in a variety of game, sport, and dance activities representing different cultural backgrounds.
DOES	10	6. Participate cooperatively and ethically when in competitive physical activities.
DOES	10	7. Participate in several outdoor pursuits indigenous to the geographic area.
KNOWS	10	8. Identify participation factors that contribute to enjoyment and self-expression.
KNOWS	10	9. Compare and contrast offensive and defensive patterns in sports.
KNOWS	10	10. Discuss the historical roles of games, sports, and dance in the cultural life of a population.
KNOWS	10	11. Categorize, according to their benefits and participation requirements, activities that can be pursued in the local community.
KNOWS	10	12. Analyze and compare health and fitness benefits derived from various physical activities.
KNOWS	10	13. Analyze and evaluate a personal fitness profile.
KNOWS	10	14. Use biomechanical concepts and principles to analyze and improve performance of self and others.
VALUES	10	15. Appreciate and respect the natural environment while participating in physical activity.
VALUES	10	16. Enjoy the satisfaction of meeting and cooperating with others during physical activity.
VALUES	10	17. Desire the enjoyment, satisfaction, and benefits of regular physical activity.

NASPE PHYSICAL EDUCATION OUTCOMES PROJECT

Examples of Benchmarks—Twelfth Grade

As a result of participating in a quality physical education program, it is reasonable to expect that the student will be able to:

HAS	12	1. Demonstrate intermediate or advanced competence in at least one activity from three of the six following categories: aquatics; dance (e.g., modern, folk, country, ballet); outdoor pursuits (e.g., hiking, biking, canoeing); individual activities/sports (e.g., golf, cycling); dual activities/sports (e.g., tennis, racquetball); team activities/sports (e.g., soccer, softball).
HAS	12	2. Apply scientific principles to learning and improving skills.
IS	12	3. Maintain appropriate levels of cardiovascular and respiratory efficiency, muscular strength and endurance, flexibility, and body composition necessary for a healthful lifestyle.
IS	12	4. Use the results of fitness assessments to guide changes in his or her personal program of physical activity.
DOES	12	5. Monitor exercise and other behaviors related to a healthful lifestyle.
DOES	12	6. Willingly participate in games, sports, dance, outdoor pursuits, and other physical activities that contribute to the attainment of personal goals and the maintenance of wellness.
KNOWS	12	7. Know about career opportunities in physical education and related fields.
KNOWS	12	8. Identify the effects of age, gender, race, ethnicity, socioeconomic standing, and culture upon physical activity preferences and participation.
KNOWS	12	9. Analyze time, cost, and accessibility factors related to regular participation in physical activities.
KNOWS	12	10. Use scientific knowledge to analyze personal characteristics and participation in physical activity.
KNOWS	12	11. Evaluate (critically) claims and advertisements made about commercial products and programs.
KNOWS	12	12. Evaluate risks and safety factors that may affect physical activity preferences throughout the life cycle.
VALUES	12	13. Accept the ways in which personal characteristics, performance styles, and activity preferences will change over the life cycle.
VALUES	12	14. Accept differences between personal characteristics and the idealized body images and elite performance levels portrayed by the media.
VALUES	12	15. Derive genuine pleasure from participating in physical activity.
VALUES	12	16. Feel empowered to maintain and improve physical fitness, motor skills, and knowledge about physical activity.
VALUES	12	17. Make a commitment to physical activity as an important part of one's lifestyle.

STUDENT EVALUATION

> "Most teachers grade students relative to their classmates, not against an absolute standard: They give A's to their best students, and work down from there."
> —*Grant Wiggins,* ASCO *Update,* September, 1993.

For decades, school districts across the United States have struggled with traditional letter-grading systems that:

- provide little information about the curriculum and what was learned
- fail to show individual growth
- do not correlate with current delivery systems, e.g., cooperative learning
- demoralize those below level, ultimately affecting motivation
- are ineffective as a source for punishment.

Traditional Secondary Evaluation Device

MERCER MIDDLE SCHOOL 110 1ST SEMESTER **Performance Report** — The Seattle Public Schools
Report Period Ending: **2/07/89**

TURNER MATTHEW ALLEN **4162640** Grade **07** Home Room **115**

TERM GPA 3.86

Course Description	Teacher	Credits Earned	Credits Attemp.	Grade 1	Grade 2	Grade F	Absence 1	Absence 2	Citizenship 1	Citizenship 2	Effort 1	Effort 2	Teacher Comments
GENERAL SCIENCE I	LEAVENS	0.50	0.50	A	A	A	00	02	A	A	A	A	
CMMUNCATIONS SKILL	MC KINLEY	0.50	0.50	B	B	B	01	00	A	A	A	A	
PHYSICAL EDUCATION	JOHNSON	0.50	0.50	A	A	A	00	01	A	A	A	A	
LANGUAGE ARTS 7H	PAULUS	0.50	0.50	B	A	A	00	00	A	A	B	A	05 45
UNIFIED ARTS MS	BRAS	0.08	0.08		A	A		02		A		A	
MATHEMATICS 7H	HARR	0.50	0.50	B	A	A	01	02	A	A	B	A	
U S HISTORY 7H	PAULUS	0.50	0.50	A	A	A	00	00	A	A	A	A	05
REVIEW / REFRESHER	THOMPSON 8	0.50	0.50	A	A	A	03	00	A	A	A	A	

(FOLD)

Teacher Comments:

05 A PLEASURE TO HAVE IN CLASS
45 SHOWS CREATIVITY AND ORIGINALITY

MERCER MIDDLE SCHOOL
1600 S COLUMBIAN WY
SEATTLE, WA. 98108

> "If you always do what you've always done,
> you'll always get what you've always got."

STUDENT EVALUATION: FOUR ALTERNATIVES

1. **CHECKLIST** Once the desired card is designed, actual teacher time for completing this assessment is less than that required for narratives, but considerably longer than standard reporting forms. The sample that follows gives students and parents a comprehensive picture of the program components and the progress made.

MIDDLE SCHOOL P.I. REPORT CARD

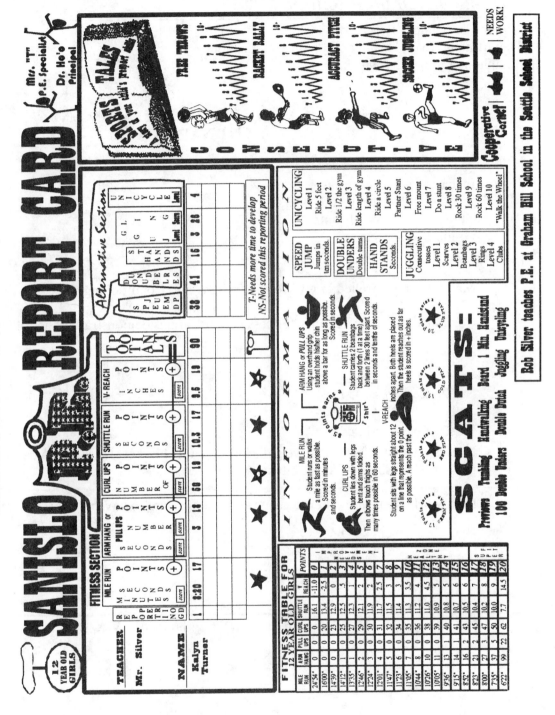

2. **NARRATIVE REPORTS** Narratives delineate student highlights and "lowlights" for that reporting period. While they are personal and illustrate growth, narratives are time consuming.

RAINIER BEACH HIGH SCHOOL

Charles E. (Chuck) Bernasconi
Department Head, Health and Physical Education
Telephone (206) 281-6090

PHYSICAL EDUCATION DEPARTMENT
STUDENT NARRATIVE

Student: Matt Turner
Instructor: C. Bernasconi
Date: October 3, 1993
Class: Wt. Training
Grade Level: Senior
Period: 2nd

Mat Turner is enrolled in my Weight Training and Conditioning class.

Currently he is involved in a "Fitness Circuit" and is demonstrating the following progress:

1. Bench Press: 135 lbs.

2. Leg Press: 430 lbs.

3. Overhand Pullups: 15

Matt is interested in gaining weight. Consequently his diet is recorded on a weekly basis with the goal of increasing his caloric intake.

Matt works well with other students and is a pleasure to have in class.

8815 Seward Park Ave. South Seattle, WA 98133

3. **PORTFOLIOS** "A portfolio is a purposeful collection of student work that tells a story of his or her growth as a learner."—*Northwest Regional Educational Laboratory*

Portfolios personalize the learning process. They provide a positive reflection of what has been accomplished and what needs to be improved upon. Parents enjoy receiving these communications with sons and daughters serving as the narrator. The library of available choices assists students with different learning styles.

Best evidence efforts may be described through (a) test scores, (b) "brag sheets," (c) outside participation, (d) homework, (e) journals, (f) video analysis, (g) certificates, and other means important to the student. These **celebrations** tend to motivate the learner toward further successes. Portfolios, like narratives, are excellent self-evaluation tools.

4. **CLUB CARDS** Club Cards evaluate students on an absolute standard. They increase student interest and, ultimately, the level of quality in a program. To earn a card the student must achieve a specified skill.

HANDSTAND CLUB

(Your age in seconds—
15-year-old = 15 seconds.)

HOT SHOT CLUB

(Consecutive foul shots
equalling your age.)

IT'S HIP TO BE FIT CLUB

(Score at or above the
85% on the
President's Physical
Fitness Test.)

(Run/jog 50 miles in or
outside of school during
one semester.)

50 MILE CLUB

(20 consecutive good
form volley with a
partner over a volley-
ball or tennis net).

VOLLEY CLUB

The design and production of Club Cards can be approached in a variety of ways. Some teachers offer prizes for the best designs while others utilize computer graphics, the expertise of art instructors or, when funding is available, outside graphics professionals.

8 1/2″ by 11″ plastic sport card sheets provide protection and a permanent means for displaying these successes in student binders or on walls.

When it comes to student evaluation, the best interpretation for what a student has learned is through multiple assessments. If the standard letter grade is paired with one of the aforementioned descriptions, evaluation becomes more meaningful and productive.

PROGRAM EVALUATION

HOWDOYOUKNOWIFWHATYOUDOISGOOD?

Answer YES or NO   YES or NO

- Does your curriculum include a variety of individual, team, and alternative activities? _____

- Are all students improving? _____

- Do the majority of students look forward to participating? _____

- Do boys and girls have the same opportunities and expectations? _____

- Are all students active the majority of time? _____

- Is there a major theme or focus, e.g., ball control, for each lesson? _____

- Are students allowed to choose among certain activities? _____

- Do staff members frequently venture out of their comfort zones? _____

- Is change evident from one year to another? _____

- Are teams selected without negative peer pressure? _____

- Does every student experience leadership opportunities? _____

- Is evaluation a part of each activity unit? _____

- Are skills taught in a safe, sequential progression? _____

- Does the teacher set an atmosphere for success? _____

- Do students understand the *why* as well as the *how* behind each skill? _____

- Is cooperation as important as competition? _____

IF ALL OF THE ABOVE POINTS ARE MARKED YES ABOUT YOUR PROGRAM ... "IT'S GOOD!"

> "I implore you to make physical education worthy of its place in the schools. ...
> Only then will we earn the additional time, facilities, equipment, and physical
> education specialists we seek."
> —*Sam Baumgarten*

In Native American cultures, one's wealth was measured on what the person gave away, not what was kept.

As physical educators, we must continue to share the wealth of ideas we create.